PS3552.A76Z68   267

GORDON
DONALD BARTHELME

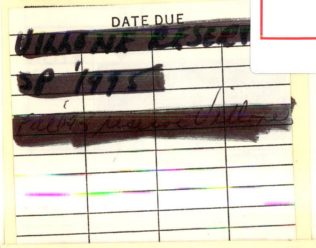

DATE DUE

Twayne's United States Authors Series

EDITOR OF THIS VOLUME

Warren French

Indiana University

Donald Barthelme

TUSAS 416

Photo by Jerry Bauer courtesy of Farrar, Straus and Giroux

Donald Barthelme

DONALD BARTHELME

By LOIS GORDON

TWAYNE PUBLISHERS

A DIVISION OF G. K. HALL & CO., BOSTON

Published in 1981 by Twayne Publishers,
A Division of G. K. Hall & Co.
All Rights Reserved

Printed on permanent/durable acid-free paper and bound
in the United States of America

First Printing

Library of Congress Cataloging in Publication Data

Gordon, Lois G.
Donald Barthelme.

(Twayne's United States authors series ; TUSAS 416)
Bibliography: pp. 217–21
Includes index.
1. Barthelme, Donald—Criticism and interpretation.
I. Title. II. Series.
PS3552.A76Z68   813'.54   81–4240
   ISBN 0–8057–7347–9   AACR2

For
Alan and Robert

Contents

About the Author

Lois Gordon received her B.A. from the University of Michigan and her M.A. and Ph.D. (1966) degrees from the University of Wisconsin. She taught for two years at City College in New York (1964–1966), and during the two years her husband served in the army, she taught at the University of Missouri–Kansas City. She began teaching at Fairleigh Dickinson University in 1968, where now, Professor of English and Comparative Literature, she teaches a variety of courses in twentieth-century literature. Her dissertation, written under Ricardo Quintana, was on Samuel Beckett. She has since published a number of articles on modern authors, including Faulkner, Eliot, Pinter, Rich, Eberhart, Roth, Miller, Jarrell, Purdy, Merwin, Bishop, Davie, Rukeyser, Gaddis, and Sorrentino. Her *Stratagems to Uncover Nakedness* was one of the earliest books published on Harold Pinter, and she has just completed a book on Robert Coover for Southern Illinois University Press. She is now writing a book on the foundations of avant-garde literature.

Preface

Despite the continuing success of the traditional novel in America and abroad, a new fictional form (and literary avant-garde) has emerged since the mid-sixties that rejects virtually all of its conventions. The movement, given a variety of labels,[1] including postmodernism, metafiction, surfiction, and parafiction, among others, includes, outside of America, Cortázar, Calvino, Pinget, Simon, Sollers, Ricardou, and Le Clézio, as well as the better-known and earlier-established Borges and Beckett. In America, it includes Donald Barthelme, William Gass, Robert Coover, Ronald Sukenick, John Hawkes, Gilbert Sorrentino, Raymond Federman, Steve Katz, and Ishmael Reed, with Barth, Pynchon, and Nabokov its earliest practitioners.

Characteristic of this avant-garde is its rejection of conventional mimetic (imitative) form. It abandons traditional linear plot and characterization, the concomitant unities of time and space, and the basic, traditional assumption that the novel can reflect and comment upon reality. In its refusal to be teleological—to be an orderly comment upon a knowable world—it takes as its subject, most frequently, the very act of writing, the difficulties of using language to reflect a reality that in itself may be unknowable.

If one considers the history of twentieth-century intellectual thought, he may speculate upon the reasons why the traditional novel, as Barth put it, is dead, on why—at least for the avant-garde—the writer can no longer create a teleological form that reflects a stable reality. While one hesitates to make such generalizations, it may be instructive to suggest that the notion of "relativity" is common to most contemporary scientific, psychological, philosophical, and linguistic explanations of reality. One can then perhaps better understand why the artistic renderings of reality have changed so dramatically.

Modern physics demolished the Newtonian idea of a fixed and

stable reality and demonstrated the relativity of time, space, matter, and energy. The new science indicated that reality includes the unseen, that it includes data that contradict the senses. Similarly, psychoanalysis demonstrated that human nature is not fixed, and that the study of it goes beyond empirical observation to the (unseen) recesses of the unconscious mind, which function outside traditional time and space. The fixed distinctions between normal and abnormal, the real and the fantastic—like those between mass and space, the past and present—were discarded. The existentialists, working with the fundamental idea that God is dead, asserted that the moral values by which man establishes his worth and identity were similarly relative and arbitrary. With the demise of absolute good and bad, man was free to create his own set of absolutes, aware at the same time of the arbitrariness of these values. The fixed (Aristotelian) notions of responsibility, courage, and heroism were now profoundly challenged. More recently, students of linguistics and semiotics have theorized upon the very relativity of language as an approximation (metaphor) of experience, in itself possibly indefinable.

Whether or not the avant-garde, and Donald Barthelme specifically, is well read in these matters is less important than our awareness that this notion of relativity (really the twentieth-century *Zeitgeist*) informs his (and their) work both structurally and thematically.

This book, the first on Barthelme, deals with his work chronologically and traces the emergence and development of specific themes; it also focuses on Barthelme's remarkable use of language. Whether he is dealing with our hypereducated society, brainwashed by packaged slogans and media-marketed expertise, with the political and social pathology of American life, or with more personal matters like the endless war between the sexes, or the father-son relationship, or aging, or the difficulties of writing (i.e., with irony as a defense against the world), he consistently treats the issue of language as a problematic vehicle with which to serve both the ordinary and creative life.

As though to offer an alternative to our immersion in fixed roles and clichés, and our inevitable imprisonment in the fixed structures of language, he subjects the written and spoken forms of language to endless experimentation and parody. Most typically, he literalizes metaphor, which shocks the reader into an awareness of both his own uncreative use of language and its rich possibilities. Barthelme evokes through his verbal arrangements, in fact, a universe—unborn until then, untapped in his reader's consciousness. He creates, especially up through *The Dead Father*, a unique form of comedy, with language as its subject, the emblem of man's relationship to other men and to the universe. It is a comedy, moreover, that is wildly funny, as it is liberating and educative. In some of his more recent work—with either its literalizations of metaphysical issues (which create a unique form of fable) or with its new dialogue forms—he creates an even more poetic and diffuse style. One may associate the brilliant verbal collage with the earlier and main body of his writing, and the more ineffable, infinitely suggestive and polyphonic techniques of poetry and musical composition with some of the more recent material.

The format of this book, after the biographical material and introductory chapter on Barthelme's technique, is to treat each volume individually, to state the themes evolving in each, and then to examine each work separately. The first few chapters devote greater space to language and form, to suggest to the reader the style that develops throughout; thereafter, the book concentrates on the issues most challenging to Barthelme's readers—clarification of the matters of linearity, point of view, meaning, and method.

I am grateful to Donald Barthelme for his kindness in reading and discussing portions of the manuscript, and to my husband, Alan, and son, Robert, for their patience and support during its preparation. I owe Warren French many thanks for his support and encouragement over many years.

LOIS GORDON

New York City

Chronology

1931   Born April 7, in Philadelphia, oldest of five children, to Donald (architect and professor) and Helen Bechtold Barthelme.

1933   Family moves to Houston.

1945–   Becomes "literary reporter" for the *Eagle*, St. Thomas
1946   High School newspaper.

1948–   Wins poetry and short story awards in *Sequoyha*, Lamar
1949   High School literary magazine.

1949   Enters the University of Houston. Studies journalism on and off through 1957. Stops in junior year.

1950–   Edits college newspaper, *Cougar*.
1951

1951   Works as reporter for *Houston Post*.

1953   Drafted into U.S. Army. Serves in Fort Polk, Louisiana, Japan, and Korea.

1955–   Reports for *Houston Post*.
1956

1956   Returns to University of Houston. Works for News Service. Writes speeches for university president. Edits *Acta Diurna*, faculty newsletter. Founds *Forum*, university literary magazine.

1959   Board of Directors, Contemporary Arts Museum, Houston.

1961–   Director, Contemporary Arts Museum.
1962

1962   Moves to New York. Becomes managing editor of *Location*.

1963   Publishes first story, "L'Lapse," in *The New Yorker*.

1964   *Come Back, Dr. Caligari*.

1965 Spends year in Denmark.

1966 Receives Guggenheim Fellowship.

1967 *Snow White.*

1968 *Unspeakable Practices, Unnatural Acts.*

1970 *City Life.*

1971 *The Slightly Irregular Fire Engine* (children's book).

1972 *Sadness.* National Institute of Arts and Letters Award. National Book Award for *The Slightly Irregular Fire Engine.* Begins teaching at the State University of New York at Buffalo.

1973 Visiting Professor, Boston University.

1974 *Guilty Pleasures* published and nominated for National Book Award. Becomes Distinguished Visiting Professor, City College of New York.

1975 *The Dead Father.*

1976 *Amateurs.*

1979 *Great Days.*

1981 *Sixty Stories.*

CHAPTER 1

The Man from Texas

DONALD Barthelme lives with his wife in New York's Greenwich Village in an elegantly furnished, floor-through (townhouse) apartment. On one wall of their connecting living room and library are massive white bookcases; at the opposite end of the room are two or three tall windows which open on to an unusually rich cluster of trees in the front yard. Two large prints (an Ingres and a Lindner), leather and chrome chairs, an upholstered velvet couch, a thick and textured area rug on the expansive parquet floor, and a wood-manteled fireplace—all in rich, earth tones—plus an occasional plant and fresh flowers, decorate the room. It appears to be very comfortable, spacious, and tidy. A long desk, with a typewriter and neatly piled materials, stands on one side.

Barthelme is tallish, and although he wears a Captain Ahab beard (less red than blond, with streaks of grey), his most striking visual features are his sharp blue eyes which, through his gold-rimmed glasses, steadily communicate through his frequent silences. His voice is rich and resonant; he has noticeably impeccable enunciation. He appears to be conservative in dress, although he is fond of cowboy boots, one suspects less for their stylishness than as a link with his Texas past.

Barthelme was born in Philadelphia (1931), a year after his father received his B.Arch. degree from the University of Pennsylvania (where his mother, "a Northerner," was an English major), and they moved to Texas when he was about two. His father, a "modern," in the sense that "he was an advocate of Mies and Corbu," "an anomaly in Texas in the thirties,"[1] opened an architectural firm and later began a long and distinguished academic career as professor of architectural design at the University of Houston.

15

Barthelme's father, interested in all forms of modern art, designed their house, "similar to Mies's Tugendhat," and Barthelme recalls: "It was wonderful to live in but strange to see on the Texas prairie. On Sundays people used to park their cars out on the street and stare. We had a routine, the family, on Sundays. We used to get up from Sunday dinner, if enough cars had parked, and run out in front of the house in a sort of chorus line, doing high kicks."[2]

Artists and architects visited often, and his father's considerations frequently were, "What was Mies doing, what was Aalto doing"—concerns "to say the least somewhat different from those of the other people we knew."[3] Yet, speaking more broadly about his childhood, he describes it as "normal, middle-class." He went to the movies frequently, spent summers with his grandfather in Galveston, and especially enjoyed, of the "many books around the house," mythology (particularly Norse), and "all the normal kids' books, like Sabatini." When he was ten, he decided to be a writer, and that was that.

Brought up as a Roman Catholic, he attended parochial schools and from a considerably early age wrote for and then edited school publications; he won a series of awards. Although "the house was filled with a lot of books, like Dos Passos, as a teenager I was buying alot" i.e., Eliot and Joyce. His father gave him an anthology of modern French poetry, which he cites as influential in his life, though not as much as his father's interest in "artistic modernism."[4]

Barthelme attended the University of Houston and had an extended involvement with the school. He studied journalism, edited the newspaper, *Cougar* (as a sophomore, the youngest to hold that post), and was managing editor of the yearbook; again, he won a number of awards. His articles for *Cougar* (frequently under the penname "Bardley," and with personae named Pitkin) were on school issues and cultural events, but mostly they were movie reviews. One essay, for example, was "A Modest Proposal for Short Tables," in which he answered the complaint that the cafeteria tables were too short for the sororities, by proposing sororities small enough for the tables.

Barthelme also worked as a reporter for the *Houston Post*, where he was known as the resident Damon Runyon scholar.

He wrote on all cultural events, from piano recitals to acrobat performances, again reviewing films regularly. In 1953, he was drafted, and the day he arrived in Korea, much as might happen to one of his characters, the truce was signed. He then edited an army newspaper. After his discharge he returned to Houston and again worked for the *Post* and joined the public relations department of the University of Houston, where he wrote speeches for the university president (one of his fictional characters, similarly employed, writes "poppycock" and sometimes "cockypap"), and he took "as many courses as I could" with a young philosophy professor (now at Yale), Maurice Natanson, whom Barthelme singles out as a key figure in his life.

His professional life during the next few years is interesting because of his close association with a variety of artists. At the university he had been editing the faculty newsletter; then he founded *Forum*, a literary magazine, and published Joseph Lyons, Roger Callois, Bateson, Fiedler, Sartre, Kenner, and Robbe-Grillet (1956). He has spoken of this as a time when he especially read a great deal—not only for material to publish but also in the fields of philosophy, psychology, anthropology, and history. He enjoyed, in addition, doing the layouts and design work for the journal ("I love typography"). He then joined the Contemporary Arts Museum in Houston and—when he was only thirty—became its director. The following year he moved to New York and became managing editor of Tom Hess's and Harold Rosenberg's art and literary review, *Location.* Here he published Gass, Bellow, McLuhan, and Koch. His first national publication appeared before this in *Harper's*, a review of the 39th *Annual of Advertising and Editorial Art Design.*[5]

Barthelme did not train himself, as many young writers do, by imitating others (although he says his early unpublished work may indeed have sounded like Hemingway or Bellow), for he was always striving—and remains now—after a unique style. He was dissatisfied with his work until he was "in his thirties," and suddenly, there it was. "L'Lapse" was his first story published in *The New Yorker* (1963), and since then he has published fiction there, regularly and frequently. (He has also contributed film reviews.)

Barthelme is a careful, highly regimented writer. He sits at the typewriter seven mornings a week ("Sunday seems to be my best day, probably because I'm a lapsed Catholic")[6] and writes slowly, revising constantly. He has been known to rework pieces even beyond publication. He is said to lead a very organized life; after writing each morning, he is likely to spend his afternoons walking around and exploring the Village, visiting and drinking with friends. He likes movies "as relaxation, as entertainment," and every kind of music. He enjoys travel, especially abroad, and he smokes a great deal. He names as the contemporary writers he finds most interesting, in addition to the German Becker and Handke, Beckett, Koch, Ashbery, Gass, Percy, Nabokov, Pynchon, Paley, and Barth. Among the writers of the past he lists Rabelais, Rimbaud, Kleist, Kafka, Stein, and Flann O'Brien. He has a daughter, Anne (born in 1965), for whom he wrote *The Slightly Irregular Fire Engine*, and whom he apparently consulted faithfully in its preparation.

Barthelme does not seek out celebrity, and he appears to be shy. He dislikes public and literary gatherings, although when he made his acceptance speech for the National Book Award, his speech was so witty that many present apparently thought it also should have received a prize. He is reluctant to talk about his life, though less so to discuss his work—or more precisely, specific characters or even words. Occasionally, he reads his work on college campuses, and since the early seventies he has done some teaching—initially "to get me out of the house. After ten years in a room you begin to get a bit flaky."[7] Now, he meets with his City College writing students in his apartment.

Since so much of his work deals with language, one is tempted to draw from it a "credo." The best statements on his aesthetic, however, may be gleaned from "A Symposium on Fiction," published in *Shenandoah*:[8]

. . . painters had to go out and reinvent painting because of the invention of photography and I think films have done something of the sort for us. (26)

There is a realm of possible knowledge which can be reached by artists, which is not susceptible of mathematical verification but which is true. This is sometimes spoken of as the ineffable. . . . And I believe that's the place artists are trying to get to, . . . somewhere probably between mathematics and religion, in which what may fairly be called truth exists. (11)

One does not choose to be a "conventional" writer or "experimental" writer. One writes as he or she can. It's not a conscious choice. . . . One of the funny things about experimentalism in regard to language is that most of it has not been done yet. Take *mothball* and *vagina* and put them together and see if they mean anything together; maybe you're not happy with the combination and you throw that on the floor and pick up the next two and so on. There's a lot of basic research which hasn't been done because of the enormous resources of the language and the enormous number of resonances from the past which have precluded this way of investigating language. (15, 20–21)

CHAPTER 2

The Green Billiard Table – An Introduction to Barthelme's Fiction

"The per-capita production of trash in this country is up from 2.75 pounds per day in 1920 to 4.5 pounds per day in 1965, the last year for which we have figures, and is increasing at the rate of about four percent a year. . . . We may very well soon reach a point where it's 100 percent. Now at such a point, you will agree, the question turns from a question of disposing of this 'trash' to a question of appreciating its qualities, because, after all, it's 100 percent, right? . . . We want to be on the leading edge of this trash phenomenon, the everted sphere of the future, and that's why we pay particular attention, too, to those aspects of language that may be seen as a model of the trash phenomenon."[1]

"My nourishment is refined from the ongoing circus of the mind in motion. Give me the odd linguistic trip, stutter and fall, and I will be content" (*SW*, 139).

ANY discussion of Donald Barthelme's comedy necessitates the backdrop of contemporary thought, because Barthelme's characters, and their world, are among the most sophisticated in literary history. Freud, Fellini, Einstein, Roland Barthes—as well as Norman Lear, Pepsi Cola, John Wayne, and *Cosmo* magazine—such is the milieu of Barthelme's people. Their everyday vocabulary includes Heidegger's angst, Bachelard's poetic space, Sartre's "other," let alone the vast legacy of literary, anthropological, psychological, historical, and scientific thought—and the prodigious jargon of T.V., ads, current events, pop art, and culture. Barthelme's people are hypereducated, wild consumers of information, and devotees of every possible "how-to" formula.

If literature at one time presumably reflected life, Barthelme reverses the formula. His figures have in great part become the media, the art and slogans—the words—about them. They mouth technology, although they are utterly ignorant as to what it means; they explain everything and approach every experience with strategy and skill, with the statistics of management and survival, or the rationalizations of historical precedent. They accept roles—is it not one's greatest goal to be Mick Jagger or Blondie, the Brut man or Breck girl?—and they admire expertise, as though it had divine authority. Indeed, they give credence and praise to authorized texts and media personalities, as they once did to God.

Similarly, if literature until our time—in its focus upon character—reflected growth from ignorance to insight and measured the gap between seeming and being, Barthelme's fiction, *when* it concerns people, abolishes any such dualities and growth of character. ("Insight," as we shall later discuss, involves the reader, rather than the characters.) Barthelme says (or at least one of his characters does) that the meaning of books is *in* the lines, not in the spaces between them, a pithy analogy of his characters' programmed approach to experience. Most of his people are beyond questioning the difference between what they are and what they could be. They are so much the product of modern expertise regarding "identity," such authorities on Freudian or Jungian thought—and all the rest—that they speak and act this out in their very lines, in the very jargon of contemporary expertise. The inner and outer worlds, once a fascination for the literary artist, have now atrophied, and what was once an inner void (enigmatic, neurotic, or mythic)—at odds with act or spoken thought —is now identical with the slick jargon of conscious speech.

Barthelme has been called a surrealist, but apart from the fact that he is both hilariously funny and an implicit social critic, as the surrealists were not, he goes one step beyond surrealism, which externalized or concretized the inner world. For Barthelme, the one-time, inner, mysterious world—if it exists at all—is at one with the supereducated, supersophisticated outer one.

His people often appear as robots, or zombies (in fact, the title of one story) in a world without specific definition or locale. Lacking flesh and blood, they appear in a sense to be just forms of people or meaning, like skeletal outlines of sentences, or contours of words that lack substance. One rarely identifies with them.

But, as we shall see, one does identify with these odd and abstract figures linguistically. Although they may initially appear as word constructs and assemblages of language and information, with no emotion or felt-experience attached to their words, it is in Barthelme's "dislocations"—really his unique way of "characterizing" them—that they develop; they become purveyors of extraordinarily odd and unusual linguistic patterns. It is at this point that the reader, rather than the speaker, gets swept up with their infinitely suggestive language, with the spaces and movement between and beneath their words. Their odd juxtapositions of fragmented information, literary materials, and intentionally vague and open-ended statement and metaphor, present a world of potential connections which, while seemingly inaccessible to the characters themselves, are imminently available to the reader. This double vision toward language—as anesthetizing ("blanketing") and liberating—and the comedic form in which it is shaped, are uniquely Barthelmean.

In focusing upon his figures (rather than the reader's creation of their world), we might well consider as Barthelme's diagnosis of the contemporary malaise a term he uses in *Snow White*, a word which, interestingly enough, expresses the goals of many in our society—"equanimity." Modern man, Barthelme seems to be saying, the mass consumer, is stuffed with roles, words, and expertise; as such, he has pretty well achieved this goal. But to Barthelme, equanimity is paralysis.

Essentially both hollow and stuffed (starved of real feeling while overindulged in slogans), modern man is the offspring of T. S. Eliot's hollow man and waste lander, buried under the very thing Eliot yearned for—tradition, systems of belief, meaning, and explanation. It is as if the ritual Eliot wished us to pursue had completely lost its substance, and in our compulsive and habitual search for "meaning," we had gained the words and the process for search, but lost any significance that might have attached to either. We have lost our residual roots with humanity and instead become monsters of information, like computers.

Such a portrait of modern life may indeed reflect a disjointed and fragmented contemporary condition—and perhaps this represents a new sort of mimesis. Though Barthelme never admits it directly, there is implied social criticism in all his work. If a potentially serious or humorous situation elicits only a concatenation of fragmented, textbook responses, and jingles, or soap opera phrases, then one has indeed lost all connection with the affective life, indeed with life itself. If all one has to do is push a button in his head to find the proper words of condolence, love, friendship, and loneliness, then obviously something is gravely wrong. Furthermore, Barthelme's juxtapositions of serious and lighthearted response, even in jingle form, reflect another target of criticism, although Barthelme is surely not the first to explore this technique. As Pope had his Belinda equally concerned with "billet doux and Bibles," so too Barthelme shows us how, with the grave and trivial jumbled, people have lost their sense of priorities. Everything has become equally meaningful, traumatic, and alas, meaningless.

I *Language and Technique*

Such a portrait of human nature necessitates a flexible language, and to be sure, Barthelme's characters at times sound jazzy, like Antonioni characters, like John Wayne, or even Mr. Clean. In the same sentence they may recite the dubious abstractions of technology, the slogans of popular magazines, the latest gourmet recipe, or they may speak with awareness and assurance of their mythic potential and an instant later mime a line out of Freud announcing their limitations.

Barthelme's technique is to intentionally interrupt the flow of the story, to expand and dissolve meaning by contradictions, retractions, and any number of other means. This shifting from one voice of authority to another, or manipulation or literalization of metaphor or cliché, or creation of open-ended and seemingly nonfixed significations, is noticeably *dislocating* (or disorienting), and indeed this is the first of Barthelme's most striking characteristics. (More accurately, it is his "second"; first, and foremost, he is very funny.) The moment, for example, we locate his figures as characters out of *The Waste Land*, he switches gears, and we are in the world of cartoon, or a fifties love song, or any number of other real or fantasied worlds. These then serve not only as comments in themselves but also as vehicles that reinforce, or open up, or undermine, or contradict, or logically dissolve, the preceding material. Invariably, the mood or, most important, traditional reading, response, and "meaning" are challenged and diverted. Meanings, sensations, and any number of nonverbal responses flow in abundance and refuse to settle anywhere.

Barthelme is an expert in the *shapes* of meaning; he may connect people and objects and use causal logic to structure a situation or dialogue, but it is the shape of meaning, and its infinite possible connections, that he evokes, rather than fixed and final meaning. "Perception," he writes, "[is] like balls of different colors and shapes and sizes, [that] roll around on the green billiard table of consciousness" (*SW*, 129). He rejects centrism of any sort—of character, dialogue, event—and his disjunctures and dislocations function to open up the world of meaning to his reader. His world is hence full of the details of ordinary life, but his juxtapositions are—in traditional terms—curious and even bizarre, as are his admixtures of violence, sentiment, sexuality, and any number of ordinarily disparate and incongruous moods.

Barthelme brings a metaphysical quality to his work as he mixes the extraordinary (from the grotesque to the exotic) with the ordinary and clichéd, but of course he rejects the strict logic of seventeenth-century wit that ties together its evocations of disparate experience.

One of his favorite techniques to open up the world of meaning and to enhance the fluidity between the word and what it evokes is his use of wildly anomalous or unexpected words in the midst of hackneyed phrases: "You can take your love and shove it up your heart." Or, "The young people today are doing a bloody great lot of *cooking together before marriage* . . . shamelessly, night after night" (*GP*, 41). He creates purposefully vague symbols and metaphors and then extends them in the traditional form of poetic conceit: "[the book] was hard to read, dry, breadlike pages that turned, and then fell, like a car burned by rioters and resting, wrong side up, at the edge of the picture plane with its tires smoking" (*SW*, 105). The scheme, he writes elsewhere, "oozed out over the floor of the living room into the dining room.

Then it ran into the kitchen, bedroom and hall. Plant life from the bursting nature outside came to regard the plan. A green finger of plant life lay down on top of the plan" (*SW*, 152).

Barthelme loves oxymorons and negative lists:

Rose Marie made a list of all the people who had not written her a letter that morning:

> George Lewis
> Peter Elkin
> Joan Elkin
> Howard Toff
> . . . .
> *and many others*

and he even includes the name of one of his own fictional characters, "Sue [Ann] Brownly" (from "Me and Miss Mandible") (*CBDC*, 45).

He uses well-known literary or pop allusions, or statistics, or scientific jargon (or jargon from dozens of sources) either to boldly interrupt his preceding material, or to only slightly color it or widen it with the most subtle contrasts in mood or style. Snow White, very much transformed into the sixties woman in need of liberation, is addressed: "The *horsewife*! the very base-bone of the American plethora! . . . Without whom the entire structure of civilian life would crumble! . . . Were it not for her enormous purchasing power and the heedless gaiety with which it is exercised, we would still be going around dressed in skins probably, with no big-ticket items to fill the empty voids, in our homes and in our hearts. *The horsewife*! Nut and numen of our intersubjectivity!" (*SW*, 99).

He writes sermons, trivializes, breaks up syntax, changes parts of speech, creates new words and spellings, and puns (at times shamelessly): "*Jean-Paul Sartre is a Fartre*" (*SW*, 66). In an absolutely wacky trial scene in *Snow White*, a policeman is called to testify: "'*Shield 333 to the stand!*' 'Come along, fellow, come along. Do you swear to tell the truth, or some of it, or most of it, so long as we both may live?' 'I do.' 'Now then, Shield 333, you are Shield 333?' 'I are.' . . . 'And your mission?' 'Prevention of enmanglement of school-children by galloping pantechnicons.'

'And the weather?' 'There was you might say a mizzle' " (SW, 162–63).

Barthelme frequently juxtaposes the serious and the trivial. A newly divorced man is asked—by "friends"—about his marriage: "whether she wept when you told her, whether you wept when she told you, whether she had a lover or did not have a lover, . . . whether you kept the television, . . . the disposition of the balance of the furnishings including tableware, linen, light bulbs . . . the baby if there was a baby, what food . . ." (CBDC, 59).

He retracts what he has just said, or interrupts his story to interpret or philosophize, or even ask the reader how he is enjoying himself. He juxtaposes two or three, or even more, literary styles within a paragraph, and he piles irony upon already endless irony until any point of reference is entirely lost. He clothes the forms of meaning (or interrupts familiar cadences) with metaphors that resist logical extension. "[My father] knew some things that other men do not know. He heard the swans singing just before death, and the bees barking in the night" (SW, 28). He literalizes metaphor: " 'Now get up and go back out to the smokeroom. You're supposed to be curing a ham.' 'The ham died,' she said" (CBDC, 19).

Barthelme manipulates the traditional forms of typography and even the old-fashioned form of the novel itself, and includes spaces, black boxes, old prints, and engravings (which also have his own Kilroy-was-here kind of trademark) in the text. He is the master parodist of spoken and written language, and he loves long lists of any sort. Snow White runs the gamut of styles from the prose of social science and philosophy to that of comic books, cartoons, and film, from the language of business and technology to that of advertising and hip lingo, from flat, vulgar street talk to inflated political, academic, and even church diction. It parodies any number of authors (and even song writers) and alternates in gradations of tone from mock epic to mock fairy tale.

The question arises as to what function, in precise terms, these dislocations and disjunctures have, and how the reader responds to them. Barthelme's people, as we have said, have little insight into the way they incorporate and parrot the vast published and media sources that saturate their society. Most of them are not even mildly aware of how these define both their vision of the world and their very identity. Barthelme's continuous manipulations of language function *simultaneously* to alert *us* (rather than change the speakers) to the stilted, unfeeling, and inauthentic quality of their programmed and fragmented language, and at the same time to open wide the vast resources of language and the way fresh meanings—often even vague and approximate ones—can attach to words. When in *Snow White*, for example, Jane and all the men learn that their respective lovers have rejected them, they express what should be an emotionally charged experience with the same phrase. We have been left, they all say, "sucking the mop." The reader immediately connects this with "holding the bag" and realizes how clichés (in other circumstances, paraphrases or respected quotations) are in fact his predominant way of connecting with the world. And yet Barthelme's transformation of the cliché "holding the bag" into the more distasteful "sucking" and "mop," while still a cliché (since everyone in the novel uses it), is surely more graphic, inventive, and "authentic" than the cleaner paper bag sense evoked in the original (literalized) metaphor (whose "holding" also evokes a more passive role than "sucking").

Barthelme exaggerates the mass anesthetization of contemporary life through his bombardment of similarly inventive phrases, as well as juxtapositions, manipulations, and plays on odd, related, and seemingly unrelated materials. His extraordinary ear for the sounds of language and his parodic mastery of its spoken and written forms, elicits from his reader enormous laughter (and insight). As a matter of fact, he teases us into source hunting, and when at last we think we have hit on meaning, he shifts gears, and we are left with a sense of how silly we are, in fact miming his figures in looking for fixed, authoritative explanations. What is wanted, and what the author gives us—with no holds barred—is the delightful play of language between, under, above, and through the spaces around his words. Even his occasional use of gibberish and wonderful verbal and visual slapstick serve a similarly cathartic function in pushing us away from our cerebrations to connections with a new world of language and response, our ultimate reality.

Finally, Barthelme creates a spatial form close to collage or sculpture, where structure becomes more important than content.

(Some of his most recent work, beginning with *The Dead Father* —in a unique "dialogue" form—incorporates techniques of poetry and music to create an even more diffuse and open-ended form.) Fragmentation, multiple points of view, a literature that begins with traditional meaning, which is then undercut or overlaid with additional statement, then mixed or split apart or truncated, and then given metaphoric transformation—all function to create portraits that shift, in traditional terms, between meaning and non-meaning, with mixtures of what would conventionally be called the banal and fantastic, the comic and horrific. Because of the open-ended quality of his language—which always begins with a logical albeit extraordinarily unusual connection before it splits and widens into its several, moving parts—one never feels he "finishes" a Barthelme story, and this is perhaps his next most noteworthy characteristic.

One can already project from these generalizations that Barthelme is very much in the avant-garde—in the so-called post-modern movement. He rejects traditional chronology, plot, character, time, space, grammar, syntax, metaphor, and simile, as well as the traditional distinctions between fact and fiction. What used to organize reality—time, space, and the structure of language—is now often disjointed, and *language*, and the difficulties in "using" it, becomes the very subject of his art. Most obvious is its antiteleological function—its refusal to be an orderly reflection of, and comment upon, a stable, external world.

Barthelme's collages lack, as do all collages, a fixed perspective and meaning. His people—patchworks of and variations upon the world of literature, history, art, and the media—are shifting surfaces of any and all of the meanings we can bring to them as they strike a chord (literary and otherwise) in us. Since Barthelme reflects in a sense the phenomenological world continuously unfolding, and the ways language reflects that free and open-ended world, it is *reactions*, rather than "meaning," that he elicits, and these shift continuously. As in sculpture or collage, "meaning" lies in our perception of the varied relationships of the medium to space and time, and if it is his extraordinary arrangements of words that create the collages, it is their interplay with the variety of our verbal and nonverbal responses that organizes our relationship to time and space, the flux of experience. Yet once we articulate our response, that flux has been touched (organized and hence changed)—but only for the moment. One always has the sense in "interpreting" Barthelme, that our words, like his characters' words, like reality, are only temporarily stayed. In an instant, they separate and return to the larger flux.

This is, of course, not to say that his books lack meaning, but they do lack, as Merleau-Ponty says of life, a meaning "we can hold on to." One could well substitute "words" for "life" in the following: "It is futile to wonder what life means or if we perceive a world. Just that the world is what we perceive. We must laugh in the face of the provisional. Not that life has no meaning but meaning is none we can hold on to."[2]

II *Philosophical Implications*

At this point one may well speculate upon how Barthelme's work, with its emphasis on language, reflects contemporary thought. It is, I think, as if Barthelme had pushed the existential position to its furthest limits. If man's dilemma is that there is no inherent value in the universe, and he must hence embrace a "role" and be true to it to be authentic—whether that role is through the media, like television or film, or the respectable, authorized texts, say of philosophy—then one is virtually fated to becoming a nonbeing, an abstraction of the sort Barthelme parodies. It is as if Barthelme had observed that such a commitment to *any* role brings with it a ready-made script, and hence, built-in mechanization. To be a good parent is to '*be*' Dr. Spock's *Baby and Child Care*. To be a good lover is to master the variety of authoritative (and illustrated) manuals. "Identity" is really just a costume, an act, a role, a "bit."

John Barth, in an early novel *The End of the Road*, pokes great fun at a character Joe Morgan, who is absolutely faithful to his Sartrian position. He mouths "authenticity" with religious fervor and is totally logical in everything he does and says; but he is totally inhuman in ignoring the emotional life, and ultimately he contributes to his wife's literal though absolutely ridiculous death. Roles, then, and integrity and good faith, all involve fixed patterns of response, which Barthelme indicts for their strangulalation of one's vitality and, in a word, one's pleasure in living, his ultimate freedom. But where did the existentialists go astray?

It's not that they were wrong in having us "act," in order to define ourselves. Nor were the Freudians wrong in urging acknowledgment of the unconscious side of self. What is wrong is the limited information and language inherent in *any* system of thought. "Fragments are the only forms I trust," says one of Barthelme's figures, and this may refer not only to the verbal collage Barthelme so often writes, but also to the fragmented authority of all scientific, psychological, philosophical, etc., systems. Any explanations are limited, rather than totalizing. Parts of them may be right, or they may be right under certain circumstances. Any single explanation can be no more fixed and absolute than reality itself. (Postscript: Is the intention behind "Existence precedes essence" any the less absolute and unattached to a known reality than the intention behind "God exists"?)

The language that conveys these explanations also prohibits one from embracing two, three, or even more, alternative and perhaps contradictory styles. We accept a single, or perhaps double, script, and once again become buried within it. We observe the words, what Barthelme calls the "sludge," and cherish its blanketing effect, as if it had some ultimate protective function. We substitute the expertise of texts and the forms of language for divine authority.

III   *The Paradox of Language*

The obvious alternative to accepting these patterns, these wholesale definitions of self, is to use language freshly, to enjoy it as the only free act one has in the universe, truly our only barter against annihilation. Yet the same paradox that underlies existentialism underlies the use of language. Just as there are no absolutes except death and one must live with certain personal values *as though* they were absolute, so too one must use language to articulate the ultimate flux both inside and outside, *as though* one could define his universe and himself.

It is here that we get to the most interesting part of Barthelme's work, and most of his writing deals with just this—the word as an emblem of man in the universe, the way we separate ourselves from the universe in words, how we strive to define what we all think is that world out there, and ultimately how very feeble (though often joyously so) we are in our efforts to do so. Although the word is not our creation, it is our means of realizing consciousness (as the modern Cartesian might say: "I speak, therefore I am"), but our consciousness is always pluralistic. Words, like roles, both constrict and construct our lives.

The problem is this: the word—as word—inherently means nothing. In *The End of the Road* again, Barth has a great deal of fun showing how all meanings are arbitrary and yet necessarily revered as though they were absolute: "... the symbol x can represent anything we want it to represent, as long as it always represents the same thing in a given equation. But *horse* is just a symbol too. ... I mean, if you and I agreed that just between ourselves the word *horse* would mean *grammar book*, then we could say 'Open your horse to Page Twenty,' or 'Did you bring your horse to class with you today?' ... The significances of words are arbitrary conventions."[3]

Barthelme is also aware that despite their limitations, words are our single connection with the universe, our single way of communicating and touching the world. His very difficult task (and his great achievement)—and this is at the heart of all his dislocations—is to use language in fresh ways and to ultimately create new combinations and wring fresh meanings out of them. Thus, while many of his stories deal with the problems inherent in using language (and his subjects include the sterile function of irony and the frequent failure of writing), some consist of totally unique combinations of words, or juxtapositions of seemingly unrelated materials within totally new spatial patterns. By the time he gets to *Great Days* (1979), he modulates language as musical phrase, and connections are established not so much through linguistic and thematic exposition, variation, and explosion, as through more subtle tones and harmonies, through only the most delicate recurrences of, say, concrete image, color, or gesture, through the evocation of mood at the base of most utterance. At this point, Barthelme is also concerned with more basic issues, like time and mortality. In his most recent work, he appears to have created more human figures than earlier, people with whom one even feels a certain personal kinship.

Thus, we tie together the two main strands of Barthelme's work—those pieces that deal with people and experience, and the works about language. Words, as we have been discussing them, are really just as problematic as roles, in the dilemmas they raise. Just as most efforts to define the self promise failure—because the script imprisons and anesthetizes—so, too, the most imaginative efforts to use words often end in failure (Barthelme's favorite word to describe the artist), since words too have a built-in "script" or meaning and are limited pretty much by their dictionary meaning. Words are, in effect, very much like actors who, under certain circumstances and with proper costuming or context, or the right audience, take on signification. But sometimes they fall flat and really don't work at all. Indeed, even in our most successful efforts to express *feeling* in words, "something is lost in the translation." Words replace emotions and, in a sense, we're left mixing apples and oranges.

Yet, as Barthelme illustrates in "Sentence" and "Bone Bubbles," words *are* our only link with the universe which, at moments—like all our other systems of decoding, from science to philosophy —can bind and "signify"; but they do so only temporarily and arbitrarily. Nothing is "final" or "true." Barthelme can hence write about language both the following: "Strings of language extend in every direction to bind the world into a rushing, ribald whole" (*UPUA*, 11); and, "Why does language subvert me? . . . whenever it gets a chance? What does language have against me? . . . What do 'years' have against me?" (*UPUA*, 139).

In "Nothing: A Preliminary Account" Barthelme writes an elegant and rhapsodic, funny and serious essay on "Nothing." With the punctuating refrain "hurry on," he tries to define his term—in an unending list of negatives—and he ends (or at least "stops") by negating his subject and rather passionately embracing life:

Our list can in principle never be completed, even if we summon friends or armies to help out (nothing is not an army nor is it an army's history, weapons, morale, doctrines, victories, or defeats—there, that's done). And even if we were able, with much labor, to exhaust the possibilities, get it all *inscribed*, name everything nothing is not, down to the last rogue atom, the one that rolled behind the door, and had thoughtfully included ourselves, the makers of the list, on the list—the list itself would remain. Who's got a match?

. . . But if we cannot finish, we can at least begin. . . . Nothing is what keeps us waiting (forever). And it's not *Charlie Is My Darling*, nor would it be Mary if I had a darling so named. . . . What a wonderful list! How joyous the notion that, try as we may, we cannot do other than fail and fail absolutely and that the task will remain always before us, like a meaning for our lives. Hurry. Quickly. Nothing is not a nail. (*GP*, 164)

Barthelme is wonderfully interesting and funny: more important, he is remarkably liberating. Our pleasure comes not in figuring out how his people use words, or the sources of his parody, but rather we revel in his dazzling and endlessly provocative verbal textures. He may be aware that language constricts and that the mind tends to operate in structures, but he is unique in creating for us through his wonderful elegance the great and abundant world. He demands a sophisticated reader, for the better read and more sensitive to language and style one is, the more fun he will have, since Barthelme seems to have read everything. Unlike Eliot, however, whose literariness was didactic and in many ways, an end in itself—because it pointed back to a time of former value—Barthelme's vast information is but his means of stimulating us to a recognition of the limitations as well as the meanings of past formulations. Ultimately, Barthelme wishes us to break free and take pleasure in the world his thick textures evoke.

IV *Comedy*

In certain ways this is a unique brand of comedy; in others, finally, it is not. As we have said, Barthelme seduces us to pick up on his vast expertise and begin source hunting. But he inevitably sidetracks us to the textures of language so that we act out—only up to a point—exactly what he is parodying, the foolish rituals of fact finding and authority worship. Yet, despite all our protestations about his uniqueness, art is art, and Barthelme's work is not entirely removed from traditional comedy.

If exaggeration lies at the heart of this form, Barthelme's continuous verbal dislocations function not only to transmit his extraordinary vision of the contemporary world but also to separate us from his characters. They stop us from obsessive intellectualizing, and, as we discussed earlier, in their sheer magnitude they prohibit us from identifying with his figures. One is thus free to (in fact) howl at their ridiculousness.

But Barthelme also has the compassion of the comedic artist, and he makes the world more manageable for his reader—more comfortable and even more comprehensible. His stories may not "finish," and the traditional happy ending may be absent, but they do awaken in us a fresh awareness and delight in the multitudinous textures of language and experience. Finally, then, Barthelme educates, as he lifts us out of whatever monistic grid we identify our lives by and helps us to discover our own freedom.

One final irony: Barthelme's literature may really do what literature has always done (and perhaps Hamlet's actor was wrong when he said it holds the mirror up to nature), for literature has always been selective, and through the writer's organizing process, reality has always been distorted. (Even Zola's manuscript was not photographic.) Barthelme, like all the great writers before him, creates a context for our imaginations to function within. Perhaps the major difference is that his context, like our reality, has simply widened and become open-ended.

CHAPTER 3

Come Back, Dr. Caligari

THE first collection introduces many of Barthelme's themes and landscapes, most prominently the spiritually weary, contemporary world, brainwashed by popular culture and the media ("Viennese Opera Ball"), a society of people looking for "the right words" ("Florence Green") and specific scripts with which to duplicate an identity ("For I'm the Boy," "Big Broadcast," "Hiding Man," "Margins"). The theme of failed marriage recurs ("To London and Rome," "Broadcast," "For I'm the Boy," "Will You Tell Me?" "Piano Player"). Another subject, which Barthelme will pursue, is the problem of using words, because "signs" sometimes "lie" (the remarkable "Me and Miss Mandible"). The artist as subject, in his personal and professional life, is the focus of "Shower of Gold" and "Marie," two of the volume's best stories which treat, in a consummately humane and wildly parodic fashion, the contradiction of "the absurd" in theory and reality.

I "Florence Green Is 81"

"The aim of literature is the creation of a strange object covered with fur which breaks your heart."

Barthelme explodes linearity of language and event, and splices characters, in order to capture the disintegration of value in both the contemporary world and individual consciousness. Love, lentils, children, toilets, and Texaco merge as equal priorities in a world only occasionally and peripherally acknowledged as one of war, loneliness, sexual desire, and professional yearning.

Barthelme, in addition, is concerned with the language that

defines our world and minds, that conglomeration of catchy and hypnotic slang that swallows both serious and fashionable subject matter. As he focuses upon the rhythms that compose the contemporary psyche, his language slides in and out of meaning, like—to borrow two details of the story—Mandrake's piano and Joan Graham's gazpacho. Clichés, inadequately understood abstractions, fragments of anachronistic, woolly dreams of contemporary American life, and eminently quotable tidbits ransacked from the literature of the world, are jumbled together and packaged in easy slogans and matchbook and media rhetoric.

Words and more words: such is the junk and value of our lives. As the narrator-writer puts it, in a startlingly honest statement: "We value each other for our remarks"; "on the strength of this remark," he goes on, "love becomes possible." Nevertheless, if he is going to talk to us, and if we are to understand him, author and reader must make their way through the sludge of verbiage that envelops them and "free associate," "brilliantly, brilliantly, to [be] put . . . into the problem."

The "problem" is this: Florence Green, "a small fat girl" of eighty-one, who has 300 million dollars and blue legs, sits before her dinner guests and complains of a toilet that malfunctions. The narrator, a would-be writer (Baskerville), who aspires toward Florence's continuing patronage, is troubled by her mysterious statement: "*I want to go to some other country*" (our first of many askewed associations with T. S. Eliot). As preoccupied with a sexy girl at the dinner table as with Florence's drop-dead statement, the narrator describes the evening (which includes Florence's falling asleep "untidily") in a rambling assemblage of non sequiturs. In the back of his mind is his growing anxiety that he will not impress this arbiter of contemporary taste and values; interspersed, in addition, are his own self-mocking and somewhat self-aggrandizing comments. About Florence Green, who provides, after all, the title of the story, there are only occasional comments: she is rather ridiculous, spoiled, and possibly senile, the matriarch who supports both war and art (really the narrator's two main concerns). At the same time, she is a wonderfully appealing and somewhat enigmatic woman who, despite her enormous vanity and eccentricities (she has a room filled with a cane collection), has driven men to write poetry for her.

Barthelme's particular brand of box-within-box satire on any number of subjects serves not only to equate the trivial and serious (to reflect how everything has become equally meaningless), but also to equate the very identities and activities of his characters. Ultimately, one has an impossible task "characterizing" anyone—and this is perhaps the point. Both Florence and the narrator, for example, prize "uniqueness" and both fear "boredom." The narrator relates how, many years before, Florence vomited upon seeing the atrocities of Buchenwald (in *Life* magazine). Although she didn't know what "*exterminated*" meant, she raced to a resort for solace. Now her life, devoted (at least tonight) to toilet-repair-inflation and recollections of the good old days with her oil-baron husband, is boring, and she would go away. Although war is mentioned in the same breath as vegetables, its reality fills the story. Can it be that Florence will go away (again), because the atrocities of the contemporary world are overbearing? Or is toilet repair overwhelming? Is she bored with her life and guests? Is she bored with the world situation? Or is she simply looking for some new words to say—because words *are* one's identity? ("On the strength of" our remarks, "love becomes possible.") All Barthelme gives us is this: "She is afraid of boring us. She is trying to establish her uniqueness." At this point, let us remark not only on the impossibility of "characterizing" Florence, but on the extraordinary difficulty of understanding what the simple and frequently used words "bored" and "unique" mean.

About Florence's desire to go away—and her earlier escape to a resort—Barthelme, again, refuses to comment. But traditional readers that we are, we trust the narrator's point of view and share his alternating scorn and respect for her. Florence invites moral interpretation, and to prod us on, Barthelme even plants a line from Husserl in the story that fits our bill: Florence has "not grasped the living reality, the essence." Yet, while this might neatly fit within the well-made story (and alienate us from Florence), Barthelme undercuts its authority at once. Indeed, if we impose any such fixed meaning, it is we who will not have grasped the living reality, which is that there is no such thing as *the* living reality, at least attainable through language.

Let us turn to one of many examples. Although Florence appears to attach equal importance to trivial and tragic concerns, so does the narrator. If this were traditional satire, the narrator, who at points enlists our respect, would stand as a foil against Florence. Instead, after drawing us to his side, he reacts in an equally indiscriminate manner to the reality about him. He recurrently qualifies his own positions to the point of contradiction. Thus, if he is the ironic voice, he is ironic about his own irony. As a result, we lack a consistent foil against which to construct a standard or central focal point. If Florence's evasion of reality for the "unique" *seems* a cop-out, the narrator, in his own statements about "uniqueness" and "boredom," evades characterization, as he wavers erratically between integrity and opportunism.

First, he would be *honest* in his writing (presumably an indictment of war). Yet, comparing himself to a psychiatrist's patient, he admits that he would be *manipulative*, striving "mightily to establish" his "uniqueness." He explains, in addition, that he writes to *amuse* and not bore. He then undercuts this with the conjunction "or" which, in context, neither qualifies nor contradicts, which is its function: "Or for fear of boring you: which?" Finally, he admits, "I adopt this ingratiating tone because I can't help myself." What has happened to the fearless antiwar commentator? He then answers a claim that writing should not be discursive by defining it as "portages through the whirlpool country of the mind" and adds, "Mostly I make remarks."

It is almost impossible to organize this mishmash of confessional material. Is the writer honest? playful? a liar? neurotic? confident? condescending? Is he socially committed? One is also dazed trying to figure out whether the narrator is indeed Baskerville and, in any case, if one can trust him. After all, while he is maintaining his integrity, he is also nervously jogging his memory for impressive comments other people might have made at a dinner party. He even admits, with self-mockery, how he has sold out professionally: he edits an interdisciplinary journal (with his left hand!), "The Journal of Tension Reduction," which pampers the contemporary need for self-help information with "learned disputation[s], letters-to-the-editor, anxiety in rats."

Yet this is really only the beginning of our confusion. If both Florence and the narrator are/are not, for example (in traditional "moral" terms), responsible/irresponsible, in their aspirations toward "uniqueness," Barthelme plays with several other levels of irony, so that by the time we finish the story we haven't the slightest idea what self-confrontation, or evasion, or being "committed" and "having integrity" mean. First, it seems as if the speaker mocks and upholds *both* self-knowledge and self-evasion. He says (possibly of himself): "Oh Baskerville! you silly son of a bitch, how can you become a famous writer without first having worried about your life, is it the *right kind* of life, does it have the right people in it, is it *going well*?" Further, the narrator connects and equates introspection with middle-class chic: in Santa Ana, California, "100,350 citizens nestle together in the Balboa blue Pacific evenings worrying about their lives." What *is* the narrator's point of view? Where has our author, Barthelme, disappeared to?

War, toilets, discursiveness, essence, Fleischmann's gin (the antidote to angst: "I favor the establishment of comfort stations providing free Fleischmann's . . . on every street corner"), psychiatrists, writing, and war: where are we? Barthelme tantalizes us with meaning; his story is indeed a "portage" through the "whirlpool country of the mind." By the time one finishes, he has difficulty pinpointing anything or anyone. The final effect is curiously like a Cubist painting, montage, or mobile. No single surface, in terms of character, event, indeed words or their meaning, is fixed. The "colored doctor" at the dinner table (is he Mandrake the Magician and the pianist on Florence's vacation?), is also the proposed colored doctor for a novel. (Does life create art, or is it the other way around?) The doctor (psychiatrist) is the writer's audience, absorbing the author's "fantastications," while acting out his own. The narrator's search for uniqueness is everyone's search for uniqueness; Florence herself writes poems and is their subject; it becomes increasingly more difficult to separate the dancer from the dance, that is, who, during this party, is author, and who is guest. The narrator gets a "promotion" and a "discharge" from his writing school (his "orders"), and words are surely a major "war" Barthelme writes about. Ultimately, the narrator is Baskerville, the soldier, the doctor, the poet, Florence, the sexy Kathleen (whose name is really Joan Graham), Pamela Hansford Johnson, and Onward Christian. We move full circle, patients and writers alike, all looking—in our compulsive search for and belief in the "right word"—for non-boring experience, for "total otherness." Ironically, however, we avoid our true "uniqueness," the total "otherness" we basically are—which could be ours if we would just recoup the instinctive life or those ideas and words that are truly ours, beneath or between all the packaged words and slogans. Unfortunately we remain, in grand philosophical terms, as well as in linguistic and concrete everyday terms, "all involved in a furious pause, a grand parenthesis."

Finally, then, in "Florence Green," there is no center or final resting point. Everything has been refracted by the narrator's uniquely personal perception of experience, all colored by his conflicting public and private values—this necessarily filtered through the limited and yet necessary forms of language. The final object created is indeed all of the story's seeming contradictions and shapes of meaning (which ultimately never coalesce)—Husserl's living reality, an essence which is a general discursiveness—free associations and portages through the whirlpool of the mind, a truly unique work of art, "a strange object covered with fur."

II *"Will You Tell Me?"*

A number of Barthelme's stories are *tours de force* in linguistic virtuosity, where, although syntax and sentence structure remain traditional, meaning is continuously challenged and widened by juxtapositions of odd, banal, literary, or technical diction; at other points, ordinary language is violated by bizarre and fragmented action. Space and time may be dislocated to reinforce the distortions of traditional language or narrative pattern. Here, in what appears to be a very simply told story, Barthelme outdoes Ionesco and his colorless Mr./Mrs. Smith/Martin people in *The Bald Soprano*. Identities merge; banality and horror are interchangeable; everything is equally meaningful and hence meaningless. Specifically, everyone is everyone else's lover, child, threat, and even nemesis.

III *"The Piano Player"*

Similarly, here is the typically fashionable and bored suburban couple in an exaggeratedly affluent background. Barthelme exposes the silly hollowness, indeed, the almost grotesque and ghostly quality of the contemporary family. Forms of meaning or structure (i.e., marriage) are present, in language as in life, but details and linguistic variations again prevent anything whole or substantial beneath from finalizing.

The identical and shallow inner and outer worlds of the mother, for example, are concretized, as she pleads that her dreary mental and physical condition (like her children's) will improve if only she can have a fancy car to take her to hobnob with intellectual celebrities: "If you gave me a TR–4, I'd put our ugly children in it and drive away. To Wellfleet. . . . I want to talk to Edmund Wilson." Throughout, Barthelme literalizes metaphor (his trademark), as in the frequently quoted: "You're supposed to be curing a ham," followed by "The ham died."

IV *"For I'm the Boy Whose Only Joy is Loving You"*

"We can discuss . . . the meaning but not the feeling."

The elegantly named Bloomsbury, accompanied by the also formally named Whittle and Huber, is returning from the aerodrome; his estranged wife, Martha, has just flown the coop. Conversations among the three men draw a bitter (and wildly funny) picture of empty marriage, sex, and even friendship. Once again, these people can articulate anything; what they lack is feeling: "There's little enough rapport between adults" without "clouding" the "issue" with "sentiment," they say.

The story, filled with sardonic manipulations of familiar literature (from *Hamlet*'s "what manner of man is this!" to *The Waste Land*'s "[Tell me] whether she wept when you told her"), is remarkable in style. Barthelme manipulates, for example, two entirely different literary techniques to portray the common emptiness of human relationships—an elegant Jamesian style in which Whittle and Huber figure, and the more earthy Lawrentian lower-class idiom, in which Bloomsbury recites his sexual encounters with both his wife, Martha (who would rather spend the night with words—Mallarmé's), and his lover, Pelly: "An' what a fine young soft young warm young thing you have there Pelly on yer bicycle seat." (Pelly's husband literally prefers bringing his T.V.

to bed rather than her.) Not only is contemporary language incapable of communicating feeling, but the old standbys, even the language of fairy tale, are equally disfunctional: "Ah Pelly where do you be goin'?"; his Little Red Riding Hood answers, "I" grandmather's." Regardless of linguistic mask, an emptiness fills all the love nests—for Bloomsbury and Martha, Bloomsbury and Pelly—knock offs, in name alone, of Joyce's Molly, Polly, and Bloom.

The story is very funny, beginning with a takeoff on the *Casablanca*-type airport scenario. The only catch is that Bloomsbury's friends are not sure if they have been "required" or "invited" to come along (as a guard against "privacy" and "thus weeping"). Barthelme focuses on their cold formality and bland self-awareness. Bloomsbury says, his "friends . . . were as men not what he wished them to be," and he adds, "it was [also] very possible . . . that he was not what they wished him to be."

He knows, for example, that they care most about his money and that one has even made a grab for his wife. Whittle and Huber speak with only the *form* of caring; any real feeling is missing: "Customarily . . . ribald," they "nevertheless maintained attitudes of rigorous and complete solemnity as were of course appropriate." Barthelme pushes to an absurd degree our role-playing and the way language reflects our blind adherence to scripts. Can Bloomsbury's friends, for example, still be "family friends" if the family has split up? Whittle sounds like a semanticist and lawyer: "The family exists . . . as a legal entity" "whether or not the family *qua* family endures beyond the physical separation of the partners." Such dialogue is often interrupted by a familiar literary line or a song, which thickens Barthelme's irony and adds to the bitterness of his portrait. Bloomsbury can only say of his friends (from *The Student Prince*): "Golden days . . . in the sunshine of our happy youth."

In one of the most memorable sequences, they question him on the "extinguishment" of his "union," the details of the breakup. In efficient list fashion they say: "It would be interesting I think as well as instructive" to know "at what point the situation of living together became untenable, whether she wept when you told her, whether you wept when she told you . . . whether she had a lover or did not . . . , the disposition of the balance of the furnishings including tableware, linens, light bulbs,... the baby if there was [one]... in short we'd like to get the feel of the event." To be "instructed" is to get the "feel"; light bulbs are as important as babies.

Huber, who has never married, says he knows the "exquisite pain" of breakup. (He had an affair with a Red Cross worker named Buck Rogers, after which he literally jumped from the Chrysler Building. Again Barthelme literalizes the metaphor: what could be more appropriate after a sad affair? Here, he goes on to admit—and this dislocates meaning—he got "a wonderful view of the city.") Thus, when he is asked, "How would you know . . . you've never been married," his answer is grim: "I may not know about marriage . . . but I know about words." In a final, sardonic touch, Barthelme adds that he was "giggling" as he described his pain. They all comment on life, rather than feel it; forms of language have substituted for experience.

At the end, Barthelme turns whatever "meaning" we may have grasped thus far against us. Up to this point, we think that Bloomsbury has more "feeling" than his friends. Yet when he is asked, "How does it [the breakup] feel," he replies: "What is *it*?" Reflecting on how one is "trained" to confront the inevitabilities (i.e., divorce), Bloomsbury also says (with playful echoes of Husserl): "It was interesting . . . that after so many years one could still be surprised by a flyaway wife" (shades of TWA). And he continues: "Surprise . . . that's the great thing, it keeps the old tissues tense." His response (his language) is so alienating, it is not surprising that with this dramatic move *away from* feeling—his friends move *toward* it, with a vengeance. Now, when they want to know what he feels, he answers (with playful echoes of Gertrude Stein and Wittgenstein): "The question is not what is the feeling but what is the meaning?" They try bribing him and beat him with a cognac bottle and tire iron, at which point he is transfixed by the memory of a Tuesday Weld movie (whose name, like Rock Hudson's, must surely inspire), after which he felt like "a good man." (Media creates identity and morality.) Bloomsbury has obviously had a more intense emotional experience from the movie than from his divorce. But art is short, and life long, and Bloomsbury is now depressed. The two friends, beating him for meaning, confuse his bloody response with feeling. In fact, what they get is "all sorts of words." Indeed, contrary to the popular saying, one *can* get blood—not feeling—from a stone, a final irony.

V *"The Big Broadcast of 1938"*

"Are you tuned in?"

Orson Welles's 1938 radio drama "The War of the Worlds" was so lifelike that people actually took to the streets to protect themselves from what they believed was an extraterrestrial invasion. Barthelme's "Broadcast" pursues the way life is modeled after art, specifically the media—radio, film, magazine romances—and their various forms of soap opera. If life fails—i.e., a marriage collapses—it is due to the failure of script; should the role model for our "parts" age or die (the actor, a "legend," like a god), a new one must be created. The media alone provide our culture heroes, our scripts—our lives. Life is but an arrangement of words to be enacted.

We meet Bloomsbury again, now divorced from Martha. He has given her the house, in exchange for a radio station where, in addition to playing music (he plays "The Star-Spangled Banner" "hundreds of times a day" because of its "finality"), he presents two kinds of talks. The first, for mysterious and private (i.e., creative) reasons, involves his endless repetition of a single word—like "nevertheless." The second involves commercial advertisements, all directed to Martha; these consist of long recollections of their courtship and marriage. They are apparently spoken to woo her back.

One day a "girl or woman" of "indeterminate age," in a long, bright red linen duster, which she takes off to reveal fifties-style toreador pants and an orange sweater (she is also wearing harlequin glasses), visits the studio. After brief verbal sparring, regarding why he is looking at her ("It's my you might say *métier/ Milieu/Métier*"), we learn that she was the former president of the Conrad Veidt fan club. Now, however, she laments that Veidt's death has caused the death of a "vital part" or her "imagination." Again they argue about words, discuss their attraction to one another (she's been told she resembles the actress Carmen

Lambrosa), and before we know it, the woman is revealed as Martha. (Is she really, or does Bloomsbury simply see all women as Martha?) This Martha does indeed seem wooed by Bloomsbury's ads; she even takes up residence there and sleeps under the piano.

The difficulties of Bloomsbury's marriage are further revealed, and once again the trivial and significant are horrifically and hilariously juxtaposed: their problems in adequately freezing the ice cubes are given as much attention as their sexual incompatability, unwanted child, and marital infidelities. Ordinary metaphors that one might use about a relationship are literalized —i.e., the proverbial mother-in-law "lay like a sword between us," literally, in the bed.

Interestingly, in the present time of their meeting, they still act out the same problems and hurl the same abuses at each other, mostly over sexuality and language. As the story ends, their roles (or what Barthelme has once again tricked us into believing are their "roles") are reversed. She would "come back" to him (is she more taken with artifice, his ads, than reality?), but he has lost interest (because he now realizes she is his wife, and he can only respond sexually to an illusion of the Hollywood type?).

In the light of this story, Barthelme's title *Come Back, Dr. Caligari* is clarified. What the modern world seems to need, Barthelme implies, referring to the movie *The Cabinet of Dr. Caligari*, is a Caligari, a giver of roles, a programmer of people, whether the roles are mundane or monstrous. Hence, all of the scriptwriting, playacting, and absences of "identity" in these stories.

Specifically in this story, it is doubly ironic that Veidt should have been a kind of Caligari to Martha. First, in the movie, the Veidt character is only a psychotic who imagines himself to be controlled by a legendary figure, Caligari. Second, the legendary status Martha has given Veidt as "handsome and sinister" has been created entirely through celluloid, through Veidt's movie roles. Yet, despite this last irony, Barthelme further implies that for one to function in the everyday world, he needs role models; he must mimic an actor who is himself only an interpretation, a reading of someone else's words.

In such a world, with God thus dead, Bloomsbury (whose name we associate with the literary group) seeks out his own mythology by writing, producing, directing, and acting in his ridiculous radio show. With no ready-made word supply or dialogue (for his role as "husband" or "lover"), he tries to create one. He uses his favorite (chic and utterly hackneyed) words to create a reality: "assimilate," "alleviate," "authenticate," "ameliorate." Barthelme explains: he singled out "for special notice . . . some particular word . . . [and repeated it] in a monotonous voice for as much as fifteen minutes." (And Barthelme adds, to fracture meaning: "*Or* a quarter-hour"—which, of course, is fifteen minutes.) But Bloomsbury's intention in repeating these words remains private; although exposed to the audience, "the word would frequently disclose new properties [and] unsuspected qualities." (Is this true for all writers and their words?)

With no ready-made "action" or "pattern" to his life, Bloomsbury chants his ads. (What better means of creating rituals by which to structure a life?) Perhaps if he repeats sufficiently his recollections of his marriage with Martha, he can create a myth to which she will at least subliminally acquiesce (and then be anesthetized to meaning or content).

What is, of course, odd but amusing is that these commercials in mock-romantic, narrative style provide the *form* of life and adventure story, with touches of chivalry, sacrifice, and honor. But their details betray a grotesque reality about their marriage. Although he may act out the Sir Walter Raleigh role, he is in fact an infantalized and castrated male: "I remember the time you went walking without your shoes, . . . I got down on my hands and knees and crawled in front of you. . . . Afterwards you treated me to a raspberry ice, calling for a saucer, which you placed, daintily, at your feet. I still recall . . . the way the raspberry stained my muzzle. . . . We had our evening quarrel. . . . The subject, which had been announced by you at breakfast and posted on the notice board, was *Smallness in the Human Male*."

This reminds us of Pinter's and Beckett's couples (in plays like *A Slight Ache* and *Happy Days*), but where these writers reveal the terror and pain beneath ordinary word games and daily routines, Barthelme omits any distancing between what his figures seem and are. His people are unique in their abstract weirdness; they blindly and totally live out the *structure* of marriage (life) without demanding any substance. Hence their words have the form of meaning (the substance) but are continuously drifting off into distracting particularizations or amplifications that leave behind their essential, conceptual meaning. An argument is an argument as long as it follows that *form* of discourse. At one point they make freezing ice cubes a cause célèbre; and somewhat reminiscent of Beckett in his sucking stones sequence in *Molloy*, Barthelme devotes two pages to their "procuring," "conceiving," "whelping," "genesis," and "parturition" of ice cubes.

Nevertheless, unlike Pinter and Beckett, Barthelme's final effects are always funny. Appropriately, the story ends with the melodrama suitable to Barthelmean soap opera. Bloomsbury doesn't die; he sort of fades away. His great amatory loss is mirrored by the stoppage of his electrical current. The universe is indeed just: "That was the end of this period of Bloomsbury's, as they say, life."

VI   *"The Viennese Opera Ball"*

That this party at the Waldorf-Astoria (a parody of the annual ball in Vienna) should be called the "Viennese Opera Ball" is just as pretentious as the conversations captured there. There is no dancing, as "Ball" might suggest (although both Lester Lanin and Meyer Davis are presumably playing their very classy music), and even the romantic excesses associated with Viennese opera are totally alien to this group. This "Ball" is just an excuse for a large cocktail party, where Barthelme plays theme and variations upon the silly words and mere rhythms of meaning that dance about the room.

Once again he juxtaposes meaningful and trivial chatter, mouthed by the indistinguishably undistinguished, chic and mod, successful and affluent guests. This he does in a fabulous evocation of radically different subjects and styles—of obstetricians, financiers, fashion writers, anthropologists, and emptyheaded models. Paced at top speed, the barrage of wildly disparate subjects assaults the reader—on the techniques and instru-

ments of abortion, the Jumbo tree and its resemblance to the
elegant monkey and bison, the financial status of the American
Machine Company, the "*art* rather than *sheer force*" of penile
stimulation, Edward Stone's buildings in Islamabad, the size of
black bands on both widows' and widowers' calling cards, Abbey
Lincoln's stature as a great jazz singer, and so on. Surgery, travel,
modeling, mortality, forceps, and freedom: these are one's concerns, and they share equal billing in one's life.

The story is not only funny because of Barthelme's measured
juxtapositions, but it is also strangely interesting. In eavesdrop-
ping on these chic, contemporary New Yorkers—walking versions
of *Fortune*, medical journals, anthropology texts, fashion magazines, biographies, and dictionaries—we must admit (if we are to
be honest) we save ourselves time from our own reading. Typical
of so many of his stories, this one is weirdly informative, as at the
same time, it is thoroughly mocking. Barthelme allows us, in
fact, in our greed for information, to identify with his figures—
but only briefly, owing to their exaggeration.

Barthelme once again literalizes and/or plays with metaphor:
"The devil is not as wicked as people believe, and neither is an
Albanian"; "An abortionist [should] empty the uterus before . . .
[the patient] has retinitis"; "the members were ruptured arti-
ficially and a Spanish windlass applied." Finally, if we look closely
at the story, we can discern a few motifs that underlie much of
the sludge—on violence, art, force, and mortality. Serious lines
emerge from time to time—i.e., Baudelaire's "Mortality is the
final evaluator of methods." But if—to Baudelaire—death justifies
life in the existential sense, to Barthelme one can never be sure,
for he pokes fun (but serious fun) at everything we do and
think, including such highfalutin and serious pronouncements.
Barthelme, to be sure, is in it for the fun, and humor always wins
out. Immediately following Baudelaire's line is: "An important
goal is an intact sphincter."

VII   *"Me and Miss Mandible"*

Structuralist, phenomenologist, and deconstructionist critics
alike can have a heyday here where, like a master chessman,
Barthelme plays out the story's key line: "We read signs as prom-

ises" but "some of them are lies." Focusing essentially upon the arbitrariness of *both* "seeming" and "being," he goes beyond the disparity between what appears (in signs) and what is then interpreted (as fact or illusion) in order to show how virtually everything is sometimes true but sometimes false. One's roles and even the tenacity, or veracity, with which they are held, is similarly true/false, real/unreal. The "authority" both behind and presumably inherent within the word, the interpreted act, the relationship, perhaps life itself, is arbitrary. This most playful and imaginative story begins:

Miss Mandible wants to make love to me but she hesitates because I am *officially* a child; I am, *according to the records*, according to the gradebook on her desk, according to the card index in the principal's office, eleven years old. There is a *misconception* here, one that I haven't quite managed to get cleared up yet. I am *in fact* thirty-five, I've been in the Army, I am six feet one, I have hair in the appropriate places, my voice is a baritone, I *know* very well what to do with Miss Mandible if she ever makes up her mind. (Italics mine)

Our man-child, Joseph, has returned to Horace Greely Elementary School to learn exactly where he went wrong. He was brought up to believe in signs and to believe that the promises of life would materialize: "Everything" in life, he says, "is promised . . . most of all the future." Furthermore, "everything is presented as the result of some knowable process." As a result, he followed all the prescriptive steps; his life was not of his choosing but of following the "clues"—"diplomas, membership cards, campaign buttons, a marriage license, insurance forms, discharge papers, tax returns, Certificates of Merit." But no one prepared him for the fact that "arrangements sometimes slip, . . . errors are made, . . . signs are misread."

His life went awry as he misread two very important signs, the first involving his marriage, the second his career. His wife had "beauty, charm, softness, perfume, cookery," and so, he thought, he "had found love." But his wife, who read in him the same signs that now Miss Mandible and the other girls read (i.e., a woman "would never be bored"), in fact left him "for another man." Too, as an insurance claims adjuster, he followed the company's motto: "Here to Help in Time of Need," but when he awarded a settlement of $165,000 to a claimant who without his aid "lacked the self-love to prize her injury so highly," Henry Goodykind (note his name, as sign) fired him. He failed to understand the double message in his company's motto.

Now he sits in the classroom trying to get to the source of life's "conspiracy," trying to learn the rules of life: "All the mysteries [of life] that perplexed me as an adult have their origins here." His main questions are "Who decides?" and how does one apply those rules to life (specifically in his interpersonal relationships which, as Miss Mandible and her texts assume, alone make the rules relevant)?

What he learns, or at least we do, is that the promises we're given don't always come true, and this is a lesson necessarily learned *after* the fact. "It is the pledges that this place makes to me, pledges that cannot be redeemed, that confuse me later." He learns that all signs (and therefore rules) and the interpretation of them (like all roles) are arbitrary. This he calls the "whimsy of authority" and adds: "I confused authority with life itself."

Meaning, in fact, is locked in *outside* of one's experience—synchronically, rather than diachronically. It is only after the fact, chronologically after his role as soldier, husband, and employee, that he has any perspective on his life. Written in the form of a diary, it is only in the present moment that he can say: "Placed backward in space and time, I am beginning to understand how I went wrong, how we all go wrong."

His present then consists of mysterious signs, which will make sense to him only after he lives through them. Reality can be articulated and placed in the construct of words, sentences, and interpretations, only *after* one has "finished" the experience. The logic that organizes words, like one's so-called comprehension of life, is not necessarily appropriate to the experience; it is a part of it, while not particularly descriptive of it. Any role he plays out, furthermore, will be as arbitrary and "meaningful" as any other he might have chosen. Hence, he can make an easy transition from insurance adjuster to student. As he says: "The distinction between children and adults" is "a specious one. . . . There are only individual egos, crazy for love."

Miss Mandible tries to teach the children how to interpret signs or roles—how to apply their "knowledge" to real life situations. From her text "Making the Processes Meaningful," she is advised that children will enjoy fractions if the subject has social significance. One student mockingly illustrates the inappropriateness of such an approach: when Bobby Vanderbilt "wishes to bust a classmate in the mouth he first asks Miss Mandible to lower the blind, saying that the sun hurts his eyes. When she does so, *bip!*"

While the teacher's text—and the applicability of the logic of common fractions to everyday experience—may be laughable, other "literature," even popular magazines, contains messages or signs which, when interpreted, may or may not lie, but which indeed effect life, and this leads to the very funny conclusion, and Barthelme's ingenious treatment of how "art" or the media create life.

To begin, within this sixth-grade class, with its geography, history, and common fractions, there are numerous signs that lie. Each morning as the students face the American flag, our most obvious, misleading sign—the thirty-five-year-old Gulliver who is perceived as eleven (and who speaks as an eleven-year-old might: "Me and Miss Mandible")—pledges allegiance to both Miss Mandible and Sue Ann; as they all lift their geography books to read, he lifts his clandestine journal. The major sign in the classroom, totally ignored by the authorities, is its atmosphere of "aborted sexuality": the class is "a furnace of love, love, love."

Not only is Miss Mandible confused about which sign to respond to in her student/sex-object, but the narrator has his second eye on eleven-year-old Sue Ann, who actually "reminds him of his wife," just as Miss Mandible seems "like a child." Frankie Randolph, another young girl (note how her name as "sign" misleads) is also attracted to him, and Bobby Vanderbilt, hard at work transferring his libido into peculiar oral imitations of racing cars, is making a record called "Sounds of Sebring."

One day Frankie gives our narrator a copy of *Movie-TV Secrets*, after which the jealous Sue Ann thrusts seventeen more magazines at him, with their variety of infinitely suggestive articles on Liz Taylor, Eddie Fisher, and Debbie Reynolds: "Isn't It Time to Stop Kicking Debbie Around?" "Can Liz Fulfill Herself?" among many others.

Joseph has been examining a rather compromising photo with

the caption: "The exclusive photo isn't what it seems." The
"facts," it continues, are otherwise. He, however, is not convinced.
To him, the picture (the sign) and his interpretation, are one:
"I am happy," he says perhaps facetiously, "that the picture is not
really what it seems"; "it seems to be nothing less than divorce
evidence."

An ad juxtaposes less ambiguous signs, although their connection with "reality" is questionable. "Hip Huggers," or "padded
rumps," offer eleven-year-olds "appeal" in their "hips and der-
rière, both." Realizing the unified message here between picture,
caption, and inevitable interpretation, Joseph adds: "If they cannot decipher the language the illustrations leave nothing to the
imagination."

What follows is riotous. Amos Darin (because he is prepubes-
cent? because he is stimulated by the ads? because he wishes to
be Eddie Fisher?) draws a dirty picture in the cloakroom that
is, the narrator says (with the expertise of a thirty-five-year-old),
"sad and inaccurate." "It was offered," he continues, "not as a
sign of something else but as an act of love in itself." (But this
is our narrator's "reading.") This, in turn, is followed by (does
it stimulate?) an acting out in the cloakroom of the Fisher-
Reynolds-Taylor triangle: "Sue Ann Brownly caught Miss Mandible and me in the cloakroom, during recess, and immediately
threw a fit . . . certain now which of us was Debbie, which Eddie, which Liz."

Although he tries to convince the authorities of his responsibility in this act, they continue to read him as an innocent though
wayward child who will simply have to see a doctor. As to Miss
Mandible, and Barthelme literalizes his metaphors shamelessly,
she has been "ruined but fulfilled." Having read him as a thirty-
five-year-old healthy male, her "promise had been kept." She indeed now knows "that everything she has been told about life"
is "true." At the same time, she "will be charged with contribut-
ing to the delinquency of a minor." At the end, preparing to de-
part, our narrator receives a gift from Bobby Vanderbilt, the re-
cording *Sounds of Sebring*—perhaps to help him in what Bobby
still reads as his eleven-year-old peer's confusion amid the mysteries of sex.

VIII   *"Marie, Marie, Hold On Tight"*

Because the pleasure of reading Barthelme lies so much in his wit, one is self-conscious in merely focusing on his "situations." This is particularly true here, where Barthelme mixes a matter of philosophical speculation with an everyday New York happening, and the two transform into an outlandishly comic situation.

The story is this: Pickets, "pursuing their right to demonstrate peaceably under the Constitution," are marching and distributing flyers in front of a church (St. John the Precursor!) and Rockefeller Center. They are met with a few sympathizers and hecklers, and even some bullies who beat them up. What is absolutely hilarious is their cause—or at least the concrete form their cause or "revolt" takes. Barthelme literalizes their rebellion against the inequities of the human condition and the existential plight—in a picket line.

Their placards read: "MAN DIES! / THE BODY IS DISGUST! / COGITO ERGO NOTHING! / ABANDON LOVE!" Their flyers reflect their dissatisfaction and rally to action: *"Why does it have to be that way?"* "What Is To Be Done?" contains, in fact, a "program for the reification of the human condition from the ground up." All of this, by the way, is being televised and "written up" for the "important" magazines.

Barthelme is equally funny as he captures the mentality of the bystanders (i.e., haven't you ever heard of Kierkegaard? some ask). Others, the "innocents"—"possibly from the FBI"—cross the picket line and enter the church. Most of the tourists milling around Rockefeller Plaza, however, are indifferent: "It's a paradigmatic situation . . . exemplifying the distance between the potential knowers holding a commonsense view of the world and what is to be known, which escapes them as they pursue their mundane existences."

Now one may laugh at what seems to be Barthelme's parody of contemporary philosophical dilemmas, but if this sort of subject is not worthy of lofty language and concern, what is? What Barthelme is illustrating is that while content (man's condition) is of utmost significance (like "the absurd" in "Shower of

Gold"), *any* form its expression takes is inadequate, or inaccurate—indeed ridiculous (although Barthelme is good-humored, rather than mocking toward these people).

Levels of comedy expand through incongruity of situation and language and through excessive details; these undercut potentially dramatic statements that otherwise might advance the plot (indeed a *reflection* of our absurdity). When the bullies arrive, for example, "dressed in hood jackets . . . [and] tight pants"—and here Barthelme's psychologizing distracts us from our usual associations with delinquents—"they were very obviously . . . from bad environments and broken homes where they had received no love."

If, up to this point, Barthelme has been playful with the demonstrators and nondemonstrators, he shifts gears and concludes on a more serious note. One of the picketers has been physically assaulted; nonetheless, with his head bandaged, he manages to get to the "Playmor Lanes" to deliver his lecture: "What Is To Be Done?" The story concludes: "With good diction and enunciation and in a strong voice" he "was very eloquent." "And eloquence . . . is really all any of us can hope for." If ripeness or readiness was all, at another time in man's history, now—in a bowling alley, pulpit, or just about anywhere—good style is all.

The title of the story (evoking the absence of belief and love in *The Waste Land*) is significant. The speaker has an obviously important and guarded relationship with someone named "Marie." She, it would appear, has painted the placards, which are now fading in the rain, and she remains at home watching this on television. Now, as he passes a restaurant, he is reminded of something she said when at Bloomingdale's they bought her "cerise" bathing suit (the color of *The Waste Land*'s hyacinths). (Is he recalling "And I was frightened," the line that precedes "Marie, Marie, hold on tight"?) Questions of this sort, like his relationship with her, remain enigmatic, although he (and presumably she) are picketing on the "chimera of love." What Barthelme really is doing here, typical of many of his best stories like "The Balloon" and "Indian Uprising," is allowing his narrator to verbally focus on one thing—picketing, the human condition—while really concentrating on something else, i.e., Marie.

What we experience in the story (a series of boxes within other boxes) is the difficulty of pinpointing meaning in the narrator, as he tells a story about the dilemma of discerning meaning in life. Nevertheless, it is both a very funny and serious story. As Barthelme writes: "Eloquence . . . is really all any of us can hope for."

IX *"Up, Aloft in the Air"*

Very much like "Will You Tell Me?" "Up, Aloft" is another example of Barthelme's technical virtuosity. It abounds in the mockery of cliché, the burlesque of traditional technique, and the literalization of metaphor. Plot is disarrayed; sentences flow with the form of meaning, but non sequiturs intrude upon otherwise potentially logical statements. What we have often is the *form* of meaning, suspended without logical content, or *content* that lacks clear-cut context.

Divided into four sections, the story would seem to be a picaresque adventure—as Flight 309 is forced to land in Cleveland, Akron, Toledo, and Cincinnati, and a would-be macho hero, named Buck (actually, one of Prufrock's descendants) encounters and is himself an example of the lust, infidelity, indifference, and general death-in-life quality in every decadent city he visits. The trivial and tragic are juxtaposed as Buck walks the streets of Akron, equally impressed with suicidal lovers and the shape of skyscrapers, his sweet tooth, the bakery salesgirl, and the sanitation men who clean up the suicides' blood. Note how the word "green" ties all together: "From the top of the Zimmer Building . . . a group of Akron lovers consummated a four-handed suicide leap. . . . *The air!* Buck thought as he watched the tiny figures falling, *this is certainly an air-minded country, America! But I must make myself useful.* He entered a bunshop and purchased a sweet green bun, and dallied with the sweet green girl there, calling her 'poppet' and 'funicular.' Then out into the street again to lean against the warm green façade of the Zimmer Building and watch the workmen scrubbing the crimson sidewalk."

Striking are Barthelme's creations of unusual and expanded metaphors—i.e., "And the great horse of evening trod over the immense scene once and for all"; "Hookers of grog thickened on the table placed there for that purpose." Even the following has its own logic if we literalize "ill-designed": "The citizens of Akron, after their hours at the plant, wrapped themselves in ill-designed love triangles which never contained less than four persons of varying degrees of birth, high, and low and mediocre." Some of Barthelme's most frequently quoted metaphors are found here: "Bravery was everywhere, but not here tonight, for the gods were whistling up their mandarin sleeves in the yellow realms where such matters are decided, for good or ill"; "[Buck] took the hand offered him with its enormous sapphires glowing like a garage."

Barthelme literalizes a wild (green) salad mix(ture) with his "mix" of people, as he simultaneously plays on "grass" and "blanched": at a party where people are dancing, "sensuously, they covered the ground. And then two ruly police gentlemen entered the room, with the guests blanching, and lettuce and romaine and radishes too flying for the exits, which were choked with grass."

He incorporates the cornball language of melodrama to set up content (the structure of meaning) without context. In the midst of some silly instructions on how to deal with "orange and blue flames" in a 707 plane, we read: "And now, Nancy. He held out his arms. She came to him. / 'Yes.' / 'Aren't we?' / 'Yes.' / 'It doesn't matter.' / 'Not to you. But to me. . . .'" One has little idea what they are talking about.

The story is filled with puns: "Former slumwife and former slumspouse alike," enraged with their "progressive" new housing units in Akron, would call the day it all came to pass "Ruesday." Barthelme moves quickly from one literary style or form to another. There is the silly drama involving the local poet, Constantine Cavity who, in his drugstore, holds meetings of the Toledo Medical Society. (The action is continuously disorienting, for we move from the poet to the drugstore, with its "cadenzas of documents," to a long list of doctors present, including Dr. Caligari, Dr. Scholl, and Dr. Il y a, to the condemnation of the poet: "It was claimed that Cavity had dispensed . . . but who can quarrel with Love Root, rightly used? It has saved many a lip.") In another funny sequence—this time, slapstick—Buck goes into the wrong hotel room and finds a beautiful girl in bed and makes a date with her for the next day.

In the midst of all of this are serious undertones, regarding the immorality of apathy. Near the end is an interesting line, reminiscent of Prufrock's "I grow old": "I grow less, rather than more, intimately involved with human beings as I move through world life."

X *"Margins"*

Back in the world of pickets, we meet the black Carl (Carl Maria von Weber), the cultured man whose life, in part spent in jail, is advertised on his sandwich boards, and the white Edward, who tells him that the proper "presentation" on the boards—i.e., the size of the loops in the "g" and "y"—will or will not get him a job, even that of U.S. Vice-President. An implied satire on the possibility of openness between the races, the story really deals with how meaning is divorced from words. "*What* is your inner reality?" Edward repeatedly asks Carl, who replies, "It's mine."

XI *"The Joker's Greatest Triumph"*

This is whimsical in its focus on the comic-strip characters fighting crime in our affluent, consumer society. Everyone has two Batmobiles in his Bat-cave. Although the "tale" involves an encounter with the Joker (whom Bruce analyzes by paraphrasing Mark Schorer's biography of Sinclair Lewis), it focuses on the relationship of Bruce Wayne, Batman, and his friend (lover?) Frederic Brown. (Robin, now at Andover, is having trouble with his French.) Its humor derives both from its quasi-humanization of these cardboard characters in a superchic society, and from its juxtapositions of the ridiculous or fantastic and the banal: "The Batmobile sped down the dark streets of Gotham City toward Gotham Airport"; "I usually prefer Kents . . . but Viceroys are tasty too."

XII *"To London and Rome"*

In this visually and typographically interesting story, Barthelme places the "narrative" on the right side of the page and a gloss on the left. "To London . . ." is a satire on contemporary marriage, about people who accumulate things to assure themselves they are alive.

Their purchases, starting with a Necchi sewing machine and including a mistress, a big house, a piano, a Rolls Royce, a race horse, and finally a hospital that treats horses and Viscount jets, is an exercise in pataphysics. The story, in addition, is filled with "pauses" in the gloss which, unlike Pinter's famous pauses (which are always a mask for terror beneath), emphasize the empty silence of the typically respectable, affluent couple, and they, the pauses, are really the subject of the story. The horror we feel in reading this comes from our locating meaning *only* in the lines and pauses, in the absence of anything beneath.

XIII   *"A Shower of Gold"*

Although this story brings back many of the weirdly abstract people of the collection, it is Barthelme's jubilant affirmation of life's possibilities, contradictions, and indefinability. Peterson, a "romantic" sculptor, goes on a television program "Who Am I?" to earn some much-needed money. The program, designed "to discover what people *really are*," is based on each contestant's personal testimony to life's absurdity. But Peterson revolts. Although he accepts the absurd condition, he realizes the contradiction of terms in articulating and embracing it. His final statement, with its echoes of Hamlet and Perseus, lacks Barthelme's typical irony and is unusually lyrical:

Don't be reconciled. Turn off your television sets . . . indulge in a mindless optimism. Visit girls at dusk. Play the guitar. How can you be alienated without first having been connected? Think back and remember how it was. . . . My mother was a royal virgin . . . and my father a shower of gold. My childhood was pastoral and energetic and rich in experiences which developed my character. As a young man I was noble in reason, infinite in faculty, in form express and admirable, and in apprehension. . . .

"Turn off your television sets" and close your texts—is this Barthelme speaking and the underlying message of the story? We live in what Joyce called a "hyper-educated" age, where, today, existential jargon is not only part of everyone's vocabulary, but it is our very identity. Not only are we walking texts of Pascal, Heidegger, Sartre, and the others, but we are the living products of T.V. lingo. Television has, after all, become the contemporary art that popularizes manners and morality, that establishes our ethical and spiritual consciousness.

Barthelme is caustic, as he belittles the cold indifference of the T.V. employee who says to Peterson: "Mr. Peterson, are you absurd? . . . do you encounter your own existence as gratuitous? Do you feel *de trop*? Is there nausea?" The catchwords of modern philosophy follow, as she continues, abstractly: "People today, we feel, are hidden away from themselves, alienated, desperate, living in anguish, despair and bad faith." She could be speaking for mouthwash or corn pads: "Man stands alone in a featureless, anonymous landscape, in fear and trembling and sickness unto death. God is dead. Nothing everywhere. Dread. Estrangement. Finitude." Lest she forget her Ivory soap-slogan mentality, she continues: "We're interested in basics"; and she adds: "*You* may not be interested in absurdity . . . but absurdity is interested in *you*" (echoing patriotic Uncle Sam posters and reversing JFK's "Ask not what your country can do for you . . .").

Peterson goes to his art dealer, who can't sell his work because of the weather. (It is the season for buying boats, not art.) He mouths sympathy with the artist's having to sell himself to television, but he babbles more Pascal and Sartre. You are estranged, he says, "from those possibilities for authentic selfhood that inhere in the present century." To cater to the public taste, he urges, Peterson should saw his sculptures in half: "two little ones would move much, much faster."

Back in his loft Peterson thinks of the President, who has encouraged the arts, and he completes a new sculpture. Suddenly a wildly absurd event *literally* occurs. The President himself runs in and cracks a sledge hammer on the new sculpture, breaking it into several small pieces. As Peterson next tells his barber-confidant about this, the barber, another lay analyst and philosopher (like everyone these days) and the author of four books, all titled *The Decision to Be* (or not to be?), diagnoses Peterson, now in Martin Buber's "I-Thou" terms, cites Pascal and others, and tells Peterson to get out of his solipsism and be more

like the President. Yet, like the dealer, he too scorns the television show as a sellout, totally unaware of how much like it
he is: "It [and he] smells of the library."

Two other wildly absurd events then occur, absurd again in
the palpable and practical (literal), not theoretical, sense—the
only "absurd" one can really fathom and articulate. A piano
player, who is a living example of a seventeenth-century engrav-
ing, arrives (with switchblades) to play a cat piano (made from
real cats) and parrot more "pour-soi" philosophy. Three girls
from California also barge in to freeload in his loft (since by
definition the artist is automatically into the free life), and although they are waiting for their "connection," they too spout
Pascal.

Peterson finally goes on the television program, where the em-
cee resembles the President, and the contestants are attached to
polygraphs to test the "validity" of their answers. Following their
displays of "bad faith" (scientifically measured), Peterson admits: "The world is absurd . . . I affirm the absurdity." Yet, he
continues, "On the other hand, absurdity is itself absurd," and recites the lengthy statement quoted above. Dwelling on the irra-
tional and pursuing through logical discourse the illogical is,
of course, ridiculous. One is rather obliged to "indulge in a *mindless* optimism [italics mine]." Most importantly, "absurdity is absurd," because ultimately it affirms the meaninglessness of life.
Peterson's answer to all of this is that one must "play."

Attacking all the living-dead in this volume, Barthelme
writes: "How can you be alienated without first having been
connected? Think back and remember how it was. . . ." In-
dicting our "socialization," education, and brainwashing by texts
and the media, Peterson affirms the human potential for great-
ness: "My mother was a royal virgin. . . ." Evoking the great
classical past, he, in a sense, is not lying as he tells of the time
man was connected to a beautiful or humanistic universe, which
he truly thought he could comprehend, a time when one's childhood could be rich, when one might grow up to be noble.

Although Peterson is aware that the world has changed, a potential for nobility still remains. Peterson bespeaks a passion for
other pleasures still very much alive in today's world—generosity,

creativity, integrity, and his own brand of optimism. Lest one forget the conclusion of "Marie," "eloquence" is all.

As much as one might like to end the discussion here, once again nothing ever "finishes" in Barthelme, and we are reminded that words (we are discussing "eloquence," after all)—any words —never truly reflect the texture of reality and one's experience: "Peterson went on and on and although he was, in a sense lying, in a sense he was not." Indeed, one cannot verbalize "mindless optimism," just as one cannot verbalize the absurd. In fact, not only may what one *feels*, in both cases, be similar, but once translated into words, both (emotional) experiences become transformed.

Furthermore, if one tries to utter the unutterable (i.e., Peterson's "eloquence"), his words may connect with associations—i.e., a mythology—that are totally anachronistic to his everyday world. Peterson's words move us because they are (in part) Hamlet's—not even Shakespeare's or Barthelme's, and they evoke a sensibility that is totally divorced from our (from *Peterson's*) contemporary world. We have our Barthelmean boxes-within-boxes once again.

Finally, the story is not only about the artist who must "play" and strive for eloquence. It is also about the urgent need we all have for authority—whether in our barber or President, our media or history and literature of the past, or our own artistic creations. It is about our passionate need for meaning—for some control over the incomprehensibility of life—and how ultimately any answer, even that of the greatest literary artist, must be shaped in sounds, and thus be removed from the very impulse that motivated it, like one's "sense" of the absurd or "mindless optimism."

A final point: if, as Barthelme illustrated in "Me and Miss Mandible," signs do sometimes lie, this extends beyond words to the richest sign of all—life itself. Words are but a microcosm of an infinitely suggestive and fluid reality. Beneath all its humor and levels of irony, "Shower of Gold" is both a proud and jubilant affirmation of artistic ambition, as at the same time it conveys the humility of the individual in the face of an endlessly provocative and irreducible reality.

CHAPTER 4

Snow White

Snow White: "I am in the wrong time. There is something wrong with all those people standing there, gaping and gawking. And with all those who did not come and at least *try* to . . . fill the role. And with the very world itself, for not being able to supply a prince. For not being able to at least be civilized enough to supply the correct ending to the story" (131–32); "It must be laid, I suppose, to a failure of the imagination" (59).

The Men: "Before we found Snow White wandering in the forest we lived lives stuffed with equanimity. There was equanimity for all. . . . Snow White has added a dimension of confusion and misery to our lives" (87–88).

BARTHELME'S *Snow White* alters virtually every detail of both Grimm's and Walt Disney's versions, especially the promise embraced by generations of children that despite all odds, one can be a hero or heroine (the beautiful, innocent girl, or the rescuing, handsome, and noble prince) and live happily forever after. Barthelme tells the contemporary Snow White story, but his heroine is never rescued by anyone. (Nor, perhaps, would Barthelme want her to be.) Her only success—if one can call it that—is her attempt to break out of the unfortunate role into which she has been born and to create her own identity.

Barthelme's heroine is the young woman of the early sixties; she has to contend with what society, her teachers, the media— and all the standard books (especially fairy tales)—have dictated as "feminine." In addition, she has to take a stand in relationship to the highly vocal Women's Liberation movement, now afoot. Snow White really belongs to neither group, for sisterhood —either of the sorority or Steinem sort—is not her bag.

Educated at Beaver College, she reads *Dissent* and Teilhard de Chardin, wears heavy blue, quilted, People's Volunteer trousers, and black vinyl pajamas. She is a gourmet cook (specializing in meringue with cannabis, and calamaretti), indulges in porno pastry and screwdrivers, and has sex regularly (with "calculated paroxysms") in and out of the shower with the seven men for whom she both cooks and cleans. (She also sees a psychiatrist who calls her "a screaming bore.") If Snow White's "style" seems a bit excessive (*à la* Big Sur), the men in her life are also stereotypes of sorts (and Barthelme always makes the "sort" extraordinary). They are similarly rich and neurotic (they literally dream the same dream); they were all born in National Parks, and they now work as window washers (guzzling beer) and also vat stirrers at their Chinese baby food factory. They lack almost any individuality, and as we shall see, they are buried in their roles as seven "men."

Snow White, then, is the product of her world and time. But like anyone who either takes on or is saddled with a well-articulated script—a fixed identity—she is in a "rut." Despite the somewhat unusual particulars in her life, she remains "Snow White" and Barthelme focuses on how any role—especially this one (to be *born* Snow White)—has a built-in scenario, not only in terms of what the world expects, but also in terms of what one expects of the world, i.e., a prince. Barthelme elaborates one of his main themes in *Caligari*: the paralysis inevitable in role playing or in the overabsorption of texts. This he brilliantly accomplishes by literalizing the Snow White story.

Snow White knows she needs a *real* liberation. She thus attempts to create her own identity, and in keeping with Barthelme's metaphor of her life as an unworkable and inadequate script, she attempts to write her own lines, that is, to author her own life (81). In fact, she writes a "dirty great poem," which sets the novel in motion.

But "identity" is always a puzzling matter in Barthelme, and perhaps, in part, this is the point. Although neither Barthelme (nor we) can be so presumptuous as to pinpoint it (after all, Snow White's "identity" is really the issue of the book), perhaps we can at least focus on tidbits of scattered dialogue and fractured events for commentary.

There is no doubt that Barthelme mocks the misguided naiveté and unreality of the legendary fairy tale we were all brought up on—with its seven plastic dwarfs and charming but colorless prince, as well as the wicked adversary figure, presumably of the same sex as Snow White. His open-ended conclusion is a comment on the fairy tale's final "happiness" (or at least "justice") for all. But whether or not Barthelme has anything in the way of a "vision" to offer at the end, and whether or not he would call the tale unrealistic in *any* age or just ours alone (implying a nostalgia for an earlier time), is more difficult to discuss. As we shall see, the novel ends with its beginning.

This is Barthelme's most elaborate collage thus far, marked by elaborate plot and linguistic dislocations, the absence of traditional characterizations or time and space unity, as well as unusual typographical variations and spellings, made-up words, and "chapters" that consist, among other things, of lists, trivia, authorial asides, and non sequiturs. It is also marked by a submerged though distinct linearity and hence "plot."

I *Approaching the Novel*

A brief look at the first pages gives a sense of its texture.

Page 3: Snow White is not the archetypal beauty or innocent; "She is a tall dark beauty," it begins, and even if we wanted to succumb to fairy-tale magic, Barthelme's next, *impersonal* word puts us off: "She is a tall dark beauty *containing* a great many beauty spots [italics mine]." He then proceeds to strip her before our eyes: "one [beauty spot] above the breast, one above the belly, one above the knee, one above the ankle, one above the buttock, one on the back of the neck." And if this precision (and the speaker's physical intimacy with the traditionally modest and virginal Snow White) were not enough, he now becomes virtually scientific: "All of these are on the left side, more or less in a row, as you go up and down," and then proceeds from this oddly objectified, very funny and intimate focus on her body, to an actual schematization of the spots, so that the bulk of the page consists of circles, and we shift into a totally visual and abstract introduction to Snow White. The "chapter" concludes: "The hair is black as ebony," followed by the traditional and trite language of fairy tale, "the skin white as snow" (although we have just seen that her skin is in fact marked with a great many "beauty spots," the "beauty" meant literally, according to Barthelme).

Pages 4–5: Although he hasn't told her this, Bill is tired of Snow White, and generally, he doesn't want to be touched. The other "dwarfs," also anesthetized to real feeling, respond to Bill in the jargon of contemporary philosophy and psychology: "We speculate that he doesn't want to be involved in human situations anymore. A withdrawal. Withdrawal is one of the four modes of dealing with anxiety. . . . Dan speculates that Bill's reluctance to be touched is a physical manifestation of a metaphysical condition that is not anxiety. . . . The rest of us support anxiety." They literalize Bill's withdrawal, and their examples of it are also public, rather than personal: "If someone holds out a hand in greeting, Bill smiles. If it is time to wash the buildings, he will pick up his own bucket. Don't hand him a bucket, for in that circumstance there is a chance that your hands will touch." Finally, they describe Bill's inability to communicate with Snow White. Their soap opera analysis, with its concretization of the metaphor "heartless," is oddly correct: "He has not had the heart to unfold those cruel words, we speculate. Those cruel words remain locked in his lack of heart."

Page 6: Snow White announces her need to hear some new words at breakfast—with "its big cardboard boxes" of "Fear," "Chix," and "Rats." They will buy anything with a catchy label. (Is "Total" more substantial than "Rats"?)

When the dwarfs hear of Snow White's unhappiness, they react as though they had been cheated or abandoned, left "sucking the mop," and their response, intellectualized again, is to throw out "new words," like (T. S. Eliot's) "murder and create." The whole thing is finally "papered over"—with echoes of "covered over," "passed over," or, indeed, "text'd" (papered) over.

Page 8: Barthelme next concretizes and manipulates the cliché that cleanliness is next to godliness, as the men go off to work, pronouncing the holy function of clean skyscraper windows: "Clean buildings fill your eyes with sunlight, and your heart with the idea that man is perfectible." This they juxtapose, however, with their true pleasure in working up high, girl-watching: "Also they are good places to look at girls from." The girls are described in abstract terms: "Viewed from above they are like targets, the plum-colored head the center of the target, the wavy navy skirt the bold circumference." Finally, what would ordinarily be reserved for unconscious thought is uttered in Madison Avenue jargon (with overtones of Freudian chic), and the "targets" and "bold circumference" take on totally new meaning: "We are very much tempted to shoot our arrows into them, those targets. You know what that means." The girls, the section concludes, with variations on *The Waste Land*, "are trying to find the right typewriter, in the correct building."

II *Plot*

Despite Barthelme's rejection of traditional fictional elements, as this may suggest, there is a skeletal plot beneath the shifting spatial planes, which one may sort out. Snow White, a twenty-two-year-old beauty, lives with and keeps house for the seven men; she has sex with them regularly although, as she says, "artificial insemination would be more interesting." ("Why are there no in-flight movies in shower stalls," she continues, "as there are in commercial aircraft?" [34].) She yearns for something new: "Oh I wish there were some [new] words in the world" (6), (i.e., other than the Snow White story): "Who am I to love?" (12). Then, in the interest of creating a new life, she writes a very personal poem, "a dirty great poem four pages long" (10), which destroys everyone's equilibrium. Each one then acts out his own response to this threatening situation: this is essentially the "plot."

Bill, the leader, for example, as we have seen, decides he doesn't want to be touched anymore, but at the risk of further complicating matters, the reader is unsure if this is due to Snow White's poem *or* to his professional failure "to make a powerful statement" at a lecture at the University of Bridgeport (51). (Barthelme, as he often does, rejects causality through linear time.) Bill's soliloquy, marked by cadences of meaning (and echoes from Eliot), diffuses into mock inflations and indefinite metaphor: "Yes . . . I wanted to be great, once. But the moon for that was not in my sky. . . . There was no wind, no weeping. . . . Perhaps they wept in the evenings, . . . each in his own chair, weeping. . . . You laughed, sitting in your chair with your purple plywood spectacles, your iced tea" (51). Bill, who, as someone explains, "pisses" away his "potential," steadily removes himself from any sort of personal interaction. He finally commits the most bizarre of crimes. After dropping the cash he was to deposit in the vault (112), he allows the fires under the vats to go out and commits the "crime of crimes," "vatricide." (In effect, he almost ruins the family business.) He also hurls two six-packs of Miller High Life into a Volkswagen.[1]

Each of the other six "dwarfs" has similarly eccentric experiences (although most of them are verbal), but common to most is a lament for the empty life, with admissions such as Clem's: "It is killing me the way they walk down the street together, laughing and talking, those men and women." Clem flies to Chicago for a break away from Snow White, where he can make "love in a bed," although "it is not Snow White that I would be being unfaithful to, but the shower" (23). (Barthelme's people always define themselves by their things.) Later (141), commenting on the absence of a prince in Snow White's life, he equates morality, sexuality, and money, and lectures on how American egalitarianism "precludes princeliness." Clem would erase all class distinctions and redistribute the literal and emotional wealth: the "poor moneyed people" with their impoverished emotional lives would then be freed from their money through divorce and new lovers.

Edward, who on occasion blows his mind with "nine mantras" and "insect repellent" (142), delivers a lecture (99) on Snow White's lack of appreciation of her role as "horsewife." (Barthelme plays on the idea that the housewife "works like a horse.") Loaded with puns and literary echoes that extend from Pope to Gerard Manley Hopkins, and a variety of tones that range from legalistic and Madison Avenue to Feminist, he begins with the "to be or not to be" issue:

The *horsewife!* the very basebone of the American *plethora!* . . . without whom the entire structure of civilian life would crumble! . . . Were it not for her enormous purchasing power and . . . heedless gaiety . . . we would still be going around dressed in skins, probably, with no big-ticket items to fill the empty voids, in our homes and in our hearts. *The horsewife!* Nut and numen of our intersubjectivity! . . . The chiefest ornament on the golden tree of human suffering! But to say [this] . . . is to say nothing at all. Consider now the horsewife in another part of her role ... sitting in her baff, anointing her charms with liquid Cheer and powdered Joy which trouble, confuse and drown the sense in odors. Now she rises chastely, and chastely abrades herself with a red towel. What an endearing spectacle! The naked wonder of it! The blue beauty of it! ... We have here ... a being which regards itself, *qua* horsewife, with something dangerously akin to selfhatred. This is the problem. (99–100)

Dan has already delivered an extraordinary lecture on the etymology of the word "screw" (30)—in hardware terms—and talked of the need to produce plastic buffalo humps (are these new career plans?) in order to get on top of the 100-percent trash phenomenon of our times. In a much-quoted speech at the beginning of chapter 2, he talks of how American trash productivity is mirrored by language, which also consists of trash, "stuffing," "sludge," and "fill-ins" (elsewhere called "dreck" and "blague") (96–98). Such language, and surely this is Barthelme speaking, serves to "blanket" us—to comfort, protect, and bury us. Dan now answers Edward's horsewife lecture by saying that their problem of zeroing in on Snow White is really very simple, and he proceeds to *define* the real woman: since when they approach her in the shower, (1) from the front she is her "two three-quarter scale breasts" "floating . . . in a red towel" or (2) from the opposite direction, she is "a beautiful snow-white arse" "floating . . . in a towel," they should realize that her constant quality—her identity—is the red towel, her packaging, so to speak. Surely they can "deal" with the new Snow White by dispensing "with the slippery and untrustworthy and expensive effluvia that is Snow White." All they have to do is "cleave instead to the towel."

Dan, in fact, has bought each man his own red towel (101). Later, after his scheme fails (although they are able to wrap their next best thing in the towels, their money, which, incidentally, they also lose), they continue to speculate on the Snow White problem and its possible solutions. Dan begins with a statement of real feeling, but it deteriorates into a commentary on how a good dinner or new leader would abolish his loneliness. Its amplifications are very funny: "I feel abandoned. After a hard day . . . one wants to come home and find a leg of mutton on the table, in a rich gravy, with little pearly onions studded in it, and perhaps a small pot of Irish potatoes somewhere about. Instead

I come home to this nothingness. . . . It is a failure of leadership. . . . True leadership would find a way out of this hairy imbroglio. . . . When one has been bending over a hot vat all day, one doesn't want to come home and hear a lot of hump from a cow-hearted leader whose leadership buttons have fallen off"(138).

Some of the men are treated briefly. Henry, who notes his own "weakness on a pad" in thoroughly objective and informational terms, and who finds Dan's history of the word "screw" crazy, decides that the only way he can "win" a girl (Snow White?)—he is sexually frustrated—is by "courting" her. He prepares himself meticulously, as all the media-rituals urge (64): "It is necessary . . . to cut my various nails, and drink something that will kill the millions of germs in my mouth, and say something flattering, and be witty and bonny, and hale and kinky, . . . just to ease this wrinkle in the groin." Hubert retains charge of their electric wastebasket (129); Kevin seems close to breaking the mold, as he speculates on the uniqueness of individual perception (129), but he quickly becomes depressed as everyone calls his ideas "dreck" and "buffalo hump."

Throughout all of this, Snow White still longs for her prince. Aware that hair is a fertility symbol, she sits at her window with her long hair (washed in golden Prell) outstretched. (She is also Rapunzel.) No prince, however, exists to climb up, except perhaps for a rock and roll bandleader, named Fred who, in his own mythic role created by Barthelme, abandons his band each spring for love. (This year the band is going to break out of *its* pattern by having Fred arrested [91].) In the meantime, Snow White has revealed her poem's theme ("loss") and its first word (not word*s*): "bandaged and wounded," which should be "run together," she instructs. (Barthelme adds the spaces to illustrate the inability of even the spoken word to reflect the written one.) When she is asked: "How is it that bandage precedes wound?" her response, initially an explanation in Sartre's jargon, reveals her true dilemma. She stays with the dwarfs because of her failed imagination, her imprisonment in her role or script as Snow White. The dwarfs' response—they totally fail to understand her —echoes the Anglican wedding ceremony, jazzed up with Barthelme's elaboration of verbs and the strangely appropriate word "dreadful": " 'A metaphor of the self armoring itself against the gaze of The Other.' . . . 'Why do you remain with us?' . . . 'It must be laid, I suppose, to a failure of the imagination. I have not been able to imagine anything better.' . . . We were pleased by this powerful statement of our essential mutuality, which can never be sundered or torn, or broken apart, dissipated, diluted, corrupted or finally severed, not even by art in its manifold and dreadful guises" (59).

Paul is the novel's prince-manqué figure. He acknowledges his blue blood and identity as prince (27), but he realizes that princeliness (and marriage, in old-fashioned terms) brings with it responsibilities, like "teeth" and "piano lessons" (14). "Probably I should go out and effect a liaison with some beauty who needs me, and save her, and ride away with her flung over the pommel of my palfrey," he says, but in fact, Paul finds the prospect of a duck-with-blue-cheese sandwich (to Barthelme, better than ham and swiss) just as appealing (28).

Paul is actually an artist, and his traditional role—if we were reading the book in symbolic terms—would be to awaken Snow White, the word, the liberated imagination. Both a poet and painter, Paul says, because he finds it difficult to fulfill a traditional role, he "would wish to retract everything . . . the whole written world" (13). He also approaches experience as though it were a verbal construct, but he would edit or erase most words. Hence, he says, fully aware of the meaning of Snow White's hair hanging out of the window and the involvement that rescue would entail: "I would especially retract that long black hair . . . [which] makes me terribly nervous" (94).

But the other men (because they know that Paul has the potential to write new words and/or change the script, and/or carry Snow White away from them?) steal his typewriter. They would have him fight the War on Poetry, but Paul decides instead to become a monk.

Before arriving at his destination (78), a monastery in western Nevada, Paul rationalizes his inability to pursue the heroic life (with shades of Hamlet, and even Ophelia, in the monastery reference). Had he been born in an earlier time, at a different place, he might have been a hero—which Barthelme concretizes, in his reference either "with" or "against" Pancho Villa. "In either case," he continues, "I would have had a horse," and a real horse, after all, he says, is far superior to the horsepower of the twentieth century. But as Barthelme plays with the *Sturm und Drang* of the contemporary hero out of his time and place (and brings back the horse as a vaguely defined symbol), he lampoons the contemporary American dream. No matter what one's personal ambition—even something as unworldly as that of being a monk —the possibility of being the subject of a great American portrait, or better yet, of being discovered by Hollywood or appearing on "Johnny Carson" is the ultimate success. "Paul stood before a fence posing. . . . 'The engaging and wholly charming way I stand in front of this fence here . . . will soon persuade someone to discover me. . . . Then I can be on television or something, instead of going to the monastery' " (78).

Paul, subsequently, for some unknown reason, escapes the Order, to "hide" with an Episcopalian entourage in Spain; he then goes on to give lectures on music to the French; he experiences another undefined "defeat" in the post office system in Rome, and he finally returns to the monastery—before taking a "leave" to return home. There (148), he admits why he has "become everything" he has become—a "voyeur"—as he sets up quarters outside the house and watches Snow White undress. Barthelme concretizes his "dancing to a different drummer," as Paul reveals that at one time he enjoyed dancing by himself with a stick. But his individuality was crushed by the judgment of "authority": a "stick-dancing critic" said he was using the wrong sort of stick. Before we consider Paul's ultimate fate following this, and his entry into the Thélèmites Order (167) (interestingly, he goes from one authority to another), we must introduce three other figures.

Although we don't know in any detail why the red towels failed and in fact had to be returned to Bloomingdale's, the "dwarfs" decide to buy a new shower curtain to woo Snow White. They "pose" in front of it all day, hoping this new object will redefine them. But Snow White fails to respond. In their typical "Newsbreak" style, they announce their decision to invite an expert in to "assess" the situation, "to make sure we have got the *right sort* of shower curtain." Indeed, the assessor, a professor of aesthetics, who tells them theirs is not only adequate but

"the best-looking shower curtain in town," provokes their greater
disequilibrium. Distracted from the "function" of the shower
curtain to its "quality" (as Paul turned from the pleasure of his
dancing to the quality of his stick), they go off in a long pata-
physical sequence to verbalize the scientific steps necessary to
determine if, indeed, this is the "best curtain": "empanelment of
shower-curtain critics, . . . census of shower-curtain-hanging
homes, the quarter finals . . . the Olympiad. . . . There was another solution: destruction of the aesthetician" (123–26). But the
word would still remain, and one could never be sure how many
people the aesthetician had shared his appraisal with, and hence
it would be necessary not only to "wipe ourselves out," but also
every potential "listener" "alive."

Snow White is still not responding. At this point they look for
another consultation, and here we must discuss the novel's last
two figures. A descendant of Tarzan's mate ("she likes to swing
from the lianas") is Jane, the "sleepie" (the groupie?) of Hogo
(Hog-O!), whose "vileness" seems generally acknowledged by
all. Hogo, their consultant, has a totally vulgar attitude toward
women, truly the male chauvinist hog. "Ruin of the physical
envelope is our great theme here." Women don't age well, he
says, so just keep "changing girls. . . . Bear in mind multiplicity,
and forget about uniqueness." Women are all the same, and they
are all just good for sex; so for "thought and feeling," he continues, be solipsistic or look to the media (75). But in Barthelme's
story (there is no Hogo figure in the original fairy tale), Hogo
has his own role to fulfill, and it is one of "vileness." Hogo defines his life like a pattern in a painting, created by someone
else: "Nothing is to become of us, Jane. Our becoming is done. . . .
The original brushwork was not mine" (128).

Jane is the fairy tale's Wicked Queen (although Barthelme
extends her identity by calling her "wicked step-mother," something in fact odd in this novel, unless she has a family we don't
know about). In addition, whereas the fairy tale presents her as
purely and gratuitously evil, Barthelme gives her a psychological
dimension. Jane must "cultivate" her "malice" more from the pain
of aging than from some motiveless and mythic evil. "I was fairest
of them all," she says. "Men came from miles around simply to be
in my power." At least she now has Hogo, and this somewhat

mitigates against her malice. Jane's life is given some detail: she speaks to her mother regularly (who schemes for her capturing a man), she enjoys morning tea (of the Chinese variety), and she spends time in her garden cultivating memories of the good old days (40).

The "real" drama—according to Grimm and Disney—only begins near the end of Barthelme's book. When Hogo sees Snow White, he falls madly in love with her ("with all my heart until the end of time" [151]). Jane is then forced to turn from her simple poison-word letters (and telephone threats—which actually represent Barthelme's point of view about opening oneself to new language and experience) to fully embrace her identity as wicked witch. Hogo has joined Paul in his voyeurism. (Paul has set up the underground surveillance installation with trained dogs and mirrors, and he spies on Snow White undressing.) Snow White, in the meantime, completely disillusioned with Paul, is initially attracted to Hogo's "dark and vilely compelling figure" (157).

Jane, left "sucking the mop" by Hogo (although she does *not* know about Snow White specifically), now devotes herself to cultivating her malice: "Now I must witch someone for that is my role." She studies the infinite variety of possibilities in her "floor-to-ceiling Early American spice racks with their neatly labeled jars of various sorts of bane including dayshade, scumlock, hyoscine, azote, hurtwort, and milkleg" (158).

But Snow White is still holding out for a prince (170); thus, when Hogo declares his love for her, she rejects him because of his inferior blood, and in so doing, she makes him another dwarf (170). Jane finally fulfills her role; she delivers a poisoned vodka Gibson, on the rocks, which *Paul* intercepts—(why must a character be "consistent"?)—yet to Snow White he is *"pure* frog."

Although Snow White has said: "Either I have overestimated Paul, or I have overestimated history" (169), Paul then ultimately rescues her, although his actions are prompted less by passion than matters of health: "The drink . . . is too exciting for you," he says, like "a film by Leopoldo Torre Nilsson. . . . If you had drunk it, something bad would probably have happened to your stomach." Thus, either accidentally, ironically, or coincidentally, Paul ends up a prince.

Paul drinks and keels over dead. Snow White's response is as

abstract and unemotional as Paul's remark before his heroic gesture: "Look at all that green foam coming out of his face! . . .
Why it resembles nothing else but a death agony" (175). At the
end, Paul's funeral is attended by Amelia, apparently Paul's
lover, who until now has only been mentioned in connection with
the theft of his typewriter. Paul, who had received a lot of Hogo's
money before he died (did he earn it from him?), is to be cre-
mated and then put in a vase, which will be placed in the ground.
Bill is hanged for his crimes of vatricide and beer-can-hurling.
The dwarfs—now with Hogo one of them—go off, and the book
ends on the note of "HEIGH-HO."

III   Interpretation

After this effort at discovering *Snow White's* minimal "plot"—
and ignoring its intersecting planes and textures—there are several conclusions to be drawn. Once again Barthelme has created
a world of people whose very identities are the texts, media, and
myths they have absorbed. (Snow White says that "the seven
[men] . . . only add up to the equivalent of about two *real men*,
as we know them from the films" [42]). So sophisticated about
themselves—in terms of science and technology, anthropology,
psychology, philosophy, and high and popular culture—when
they speak of either private or public matters, all they can do is
mouth a hodgepodge of texts, and these are always in fragments,
or on an informational, rather than personal level. Their very
actions are prompted by how-to manuals, but these sometimes
conflict with other informational sources; if there is any "conflict"
in these people, it is in a textual sense. Snow White, at one
point, explains why sex with the "dwarfs," specifically Clem, is so
boring. Clem is confused about the church's and the pleasure
manuals' definitions of sex. "Everything in life is interesting," she
says, "except Clem's idea of sexual congress, his Western confusion between the concept, 'pleasure,' and the concept, 'increasing the size of the herd.'" There are certain things, Barthelme
implies, that cannot be "explained" in concepts.
These people are so totally defined by their absorption of texts
and the media that they act out and articulate what at one time
was reserved for the enigmatic, unconscious, inner life. (Techni-

cally, Barthelme concretizes or literalizes the existential or Freudian, say, "condition" in their speech and behavior.) Hogo "explains" his attraction to Jane: "It must be atavistic. It must be some dark reason of the blood which the conscious mind does not understand" (127). Snow White, who understands both the concrete and mythic significance of letting her hair down, says: "This motive . . . is a very ancient one. . . . Now I recapitulate it, for the . . . refreshment of my venereal life" (80). When Hogo, the pragmatist, needs a show of power, he doesn't just contemplate or feel greed; he acts it out. For a big enough reward, he would turn his friends over to the I.R.S. (121).

Snow White's characters, so seemingly peculiar, so flat, and so unreal, are weirdly abstract *precisely because* they are so coldly knowledgeable about who they are (in the terms the texts define as "normal"). One searches for the inner person, let alone a visual outer one, but these people are less flesh and blood than verbal constructs, informational machines, or automatons. It is only when their programming is interrupted or set off keel, and they must shift gears, so to speak, that their troubles begin. This is, of course, the real story behind *Snow White*, since before the novel begins, Snow White has tired of her role as Snow White.

It is most fitting then that if Barthelme sees contemporary people in these terms—as brainwashed by the supersaturation of information—that he use a language that accommodates such a plethora of materials. It is also fitting that he create characters who are beyond ethical categories, who, mindful of, say, their common Freudian heritage and their mythic, potentially heroic stature, are both puny and grand at the same time. Hogo's last name is de Bergerac; Jane's, Villiers de l'Isle Adam.

Jane, the evil witch, is as "innocent" as Snow White who, in her own way, effects as much "malice" as Jane. The vile Hogo proclaims undying love to Snow White, and the Prince Paul has had a lover stashed away all along. Thus, it follows that as we shift from myth or old-fashioned fairy-tale prose to modern psychologese, or from mock-epic diction to comic-book slang—or from the inflated platitudes of political, philosophical, or academic jargon to hip advertising lingo—that the characters, as fixed "moral" figures, shift from one state to another. The "prince" and the "witch" are equally neurotic, "good" and "bad." As a matter of fact, with the dismissal of any "core identity" and the democratization of so many qualities among all the characters, not only does Barthelme dismiss any conventional questions—i.e., What is man: is he what he says or what he feels in his deepest mind (Freud)? or is he what he says or how he acts (Sartre)?—but he creates a cast of characters whose *identities* are almost impossible to decipher, where identities merge, where one has a difficult time locating the narrator (who may not only be any "dwarf," or Barthelme, but Fred, the bandleader), where Hogo can easily transform into a dwarf, and Bill may transform into a monk, as well as into Paul. It is therefore understandable that all the men may or may not be brothers, that they themselves often confuse their names, and that they share the same "love"—Snow White— and fears and dreams. In one sequence, in fact, they literally have a common dream (about "Joan of Art [*sic*]" [109]). As the characters then shift from one "moral category" or "identity" to another, so does their language, and it follows that the same character may speak in high sounding epic form or crude street talk.

With everything then shifting in this verbal collage (perhaps the analogy with sculpture or mobile would be more appropriate), we finally get to Barthelme's central concern: our anesthetization in roles and words (which he has exaggerated in his men) and our need—nearly impossible to fulfill—to break free in new words (as portrayed in Snow White). Once again, though Barthelme's figures may be unsuccessful, his readers gain the advantage through his great comedy.

As discussed in detail in chapter two, Barthelme tempts us to source hunt, to flesh out his characters' fragments with their original source material, but then with his distracting antics, we realize how foolish (and brainwashed) all of this is (and how brainwashed we are), since information and expertise constrict more than they clarify.

Throughout, in ferreting out these figures' worlds and playing with Barthelme's wonderful language, we find ourselves moving from one system of thought and response to another, which is then instantly transformed into other combinations and re-formations. Ultimately, Barthelme forces us to stand away from our cerebrations and moves us to connect with the great and rich world his language evokes. Interestingly, it is Jane who speaks to us for Barthelme of the need to break out of our limited worlds (linguistic and otherwise) in order to be free. In a variety of tones—polite, abusive, and slangy—Jane speaks about estrangement and communication, as she focuses on the word (again literalizing her metaphors). Jane has phoned a Mr. Quistgaard:

We exist in different universes of discourse. . . . It may never have crossed your mind to think that other universes of discourse distinct from your own existed, with people in them, discoursing. You may have, in a commonsense way, regarded your u. of d. as a plenum, filled to the brim with discourse. . . . But I say unto you, . . . that even a plenum can leak. Even a plenum, cher maître, can be penetrated. . . . The moment I inject discourse from my u. of d. into your u. of d., the yourness of yours is diluted. The more I inject, the more you dilute. Soon you will be presiding over an empty plenum, or rather, since that is a contradiction in terms, over a former plenum, in terms of yourness. You are, essentially, in my power. I suggest an unlisted number. (44–46)

IV *Language: Both Means and End*

With this as an overview, perhaps we might stop to pause over and enjoy some of the wonderful verbal exercises Barthelme performs to penetrate our brimming plena. There are, for example, his memorable phrases and one-liners: "*Jean-Paul Sartre is a Fartre*" (66); "SELF-REGARD is rooted in breakfast" (105); "the President [is waging a] 'War on Poetry'" (55); "The Fire Next Time Bar and Grill" (112); "Spare the bat and the child rots" (116); "The Bluetooth period of Scandinavian history" (116); "Where have [all] the buffalo gone?" (131); "Try to be a man about whom nothing is known" (18); "I'm tired of being just a horsewife!" (43); "Laughing Marys and radishes" (as opposed to Bloody Marys and celery [154]).

Barthelme has an ear for unlimited comic and pointed modulations on every sort of expression. Snow White, who finds the dwarfs boring sexually and who would rather pleasure herself, says, while in the shower (mixing perturbation, literally, with masturbation and penetration): "It is marvelous. . . . When the water falls on my tender back. The white meat there. Give me

the needle spray. . . . A thousand tiny points of perturbation.
More perturbation!" (34).

Sometimes he strings together a series of familiar phrases—out
of fairy tale, or any literature at all—and then he expands, concretizes, or undercuts a single word or phrase—or sometimes the
total concept—to explode whatever meaning has thus far co-
alesced. There is the famous recitation of Snow White cleaning
her bookcase in Bachelardian terms (37), as well as "He knows
the deaths of the heart, Hogo does. And he knows the terror of
aloneness, and the rot of propinquity, and the absence of grace"
(62); there is also the following: "We had hoped that he [Paul]
would take up his sword as part of the President's war on poetry.
. . . The root causes of poetry have been studied. . . . And now that
we know that pockets of poetry still exist in our great country,
especially in the large urban centers, we ought to be able to wash
it out totally in one generation, if we put our backs to it" (55).
Another of these very clever (and memorable) phrases is: "Men
try to please their mistresses when they, men, are not busy in the
counting house, or drinking healths, or having the blade of a
new dagger chased with gold" (15).

Sometimes he uses purposely vague symbols, like stains, flowers, horses, and ducks, that reverberate throughout the novel but
ultimately have no fixed meaning. Sometimes he begins a metaphor that seems to have a fixed meaning, but then he exaggerates
or distorts the logic behind it to push it over into vague meaning
or nonmeaning. Snow White, for example, compares the stirring
of her imagination with money (like money, imagination allows
for mobility), but she concludes with literalizations or concretizations of the metaphor: "My imagination is stirring . . . like the
long-sleeping stock certificate suddenly alive in its green safety-
deposit box because of new investor interest."

Sometimes he begins the *form* or cadence of meaning but
then incorporates a wildly unexpected term to totally alter one's
anticipated response: "The whole thing is just trembling," he
writes, "on the edge of monotony" (36). Or, "alienation has
seep[ed] in everywhere and cover[ed] everything like a big gray
electric blanket that doesn't work, after you have pushed the off-
on switch to the 'on' position!" (131). Other times, he creates
wonderfully wild analogies. Bill's presumably self-revelatory

comment begins with the following (recall that Bill does not wish to be touched): "The refusal of emotion produces nervousness. . . . If it is still possible to smite the brow with anguished forefinger then you should let that forefinger fall. . . . The concatenation of outward and visible signs may I say may detonate an inward invisible subjective correlative, booming in the deeps of the gut like an Alka Seltzer to produce tranquillity" (139).

Barthelme also concretizes the traditional pathetic fallacy. A change in one's attitude is reflected by a change in one's environment and activities, but the symbols are again vague. If, for example, it is time for Snow White to write her new poem and change her life, she is also compelled to rearrange the furniture in her house: "We noticed that she had shifted the lilies from the escritoire to the chiffonier. . . . That she had hauled the Indian paintbrush all the way out into the kitchen. . . . Poem, she said, There it was, the red meat on the rug" (10–11).

At the heart of the novel are Barthelme's repeated demonstrations of our anesthetized responses to experience—the near demise of our spirit and mind through our overabsorption of texts and information. One of Bill's comments (92–93), in mock-inductive form, is an extraordinary example of this. First, he discusses Snow White's hair in concrete and Freudian terms; then he becomes defensive and attacks her as "a goddamn degenerate"; next, he talks of loneliness in general philosophical terms; and then, he contemplates mankind in its planetary isolation. At last, he totally objectifies all considerations of human loneliness in an absurd discussion of the existential state of the planet, like the single hair. And yet, because his questions will not resolve, his words turn full circle, and he returns to his initial personal isolation. Barthelme's undercutting of the existential dilemma is touching, infuriating, and wildly funny. "Each of us is like a tiny single hair, hurled into the world among billions and billions of other hairs. . . ."

One of Barthelme's most memorable examples of the incorporation of public or informational language occurs in the following, where the scientific or medical term intrudes upon a potentially intimate moment. His punctuation is meticulous: at the movie, we read, "Hubert put his hand in Snow White's lap. A shy and tentative gesture. She let it lay there. It was warm there: that is

where the vulva is" (41). Another amusing example is the
men's communal dream, described like a movie: "like Dreyer's
The Burning of Joan of Art"; in addition, they fancy Antonin
Artaud's joining in the festivities and cooking Snow White in
sweet-and-sour sauce (109).

Even when Snow White undresses, she views her body objec-
tively and etymologically, with flourishes from the Bible: "These
breasts, my own, still stand delicately away from the trunk, as they
are supposed to do. And the trunk itself is not unappealing. In
fact *trunk* is a rather mean word for the main part of this assemblage of felicities. The cream-of-wheat belly!" (144). So too, when
she wonders, *"Which prince will come?"* Barthelme provides from
fiction, perfumes, fact, legend, and even pop music, a long list:
"Will it be Prince Andrey? Prince Igor? Prince Alf . . . Hal? . . .
Matchabelli? . . . Prince Valiant?" and she concludes: "Waiting
as a mode of existence is, as Brack has noted, a darksome mode.
. . . But slash me if I will let it, this waiting, bring down my lofty
feelings of anticipation from the bedroom ceiling where they
dance overhead like so many French letters filled with lifting
gas" (77).

What Barthelme most obviously draws is a gallery of people
who lack any real feeling, but he accomplishes this not only in
their juxtapositions of personal feeling and public information,
but also in their garbling—in terms of response—both the significant with the trivial. The dwarfs, for example, express their loss
of Snow White in a business-as-usual attitude, in what sounds
like a stock or news report; their words deteriorate into nonsense, at least so far as Snow White is concerned: "Our letters
have been returned unopened. . . . The grade of pork ears we are
using in the Baby Sing Sam Dew is not capable of meeting U.S.
Government standards. . . . Control Data is up four points. The
pound is weakening. The cow is calving. The cactus wants water-
ing. The new building is abuilding. . . . The weather tomorrow,
fair and warmer" (119). Elsewhere, we see the value of fish
equated with God and a foreign film: "Hubert remembered the
Trout Amandine. . . . extremely tasty, that trout. And Hubert remembered the conversation in which he had said that God was
cruel, and someone else had said vague, and they had pulled
the horse off the road, and then they had seen a Polish picture"

(41). The President, with his own "role" to play, worries equally about everything—from "rosebushes" to "the falling Dow-Jones index and the screams of the poor," to "Bill and the boys" (the "dwarfs") (81).

There are endless amounts of irony in any number of seemingly straightforward statements. Potentially self-revelatory comments often turn upon themselves, and "meaning" is suspended. Snow White, with echoes of Blake, the Bible, and even Chaucer, would seem to be criticizing the sham of a moneyed society which cannot produce a proper prince for an innocent and wanting girl. Yet she concludes with an image of herself sexually afire, like an oil pipe (her untapped sexuality not unlike the wasted energy that lapses from oil derricks). But what has happened to her initial contempt for material things? She says: "There is a Paul [prince] somewhere, but not here. . . . Here everyone worships the almighty penny. . . . O Jerusalem, Jerusalem! Thy daughters are burning with torpor and a sense of immense wasted potential, like one of those pipes you see in the oil fields, burning off the natural gas that it isn't economically rational to ship somewhere!" (102).

Elsewhere, she seems aware that her responses are carbon copies of the media: "The seven of them only add up to the equivalent of about two *real men*," she admits, "as we know them from the films and from our childhood." Yet, she goes on to say, "one . . . [might] have to content [herself] . . . with the subtle falsity of color films of unhappy love affairs, made in France, with a Mozart score." Indeed, she might just substitute one film image—of the "Elvira Madigan" sort—for the other (41–42).

Paul makes one of the most interesting comments in the novel when he speaks of "retracting" the "whole written world" (13). If we ignore its context and simply consider the basic idea—that we are all authors of our lives—we can draw some inferences about the book's open-ended conclusion and the questionnaire Barthelme places in its middle. Although it is a familiar idea (as Yeats put it) that we must "fill the cradles right" (create roles or personal myths by which to live), the difficulties of implementing this are obvious. One is limited by the scripts he is given, by the meanings already inherent in the language he is forced to use. One struggles to try to write his own script, against the weight of language, history, and the need one has for validation by others (whose understandings, needs, and expectations may be different). Barthelme's heroes and heroine fail at "retracting" "the whole written world," because Barthelme has no easy answers.

In the middle of the book—middle in terms of pagination, although Barthelme tricks us with an asymmetrical part 3 (part 1 begins "SHE"; part 2, "PERHAPS"; part 3, "SNOW WHITE")—he includes a questionnaire. (One almost expects a pencil included in the purchase price.) Here he literalizes the implications of the contemporary obeisance to texts and published information. Since our lives are molded upon the published word, he invites us to participate in his creation of a future "model." In a *tour de force* that mocks both author and public consumer, he asks (82–83):

1. Do you like the story so far? Yes (   ) No (   )
   . . . .
5. In the further development of the story, would you like more emotion (   ) or less emotion (   )?
   . . . .
7. Do you feel that the creation of new modes of hysteria is a viable undertaking for the artist of today? Yes (   ) No (   )

Following this and suggesting the terrible power of the media, he writes:

8. Would you like a war? Yes (   ) No (   )

In final self-mockery, he concludes:

15. In your opinion, should human beings have more shoulders? (   ) Two sets of shoulders? (   ) Three? (   )

The artist will create anything the reader wants; reality can then become a carbon copy of whatever the word dictates.

The book ends ambiguously. The dwarfs appear to be no different than when the story began: "Bill has been hanged. We regret that. . . . Bill was hanged because he was guilty, . . . and if you are guilty, then you must be hanged. . . . It was evident that he didn't wish to be hanged" (180). Now, they say, "there is a certain degree of "equanimity," for Hogo has joined the group, and Dan has become the new leader. People are people are people. On the last page, Barthelme's list provides the open-ended finale, which also reminds us that we are, after all, just reading a book—a collection of pages—where nothing happens:

> THE FAILURE OF SNOW WHITE'S ARSE
> REVIRGINIZATION OF SNOW WHITE
> APOTHEOSIS OF SNOW WHITE
> SNOW WHITE RISES INTO THE SKY
> THE HEROES DEPART IN SEARCH OF
> A NEW PRINCIPLE
> HEIGH-HO

One could "read" anything into each of these and reach totally contradictory interpretations (i.e., in the first line, Snow White's failure to find her prince *or* to provide continuing equanimity for the dwarfs; in the next three, some form of reconstruction of the myth and typical happy ending; in the last, the dwarfs' return either to the cathouse or the forest, in search of either new sex or something to jar them either back to or out of their state of equilibrium).

The book turns full circle, and one is left back at the beginning. The reader, along with Snow White and her men, returns to page one. Heigh-ho!

CHAPTER 5

Unspeakable Practices, Unnatural Acts

IN this second collection of short stories Barthelme brings back
many themes from *Caligari*, but he focuses more sharply on
society's war mentality and its blind gropings for authority and
direction. The volume also contains several stories that ring with
a personal note and several that deal with traditional themes
(i.e., old age, the father-son relationship). He pursues what has
been called metafiction, fiction on fiction, and he continues to
probe the difficulties of discovering "truth" in the world and
"meaning" in our words. As always, there is overlapping when
one connects stories with specific "themes"; to simplify, however: (1) on war: "Report," "Indian Uprising," "Game," "Picture History", (2) on the mechanized society: "Edward and Pia,"
"A Few Moments," "Indian Uprising"; (3) on society's search for
answers—in politics ("President"), art/bureaucracy ("Police
Band"), and science ("See the Moon?"); (4) on the war between
men and women: "Indian Uprising," "Edward and Pia," "A Few
Moments"; (5) on the privacy of love: "The Balloon," "Alice,"
"Can We Talk"; (6) on the word as dubious sign and the artist's
creation of a personal reality: "Picture History of War," "Balloon," "Can We Talk," "This Newspaper Here"; (7) on art (defined) and the artist's problems: "See the Moon," "Balloon," "Indian Uprising," "Dolt," "Picture History," "Police Band"; (8) on
the impossibility of defining the world or personality, the failure
of language: "Robert Kennedy," "Can We Talk," "See the
Moon?"; (9) on fathers and sons: "See the Moon?", "Picture
History of War"; and (10) on old age: "Picture History of War,"
"This Newspaper Here."

84

I   *"The Indian Uprising"*

"You gave me heroin first a year ago."
"I decided I knew nothing."

In the "Burial of the Dead" section of *The Waste Land*, Eliot captures the barrenness of modern day love in the blind and speechless Tiresias who, in response to his would-be lover's "You gave me hyacinths first a year ago," thinks:

> . . . when we came back, late from the Hyacinth garden,
> Your arms full, and your hair wet, I could not
> Speak, and my eyes failed, I was neither
> Living nor dead, and I knew nothing. . . .

Later Eliot's narrator is asked: "Do you know nothing? Do you see nothing?"; and later still he answers: "I can connect Nothing with nothing."

Barthelme captures this death-in-life quality by setting his story up like a Hollywood filming, where everything is acted and nothing is real—except the offstage "dialogue" of the actors or bystanders. What happens is that the line between the reality and unreality—of the film (on war) and the people making or watching it (the lovers)—blurs. What should be "acted," the war, becomes very real and even moves beyond the limits of the set (as the actors stage a real revolt, and at the end children are discovered as the slaughtered enemy); what is presumably real (the love between the speaker and "Sylvia") becomes as banal as T.V. melodrama. Most disturbing is the confusion of violence and banality, on and off the so-called stage.

Barthelme literalizes the metaphors of life as war and love as soap opera. His focus is not so much the precariousness of what is traditionally considered reality or fantasy, but once again, the way in which our lives are saturated and ultimately defined by the media. Love and/or war is whatever the film or history texts dictate. A key line, which occurs after three pages, establishes at least three different perspectives: "But it is you I want now, here in the midst of this Uprising. . . . It is when I am with you that I am happiest. . . . 'Call off your braves.'" This alerts us to the fact that (1) although up until now we thought the war real and indeed the subject of the story, (2) the lovers in fact may not only be witnessing or participating in the filming of war, but, most importantly, (3) everything we have read up until now—all the details about Comanches and barricades—may simply be the speaker's *reactions* (in film terms) to his frustrations with Sylvia. That is, the filming may be occurring, so to speak, only in his mind, since his mental set, his way of thinking, has been created by Hollywood, and he can only respond to experience as an actor on a set. Indeed, Sylvia may (or may not) have instigated this war by rejecting him.

But whether or not this is a private war gets lost within Barthelme's multiple focal points. He draws box within box of trite response where the violence of the world and his characters' violence are mixed. This is graphically conveyed in the speaker's description of his military barricade. The manufactured things of contemporary life (like the stuffing of ordinary language) have consumed him: "window dummies, silk, thoughtfully planned job descriptions (including scales for the orderly progress of other colors), wine in demijohns . . . gin, Fad #6 sherry; a hollow-core door in birch veneer on black wrought-iron legs; . . . a woven straw wastebasket; two glass jars for flowers; . . . a Yugoslavian carved flute. . . ." One reacts to experience in terms of things; thus, the narrator (who may indeed love Sylvia) has expressed his love for her by making the special birch table, but it is the same table he has made for all the other women in his life.

The private and the public, the significant and the insignificant —all are jumbled. After the Comanche enemy is captured (another "Tiresias" figure who "choked and wept"), the narrator and Sylvia express a chilling indifference to war, art, and love. When the Comanche is given a most gruesome torture ("We attached wires to the testicles"), he responds in literary terms: "His name, he said, was Gustave Aschenbach." What is frightening is their shared indifference to the violence enveloping them. Following the narrator's remarks on the Indian's near-castration, he says with complete equanimity and selfishness: "And you can never touch a girl in the same way more than once."

Barthelme's "set" is also interesting, although the reader may be confused as to the origin of the war occurring—South Vietnam, Algeria, the American Indians, Russia, the I.R.A., France, university student rebellions, or race-riots. Barthelme also names each street after a different national hero—"Boulevard Mark Clark," "Rue Chester Nimitz," "George C. Marshall Allée," "Patton Place[!]" One war is the same as any other. As a matter of fact, in a lighter vein, the speaker says to Sylvia, regarding their supposed adversary positions in life/battle (she is "green," he "blue"): "She wore . . . a long blue muffler." Sylvia confuses which side she is on.

This dislocation of feeling and focus—in love and war—is reflected in the first paragraph. The city is costumed for war, aglitter with absolutely inappropriate alliteration (oxymorons): the "clubs" "clatter" on "soft pavements"; "arrows" arrive in "clouds." The speaker, in the bedroom with Sylvia, asks if "this is a good life." Her answer is as much a response to her lover and the possessions that define him, as to the booty or stakes of war: "the table held apples, books, long-playing records. She looked up. 'No.' "

In his involvement with life as a verbal or film construct, the speaker is not above self-mockery. At one point (having repeated "I decided I knew nothing"), he goes back to school, to be told, in an ambivalent statement: "You know nothing. . . . I despise you, my boy, *mon cher*, my heart." Miss R., the teacher, continues: "The only form of discourse of which I approve . . . is the litany." Then she goes on to enumerate *vertical* lists of a few "hard, brown, nutlike word[s]":

> pewter
> snake
> tea
> Fad #0 sherry

She would also "run to liquids and colors" in organizing her words, a statement that rings true of our author about the original and private use of words.

The need and yet difficulty of using language in fresh and "unique" ways (recalling "Florence Green" and *Snow White*) is summed up in two passages which comment on each other. Barthelme writes, first: "Strings of language extend in every di-

rection to bind the world into a rushing, ribald whole." There
follows an illustration of these "strings" which connect the separate parts of the story, like experience, but which then dissipate
and can never again be recaptured in the same way: "And you can
never return to felicities in the same way, the brilliant body, the
distinguished spirit recapitulating moments that occur once,
twice, or another number of times in rebellions, or water." The
story dissolves as a metaphor of feeling.

II *"The Balloon"*

". . . offered the possibility . . . of mislocation of the self, in contra-
distinction to the grid of precise, rectangular pathways under our
feet."

One of his best-known stories, this is a wonderful introduction
to Barthelme's work, because it deals with the privacy of the
word, both spoken and written, and the constrictions or freedom
with which one approaches life. The "plot" is quite simple: a
balloon has suddenly appeared in New York, covering the area
from Fourteenth Street to Central Park. Had it a label, like
"Goodyear," New Yorkers could have put it into perspective, but
because it is merely suspended (for twenty-two days), it is
treated as a "situation," with a variety of responses. For seven or
so pages, the speaker describes its texture and the reactions to it.
Some people find it interesting, some argue about its "meaning";
when such discussions prove futile, some decide to enjoy it; children jump, stroll, race, and bounce on it. Others are timid or
hostile to it, or frustrated by it. Some even perform secret tests
on it to discover how to make it go away. All, however, "interpret"
it according to their own particular frames of reference (and
Barthelme has a heyday tracing the gamut of responses). Finally,
people adopt a pragmatic attitude, and the balloon becomes a
meeting place: "Marginal intersections offered entrances."
The speaker warns: "each intersection was crucial, none could
be ignored." To each person, his own "reading" or intersection
was as valid as any other one. Finally, "it was suggested" that
the virtue of the balloon was "its randomness"; it offered people
the "mislocation of the self," a way of getting out of a rut.
Although this sort of material fills seven pages, it is only in the

last paragraph that the speaker explains: "I met you under the balloon, on the occasion of your return from Norway; you asked if it was mine; I said it was . . . a spontaneous autobiographical disclosure, having to do with the unease I felt at your absence, and with sexual deprivation." And he concludes: "But now that your visit to Bergen has been terminated, it is no longer necessary or appropriate." He has removed and stored the balloon, "awaiting some other time of unhappiness, sometime, perhaps, when we are angry with one another."

On a close reading, it is clear that from the beginning the balloon (like one's story, his words, or comprehension of life) has been controlled by the speaker, meaningful to him alone (not his lover or even Barthelme). He says at the start: *"I stopped it."* *"I asked the engineers to see to it."* Our pleasure in the story lies in Barthelme's playfulness toward the human need (and yet frequent failure) to understand signs and his parody of social science jargon. In describing how "critical opinion was divided," he writes:

"monstrous pourings"

"harp"

XXXXXXX "certain contrasts with darker portions"

"inner joy"

"large, square corners"

"conservative eclecticism that has so far governed
      modern balloon design"

::::::::"abnormal vigor"

"warm, soft, lazy passages"

"Has unity been sacrificed for a sprawling quality?"

"Quelle catastrophe!"

"munching"

In another funny passage which uses the word "sullied" several times, he spoofs the reading of foreign signs. On a more serious level, he says: "It is wrong to speak of 'situations,' implying sets of circumstances leading to some resolution, some escape of tension; there were no situations, simply the balloon hanging there." And with his typical satire on the experts (and word-play on "inflation"): "Now we have had a flood of original ideas in all media, works of singular beauty as well as significant mile-stones in the history of inflation, but at that present moment, there was only this *balloon*, concrete particular, hanging there."

Barthelme has done an extraordinary thing here, only suggested in "Indian Uprising" and "Me and Miss Mandible." In this meta-fiction, another story about writing stories, he has taken Stephen Dedalus's definition of the dramatic artist who stands totally aloof from his creation "paring his fingernails," and pushed it as far as he can, to focus on the impersonality of the word itself (the "concrete particular"). He has written a story, a "distrac-tion," that really has no need for the reader as "interpreter." He has provided, in the total story, the form of meaning—here, the process of reading and apprehending reality—without a fixed, definable substance, to illustrate how form is only form, rather than meaning. The "meaning" of the balloon is really that the balloon has no meaning.

And yet the deeper irony here is that the story does ultimately "mean" something. As the balloon is to the speaker, so is the story to the balloon. Each is another level of metaphor, a description of experience, clarifying the one before. That is, first the bal-loon is the emblem or externalized symbol of what the speaker—not Barthelme—is feeling, and this is totally personal *to the speaker*. The narrator gives it only the most general (sexual) significance, and both the reader and Barthelme remain in the dark as to its precise significance. It is the speaker's balloon.

But the balloon (an absolutely wonderful life image), as it is *described*, goes beyond its emotional or sexual significance to inevitably become the "concrete particular," since the speaker's (or anyone's) communication of (felt) experience must be clothed in images, or concrete particulars, in language. As such, it is both literally and figuratively removed from life; it is a bal-loon, both as metaphor and as concrete (or imagined) reality.

Finally, the balloon, like the story, like all words, like life, expands and connects, and in its state of infinite movement, it elicits (or "means") as many things as one can attribute to it. It lacks an absolute and fixed meaning, as it simultaneously elicits a variety of responses and significations. To paraphrase Barthelme, it offers the "possibility" and the *process* of interpretation, where at "any intersection" one can react in any number of ways. The participant thus—the reader, like the lover-narrator—becomes the ultimate artist or creator, and depending upon his system, grid, or frame of reference, he constructs, or manipulates, or rejects, or simply plays with, whatever responses the balloon elicits. These then inevitably color his experience, which indeed, for the time he is involved with them, change and "mislocate" his reality. We are left with the same internal contradiction about the meaningful/meaningless nature of words, roles, and experience itself.

III   *"This Newspaper Here"*

This again deals with the writer, here an old, presumably paralyzed newspaperman who, dissatisfied with the reality he has been dealt, creates his own world from the words he puts together. Censured by authority ("If you don't like our war you don't have to come to it, too old anyway you used-up old poop"), he would enjoy whatever pleasures he can concoct. He prints a story about the "plain girl fair," whose words are comprehensible only to him, and the fair actually materializes. There he picks up a girl (his own Marie, not Eliot's), and enjoys lobster, dancing, and "gestures of marvellous gaucherie" with her.

The story is, once again, about one's creation of his own reality, through signs—"refreshing as rocks"—such as these:

(!) (!) (!)(!) (!) (!) (!)(!) (!) (!) (!)(!) (!)
❋❋❋❋❋❋❋❋❋❋ ❋❋❋❋❋❋❋❋❋
?/?/?/?/?/?/ ?/?/?/?/?/?/ ?/
[etc.]

Pages are "solid bright aching orange sometimes and parts printed in alien languages and invisible inks." Defiance (his newspaper would have "rare lies and photographs incorrectly captioned"), originality, and whimsy are the speaker's answer to the grim reaper—whose messenger (not unlike Godot's) is an eleven-year-old with a "blue Death of Beethoven printed dress and white shoes," and she would torment him with her steel-blue knitting needles (shades of Dante). He concludes with humor in his defiance. He has written, in an editorial, that the world is an error on God's part: "They hated that. Ringle from the telephone 'what do you mean the world is a roar on the part of God,' which pleased me. I said 'madam is your name Marie if so I will dangle your health in verymerrywine this very eve blast me if I will not.' She said into the telephone 'dirty old man'. Who ha who ha."

IV *"Robert Kennedy Saved from Drowning"*

Written before Kennedy's assassination, this is a series of contrived journalistic reports (apart from one detail) which create a concrete, twelve-page portrait of a man who is ultimately unknowable. Parodying both fiction's and nonfiction's professions of "truth," Barthelme focuses on the contradictory nature of "K. at his Desk," "K. Reading the Newspaper," "K. Puzzled by His Children," and so on, in twenty-four categories: "He is neither abrupt with nor excessively kind to associates. Or he is both abrupt and kind."

Barthelme's technique, at times relieved by humor, is intentionally repetitious and dull. "A Friend" cited makes a key statement in unremarkable style: "The thing you have to realize about K. is that essentially he's absolutely alone in the world." What is most captivating is Barthelme's projection of what Kennedy *might have said* about Poulet (discussing Marivaux). We have our boxes within boxes again. Kennedy's presumed wonder toward man's precarious identity and ultimate mystery has, of course, been exactly what Barthelme has rather tediously (and ambivalently) thus far reported. But because Poulet (and Marivaux, with shades of Merleau-Ponty and Bachelard) speaks for Barthelme on the richness of experience and language, it is worth quoting (as presumably Kennedy would have expressed it). We are back to issues of "Shower of Gold": Whose viewpoint does this literary criticism—with its purple prose—reflect: Poulet? Kennedy? Barthelme, or even Marivaux? The passage is this:

"For Poulet, it is not enough to speak of *seizing the moment*. It is rather a question of . . . 'recognizing in the instant which lives and dies, which surges out of nothingness and which ends in dream, an intensity and depth of significance which ordinarily attaches only to the whole of existence.' . . .

The Marivaudian being is, according to Poulet, a pastless futureless man, born anew at every instant. The instants are points which organize themselves into a line, but what is important is the instant, not the line. The Marivaudian being has in a sense no history. Nothing follows from what has gone before. He is constantly surprised. He cannot predict his own reaction to events. He is constantly being *overtaken* by events. A condition of breathlessness and dazzlement surrounds him. In consequence he exists in a certain freshness which seems, if I may say so, very desirable. This freshness Poulet, quoting Marivaux, describes very well."

The conclusion is equally cryptic. Kennedy, gasping after a dramatic rescue from drowning, utters a brief "Thank you." The mystery remains, both about Kennedy and about what words "mean." Is the "Thank you" "breathless and dazzling"? Or is it mannered and impersonal? Can the cold and dull response be "fresh," or must "fresh" necessitate a more effusive response? Is the reporter's failure to define his subject a reflection of one's own inability to "predict his own reaction to events," how one is "born anew at every instant"? So flexible and indefinable is the Barthelmean man, that he is capable of embracing both his "K." identity (echoing Kafka's Everyman), as well as the opposing, ultimately creative "Some people see things as they are and ask 'Why?' I see things that never were and ask 'Why not?'" Through both style and subject, Barthelme has concretized the "Marivaudian being."

V   *"Report"*

An anti-Vietnam piece, "Report" is a bitter attack on our progressive technological society in which war functions like a computerized process. ("The whole structure of enemy life is within our power to *rend, vitiate, devour,* and *crush.*") Morality, furthermore ("perhaps the most advanced and sensitive . . . the world has ever known"), is reduced to punched cards. Barthelme sends a "software man," the humanist, to "Cleveland to talk to the engineers," to tell them "war is wrong". There, he talks mainly with the "hardware man," the chief engineer, whose motto is "nothing mechanical [rather than human] is alien to me." In language that evokes the esoteric breadth of scientific technology, he says: "Ask us anything. Do you want to know about . . . integrated-circuit processes? The algebra of inequalities? . . . Gross interfaced space gropes? We also have specialists in the cuckooflower . . . and the dumdum bullet as these relate to aspects of today's expanding technology, and they do in the damnedest ways." Completely indifferent to human life, he discusses the survival of the poor. Grotesque speculation deteriorates into nonsense: "[With] the development of the pseudo-ruminant stomach for underdeveloped peoples . . . they can chew curds . . . eat grass. Blue is the most popular color worldwide and for that reason we are working with certain strains of your native Kentucky *Poa pratensis,* or bluegrass . . . which would also give a shot in the arm to our balance-of-payments thing. . . . The kangaroo initiative . . . eight hundred thousand harvested last year. . . . " The software man queries: "Have new kangaroos been planted?"

When the software man insists that this war is wrong, a war of "error," he is told that to stop fighting is to "lose" or "abort" a machine whose processes have been perfected: "We don't know *how.*" Pursuing the language of the war hawks, the engineer continues: "I intuit your hatred and jealousy of our thing. . . . The ineffectual always hate our thing and speak of it as anti-human. . . . If I think it up, then 'it' is human too, whatever 'it' may be."

Barthelme's humor is searing. When the engineer, who has become wildly angry with his visitor, lists the weaponry developed (as yet unused, unless "we . . . *lose patience*"), he includes "improved pufferfish toxin which precipitates an identity crisis," but he also lists "hypodermic darts capable of piebalding the enemy's pigmentation" and a "testicle-destroying telegram." He then explains why the scientists are themselves suffering from noticeable fractures. Apparently among the other "triumphs" for "the multi-disciplined problem-solving team" is the "secret word that, if pronounced, produces multiple fractures in all living things in an area the size of four football fields." Although this story was written many years before Three Mile Island, its cry against nuclear power plants remains relevant.

The story ends with the visitor arriving back "at Newark [Airport] at 7:19," and the wonderful line, as he looks over the city: "Living things move about the surface of New Jersey at that hour molesting each other only in traditional ways." Barthelme does indeed have the power to evoke a new reality in the word. In comparison with the other inventions we have just encountered, the "molesting" of "living" things is indeed mild and something to be preferred.

VI *"The Dolt"*

As though preparing for the Graduate Record Exams, Edgar, a would-be writer, worries that, for the third time, he will fail the written part of his National Writers' Examination. The supersophisticated, overeducated Edgar can write traditional fiction and pass the oral part. He knows and can parrot all the right answers (facts, definitions, and rules). But he doesn't know the questions. He can write the old-fashioned story (in fact a parody of Kleist), but even there, he has only the "end," and he adds: "I don't have the middle."

His eight-foot-tall "son manqué" enters the room wearing "a serape woven out of two hundred transistor radios, all turned on and tuned to different stations." Confronted with the grotesqueness of contemporary reality, the mechanization and cacophony of all the "answers" about life, the *narrator* intrudes to say: Edgar "couldn't think of anything. . . . I sympathize. I myself have these problems. Endings are elusive, middles are nowhere to be found, but the worst of all is to begin, to begin, to begin." The writer (Barthelme?) can discern only his own reality and pose questions. To be sure, he lacks Edgar's safe endings.

VII *"The Police Band"*

An old police commissioner—subtle and psychologically

oriented, as well as a "graftsman" with a "drug problem of his own"—decides to "alleviate tensions" in a city of people "trembling with fear." He would organize a police band to play songs like "Entropy" and "Perdido" at disruptions like race riots. Then crowds would be "washed with new and true emotion," "a triumph of art."

Although the band drilled and rehearsed its borrowed emotion in order to appropriately "wail" and "scream" its jazz, even in rehearsals it only affected a "few old ladies leaning out of high windows" and "rusty Rheingold cans and parts of old doors." When a new commissioner took over, he totally rejected the entire scheme, this "romantic idea," for the policy that "Rage must be met with rage."

Barthelme mocks many things here: from the inept humanitarianism of bureaucrats to the idea of art as social cure, from the hired hands who "perform" art, to the idea that it speaks to people. What rings out loudest is his description of the city's grotesqueness and its inhabitants' helplessness, "a drunk trying to strangle a dog somebody'd left leashed to a parking meter. The drunk and the dog screaming at each other. This city is too much!"

VIII   "Edward and Pia" and "A Few Moments of Sleeping and Waking"

Both stories are extended examples of the lifeless relationship between the pregnant Pia (in the first story) and her "lover" Edward, who travel from country to country, as though that were an excuse to live. This is the modern Waste Land without even its latent potential for change; there is nothing left but boredom and impersonality. Edward's wife is in Maine; his lover (Pia) rejects him sexually. He "put his hands on Pia's breasts" and "then he counted his money." Barthelme's extensive exemplification of their merging the significant and trivial, and their aimlessness and boredom, is terrifying: "In Leningrad they visited Pia's former lover, Paul. The streets in Leningrad are extremely wide." Again we read: "Pia told Edward that she had been raped once." Edward replied: "How would you like to have some Southern fried chicken?" What is most alarming is their dull articulation of what—for the reader—might save them: "Edward and Pia discussed leaving each other."

In the second story, with Edward now an authority on every published work on dreams (including *Madame Cherokee's Dream Book*), they spend most of their time analyzing Pia's dreams—for their sleeping life (if not the report of it) is far more vital than their waking life; occasionally, they go to films or analyze their pasts. Barthelme goes one step further here (although in linear time Edward is younger than in the first story) in literalizing the metaphoric "nightmare" quality of their waking life, which in fact is totally emotionless—a life devoted to "interpretation." Now all significant distinctions between waking and sleeping, and experiencing and interpreting, are erased. These nonquesting, text-questioning Waste Landers are paralyzed in analysis and signification.

IX *"Can We Talk"*

Somewhat reminiscent of "The Balloon" and "Indian Uprising," this story reflects the sensibility of the frustrated lover. Although his discontinuous thoughts provide the substance of the story (he recalls going to the bank, a lunch, army disasters, and fantasies of making a fortune or being a writer), underneath is his deep but undefined longing for a woman. Barthelme recreates the mood of "Robert Kennedy," as he conveys the ultimate mystery and privacy of the individual.

X *"Game"*

"Game" is an updated version of Pinter's *The Dumb Waiter*, where two hitmen—here two air force officers who can detonate the "bird" that will destroy a population—have been locked up and forgotten (for 133 days) in their (underground) quarters. Like Pinter, Barthelme focuses upon their banality, but unlike him, he creates figures like automata, like cogs in a well-oiled machine, who react to life purely in informational terms.

Not unlike Beckett's tramps in *Waiting for Godot*, the men have devised ways of passing their days, but where Beckett's figures complement and understand each other, these two are completely at odds. One spends his time playing jacks (and is extremely possessive about them) or devoting himself to self-improvement. (He is working toward a master's degree, and he studies and underlines, with his blue ballpoint pen, his *Introduction to Marketing* text from the University of Wisconsin Extension School.) The other, who yearns to play with the jacks, writes and draws on the walls, with a two-and-a-half carat diamond ring.

The two men suspect each other, for not only has each been instructed to kill the other if he acts peculiarly, but each is worried that the other will get him first (another echo from Pinter). Once again, having lost any sense of life's priorities, Barthelme's people articulate, in rote (military) manner, both their fears and trivial concerns. When they realize they have been forgotten, they draw up new agreements on how to behave with each other: "Uniform regulations were relaxed, and mealtimes are no longer rigorously scheduled."

If the story has echoes from Pinter and Beckett, Barthelme adds his own twists. Products of the perfect bureaucracy, the two men accept their uncertain fate, and in mock-Beckettian form, they utter the existential problems of waiting: "Perhaps the whole thing is . . . [a] very successful . . . experiment. . . . I do not know." Although they have been forgotten due to an "error," (unless this is an experiment or a punishment), they are, in an odd sense, quite inventive. A parody of Beckett's resourceful survivor, Barthelme's figure becomes a sort of cave man, drawing pictures on the wall and trying to explain modern civilization. In 4,500 words, he describes one of culture's great inventions, the baseball bat, the truth of which Barthelme must write tongue-in-cheek.

Despite this humor, what distinguishes this story is the characters' focus on seemingly genuine emotion. The two have trouble sleeping, and they even contemplate turning the key, "ending it all." Barthelme's conclusion, however, bitterly undercuts their desperation and any suggestion of real feeling: "I understand what it is Shotwell wishes me to do. . . . But only if he will give me the jacks." Life and death issues correlate with getting a turn at jacks. "That is fair."

XI   *"Alice"*

"Alice" lacks the bitter satire or self-mockery Barthelme frequently employs in his first-person stories about sexual longing. Here he portrays the speaker's lascivious thoughts toward his best friend's wife, Alice. An OB, who "obstetricate[s] ladies from predicaments," he affects, in the grand Restoration style, a limp so he can "endure the gaze of strangers [shades of Sartre] the hatred of pediatricians."

In straightforward and unemotional language, which is very funny, he describes the real and imagined pleasures and problems of such an affair. Where, for example, "can I fornicate with Alice . . . [and] renovate Alice?" Equally funny is the fact that this man, a victim of traditional morality that espouses fidelity, must cite, like a lawyer in court, the various "impediments" to infidelity. His litigious, factual tone, as he discusses the various sections of an unidentified moral agreement, is interrupted by his less controlled fantasies of his great sexual adventure. Ultimately all get muddled together: "there are obstacles impediments preclusions estoppels I will exhaust them for you what a gas see cruel deprivements SECTION SEVEN moral ambiguities SECTION NINETEEN Alice's thighs are like SECTION TWENTY-TWENTY ONE."

XII   "A Picture History of the War"

"Why does language subvert me, subvert my seniority, my medals, my oldness, whenever it gets a chance? What does language have against me—me that has been good to it? . . ."

With echoes from Beckett's *Endgame* Barthelme creates a surreal but very funny drama, mixing what would ordinarily be considered dream thought and behavior with everyday waking experience. Ultrachic mothers gather with their children at various park fountains and witness, as though this were an ordinary event, the bizarre, contemporary version of Anchises and Aeneas—"Kellerman, gigantic with gin," running "through the park at noon with his naked father slung under one arm." Spatial and linguistic dislocations are extended to visual ones, as Barthelme treats once again a society of people, specifically here the father and son, who are incapable of connecting on a verbal level, although a true emotional bond exists between them.

The father is a "jumping general" who participated in battles throughout history, from the time he was the Hammer of Thor, through the Civil War, to World War II. Today, he is just an old man who looks like "a radish," hopeful "that there might happen some great dispute among nations, some great anger, so that I might be myself again!" He laments that his son never joined the "incredibly romantic" life of war, although he did everything to encourage his becoming a parachutist: "I gave him a D-ring for a teething toy . . . and put him on a mantle, and said, 'Jump, you little bastard.' " He even had "expensive green-gold grenadiers from F.A.O. Schwartz."

But his intellectual son became a bridge expert, a specialist in card battles, and he authored "a Bible of bridge." Now when asked to "say something professional," he can say "♠ 6 ♡ K," or even (and Barthelme translates) "the four of fans, the twelve of wands, the deuce of kidneys, the Jack of Brutes."

Despite all of Barthelme's verbal tricks, the story has a serious undercurrent in the son's persistent questions to his father on the meaning of life, although Barthelme has his usual fun in giving him a very long list, beginning "Who is fit for marriage?" and ending "Is a human egg like a bird's?" (The "birds and the bees" have substituted for "fear and trembling.") At the end of the story, as a matter of fact, still searching for answers, the son runs up to a fireman (another child's hero) with the same list of questions. What Barthelme is saying perhaps is that it is not only foolish to expect answers, but one is forever naive to ask the same questions. The father—if we look at the story closely—has in fact been destroyed by language; he has been patriotic, he has filled the role expected of him as a soldier, he has used words ("What does language have against me—me that has been good to it?" Note his *improper* grammar), and he still has nothing. He has only grown old, and he has always been incapable of answering his son's questions.

In two grotesquely funny sequences, the son would confess to his father, but neither father nor son can understand what is being said, because they lack a consensually validated system of words to express their experience. Filled with nonsense words and neologisms, the sequences are very funny. In the first: "Bless me, Father, for I have sinned. I committed endoarchy two times, melanicity four times, encropatomy seven times, and preprocity with igneous intent, pretolemicity, and overt cranialism once each." His second confession involves his sin of wanting to communicate through language. Now his own textbook explanation—concretized—cancels out his very intent: "I wanted to say a certain thing to a certain man, . . . I opened my head . . . and proceeded to pronounce the true thing that lay languishing there . . . that felicitous trularity, from its place inside my head out into world life. . . . I propelled, using my mouth, all my muscles. I propelled. I propelled and propelled. I felt that trularity inside my head moving slowly through the passage provided (stained like the caves of Lascaux with garlic, antihistamines, Berlioz, a history, a history) toward its début on the world stage. Past my teeth with their little brown sweaters knitted of gin and cigar smoke, toward its leap to critical scrutiny." Barthelme is once again ironical about his own irony toward our contemporary compulsion to "explain"—our need and yet inability to pursue the Grail myth. Not only can one never really "know" anything, because language subverts or misinforms, but even if we could know anything, it would not help. Life, Barthelme seems to be saying here, is really only the experience of time's passage. Although father and son quote Paul Goodman's theory several times ("In a viable constitution, every excess of power should structurally generate its own antidote"), as though this could touch the pain or joy of life, time alone is the natural antidote to power. Like the old parents in *Endgame*, the father, who at one time ruled his son with a strap, is now at the mercy of his son, also both kind and unkind to him.

XIII *"The President"*

This is a *tour de force* of spatial dislocations, reflective of our dislocated sense of direction in life and our inability to connect experience with meaning, the word with feeling or event. People shift from one role to another; they faint for no ostensible reason; even the President's mother is described as both "5'2"," with "a cane" and "7'1"," with "a dog." Nothing attaches anywhere or means very much. The only things one can be certain about are these: (1) the narrator is once again with "Sylvia," (2) he feels totally dislocated in our time, and (3) life's only certainties are "Copulation. Strangeness. Applause."

The ultimate representative of this "strangeness" is the forty-eight-inch-high President, whose "darkness, strangeness, and complexity," along with his philosophical contemplations of death, have touched everyone and won him the election. In this political satire Barthelme literalizes once again our complete separation from anything meaningful: "When the President speaks, [reminiscent of the waterfall scene in *The Magic Mountain*] one hears only cadences." Barthelme portrays our profound need for a savior, even in abbreviated form.

XIV   "See the Moon?"

"I'm just trying to give you a little briefing here. I don't want you unpleasantly surprised.... Regard me as a sort of Distant Early Warning System. Here is the world and here are the knowledgeable knowers knowing. What can I tell you? What has been pieced together from the reports of travellers.... Fragments are the only forms I trust."

Barthelme performs his usual word divertissements here (i.e., "[As a scientist] there's the matter of my security check—I'm waiting for the government. Somebody told it I'm insecure"). But one intuits and is most taken with the story's strong autobiographical elements. This is "A Prayer for My Son"—a father's promise to protect his unborn child from a hostile world (the moon). It is also a sometimes funny and always serious confession of the father's life thus far.

The speaker "briefs" his child, not surprisingly, that one can "know" only "fragments," and his fragments are then enumerated. Like the narrator in "Me and Miss Mandible," he has pursued all the things one should: an honors student, he was involved *in* the world, in the army, and in public relations; he studied science, philosophy, and religion; he raised his first child, a son, in the most modern way, but the universe remained mysterious and hostile. Despite all his information, he gained no comfort. Fragments are all he can trust.

In the midst of his autobiography, he guards his identity. Involved in "lunar hostility studies," he studies the world and imagination. (Since symbolic equivalents are arbitrary, Barthelme equates the moon, traditional symbol of the imagination and the writer's ally, with man's isolation in a hostile world.) Because his investigatory instruments consist, in part, of "folded paper airplanes" (he *is* a writer), he aligns himself with great historic explorers who also had to worry about edges (i.e., the paper, the earth), like Columbus. He says, with the cadences of familiar success mottos: "Show me a man who worries about edges and I'll show you a natural-born winner."

He and Ann talk about their baby, and Barthelme parodies the logic behind whether people can "afford" a child. They discuss the *size* of their child as though he were a melon *and* in terms of their stocks: "They cost the earth, those extra-large sizes. Our holdings in Johnson's Baby Powder to be considered too." That Ann is getting enormous in size is then literalized in a long and funny comment on "getting large with battleship."

Interrupting his "story" to make the reader aware that this is fiction, the narrator says of Ann: "I'm going to keep her ghostly. . . . I don't want her bursting in on us. . . . What we need here is *perspective*." He asks the reader: "Don't go." The big show will follow: "the greased-pig chase and balloon launchings come next," an ironic reminder of the speaker's private "balloon."

More personal disclosures follow: "I was promising once," a university honors student who, like a child (on a "toy train"), went to Korea. There he literally whitewashed the area. (Barthelme, who arrived in Korea the day the truce was signed, spent much of his tour writing newspaper stories.) His most heroic act was recovering the "bawdy [as opposed to bloody] remains" of a drunk friend. When he returned to his "cha cha cha" home, he felt displaced, and (again playing on the word) he went to a *placement* office ("My percentile was the percentile of choice"), an exemplary man, "married, mature, malleable," and got a job writing "poppycock" and "sometimes cockypap" at his alma mater. (Barthelme wrote speeches for the president of his alma mater.) "Moonstruck," however, he lost his first wife, Sylvia, and after the divorce, their son, Gregory, had to be divided up. (He got the "dreaming raffish Romany part.") But Gregory, who phones regularly to ask about his "history," and who accepts anything verbal that can be neatly categorized, never took his father's (very witty) advice: "Try the Vernacular Isles. Where fish are two for a penny and women two for a fish. But you wanted M.I.T. and electron-spin-resonance spectroscopy. You didn't even crack a smile in your six-ply heather hopsacking." Actually, the trouble with Gregory stems from his "scientific" rearing, his programming by Princeton's two commercial industries: "O Gregory, that Princeton crowd got you coming and going. Procreative [Creative] Playthings at one end and the Educational Testing Service at the other." Today, Gregory thinks science will save us.

"Did we do 'badly' by Gregory," the narrator worries, and "will we do 'better'" with the unborn child? "It's wiser not to ask," he concludes and then returns to the fragments of his life. After public relations, he pursued a "kinky" career, the science of "cardinalogy," the study of his friend Cardinal Y, which led to his even greater disillusionment with philosophy, religion, and science. Despite all his scientific investigations (like testing him with the "Minnesota Multiphastic Muzzle Map"), all his measurements "miss[ed] the most essential thing. I liked him."

At the end, still fearful of failing again as a father, he projects how he could handle his son's questions about life. "Look at my wall," he could say, pointing to pasted fragments and souvenirs, "It's all there." Earlier he had expressed his hope these would "someday merge, blur—cohere . . . into something meaningful. . . . A work of art." He would give the child the stuff of his art.

He would explain to the child: "That's a leaf . . . stuck up with Scotch Tape," and aware of the difficulty of explaining the arbitrary meanings of words, he might have to say: "No, no, the Scotch Tape is the shiny transparent stuff," "the leaf the veined irregularly shaped. . . ." (Ellipses can reflect substance as accurately as words.) He might then show him three prints on the wall (including "Yeats Presenting Mr. George Moore to the Queen of the Fairies"), each reflecting the creativity, privacy, and wonder of art. Though scorned by science, this magical world of fantasy and art would be his gift to his child.

His final warning is a reminder of one's ultimate separation and alienation from the universe: "See the moon? It hates us." Yet the story ends in a mixture of tones. In what Barthelme calls a "nasty last line," he says: "In another month" the child is born. "What can I do for him? I can get him into A.A., I have influence. And make sure no harsh moonlight falls on his new soft head. . . . We hope you'll be very happy here." But the reader cannot help but associate the "A.A." reference with the father's earlier admission: "When a child is born, the locus of one's hopes . . . shifts . . . you feel it, this displacement. . . . Drunk with possibility once more."

CHAPTER 6

City Life

BARTHELME continues his visionary landscaping of society, its "brain damaged" inhabitants slouching toward 100 percent trash productivity through media and technology. A sobriety of tone predominates. *City Life*, remarkable in its richness, goes beyond particularized images of the moribund modern world to more extensive explorations of the matters of art, words, and irony, the last an inevitable but double-edged sword in dealing with such a world. "What recourse" has one, he asks in one story, if he is to remain *in* and *of* the world?

While he literalizes in several stories Jane's statement (from *Snow White*) that the sole possible victory through irony is solipsism, a victory over canceled spaces, Barthelme in fact accomplishes his ends through manipulation of multiple levels of irony. The result, to be sure, is more than an "empty plenum." Indeed, he may view irony as a poor compensation for the squalor of the quotidian, but implied throughout his work is the sense of an untapped richness in that very world, which his extraordinary language evokes. One feels an exhilaration in the magic of his art, as he propels us to embrace a world being born.

Despite Barthelme's evocations of the flux within which the artist must set his words adrift, and one's sense of the referential ambiguity in which they float, *the words remain*, connecting, separating, shifting, defining, provoking, stirring. If many of the stories literalize the problems of the ironic pose (i.e., "Kierkegaard," "The Explanation"), others ("Bone Bubbles," "Sentence," "Tolstoy," "The Glass Mountain," "Paraguay," "On Angels") illustrate the power of the individual to create and shape, to sing out into the void. *City Life* is apocalyptic in its vision of a mad, brain-damaged, technologically controlled world of palpitating

106

"muck," its inhabitants drenched with spiritual malaise. But it is also a bold affirmation of artistic creativity in the spirit of "Shower of Gold." Tolstoy, the red snow, like the last atom, will always resist classification and stir the imagination to barter, and perhaps even penetrate, the void.

I *"Views of My Father Weeping"*

Barthelme works the "signs sometimes lie" theme into such a complex series of plot details, character interactions, and mixture of styles, that one has difficulty finding a point of reference from which to begin. The only thing we're certain of is that the narrator's father has been killed by a horse and carriage, and the narrator seeks to learn what happened. Barthelme provides conflicting "information" and/or opinions regarding the accident or murder, depending upon (1) the witness, (2) the social status of the "accused" (was he an aristocrat, which implies a superiority to his driver and at least two potentially different relationships with the accuser-son?), (3) the father's "condition"—sober, inebriated, distracted.

The son, also looking for the "meaning" of his father in his life, recalls his youth, especially those moments his father wept. But just as external signs may lie (i.e., the aristocrat may be less civilized than the hired hand), internal signs (recollections) may also lie. The father is remembered in a variety of situations—i.e., even weeping over missing a shot at a "peccadillo"; and his identity is elusive. "Is he," the son asks, "another father: Tom's father, Phil's father, Pat's father?"

Interesting too is the affectless way the story is told. The son parrots literary styles—i.e., the popular detective story and the grand, nineteenth century novel. "I understand that you are looking for me," says Lars Bang, like Dashiell Hammett's Philip Marlowe. Because his words (the "signs" of his feelings) ring false, the most we can say is that he is filling a role expected of him, one created by pop culture and tradition, a grim parody of the Hamlet figure. His last word—"Etc."—underscores this, as it urges us to just assume the usual, trite conclusion to a story we've read many times before.

A final irony undercuts everything. Perhaps the son does grieve after all, his words a mask for his deepest feelings: "I bent over my father, whose chest was crushed, and laid my cheek against his." All signs can lie. Otherwise why would he bother to track down the "truth"? Why would he recall his youth? Indeed, why would he tell this story? We finish it as mystified as we were when beginning. The capitalized "Etc." encourages us to create our own "truth" from a variety of ambiguous signs.

II *"Paraguay"*

Since any name is an arbitrary sign, Barthelme is free to call his strange, lunar "silver city" (to which an explorer has been sent to lead his people home) "Paraguay." This is the world perfected by technology, a programmed and homogeneous society. Everyone has the same fingerprints, and people win awards for leveling out their emotions. To "complicate" and "enrich" life, sexual rules are imposed. So pure is life here that even the sand is sifted regularly, the sea programmed to exclude shells. Society is so efficient that "temperature controls activity," which is thereby totally predictable. For example, only between sixty-six and sixty-nine degrees does "intercourse occur." Finally, silence "is sold in paper sacks like cement," and art has been reduced to rules: quality control devices guarantee high production and proper distribution.

Yet despite this ridiculous, mechanically perfect, presumably humane albeit totalitarian society (when crime occurs, people are "chosen at random" to be punished: "everyone is liable for everything"), it is obviously a totally inhibiting world. Fortunately, the explorer discovers a redeeming element "yet not forbidden." This is the "red snow"—the concretely and symbolically fresh experience (like Wallace Stevens's "ice cream"), of exquisite texture and design, sensuous, and at once ephemeral and eternal—to be touched, enjoyed, and contemplated *before* it has been categorized. Despite everything else that buries the human spirit, like the purified sand, the "red snow" still "invites contemplation and walking about in . . . a red glow . . . [a] mystery."

III *"The Falling Dog"*

One day a dog with bad breath jumped out of a high window

and knocked down the speaker, a sculptor and poet. The story is a funny concretization of the origins of the poetic muse, of private fantasy and artistic creation. Barthelme again evokes the mystery of art and its sometimes eccentric origins.

IV *"At the Tolstoy Museum"*

About half of this consists of museum prints, most of which are untitled. Some are portraits, some group scenes; others are buildings with figures and lines superimposed diagramming fixed, Renaissance perspective, as though to indicate centrality of plot, character, and meaning. Prints are juxtaposed without regard to size, theme, or perspective, and most noticeably, they lack any context. One can assume, since they are part of the museum, that they might be useful to the archivist interested in "objective facts."

Apart from these, and a brief retelling of a Tolstoy tale, the story consists of factual and satiric statements about Tolstoy, the museum, and its visitors. Barthelme's point—if one were to ignore his recasting of the Tolstoy story—might be that Tolstoy's significance today exists only in his artifacts, in the details of his life. Nevertheless, the speaker, while reporting all this, is simultaneously impressed and overwhelmed by the power of the legend, Tolstoy. Indeed, upon finding one of his stories on file, he is moved to repeat it, and in so doing he demonstrates the eternal relevance of the artist, the wonder of an imagination that inspires in other generations imaginative fecundity.

Form and content merge. The story (both Tolstoy's and Barthelme's) is about a bishop who intrudes upon three hermits at prayer in order to teach them the "proper" words to use, only to subsequently learn, in a mystical scene, that "their prayer, too, reaches God." Indeed, in the telling of this story the narrator accomplishes the same effects he praises in Tolstoy—"beauty" and "distance."

One could remark that Barthelme demonstrates the relevance of irrelevance, or the universality of art (concretizing the synchronic and diachronic). But if there is an irony here, it goes much deeper. Although all the artifacts seem relevant only to the scholar or archivist (who reflect the modern world's definition and evaluation of itself in terms of *things*), Barthelme demonstrates the eternal power of imagination—the survival of that last atom, once again the "red snow" in the sterile world of statistics and things. That is, signs may lie and they may change, but if one is inspired, he may take the old signs (i.e., the museum prints and Tolstoy's story) and reconstruct them in new ways. The "message" does indeed remain constant: one must do his own thing for, in a sense, any prayer may "reach God." The hermit is to the bishop, as Tolstoy is to Barthelme.

The museum—with its 30,000 pictures, Tolstoy's clothing, and all sorts of trivia—becomes finally, in yet another irony, an emblem of "meaning"—of "beauty" and "distance"—of the transcendence and yet permanence of artistic vision (like the word itself), but only when *Barthelme* transforms the museum into his story. The reader then, inspired by Barthelme, inspired by the museum and Tolstoy (who perhaps took the story from St. Augustine, though "it is said to originate in a folk tale"), uses and then goes beyond fact and signs to create, within his own contemporary frames of reference and personal language, a world.

V *"The Policeman's Ball"*

Horace, one of "New York's finest," prepares Rock Cornish hen for Margot, whom he expects to "put out" tonight. Although the possibility of her rejection stirs violent images in his mind, he puts these aside, because "I must . . . be an example for the rest of the people." At the Camelot Ball, the Pendragon (who, like every other man there, Margot finds attractive) speaks on police matters with similar violent undertones. Like Horace, he handles these in terms of the public good. As Margot and Horace dance, she decides—for reasons of public welfare—to succumb: "His heroism deserves it. He stands between us" and the powers of evil. Back at the apartment, however, that "evil" is personified in the "horrors," who have literally moved outside Horace's apartment.

At the end, Margot responds to Horace as symbol (her protector, the *form* of modern prince), rather than as person, a truly disconcerting and horrifying idea. There is no connection between her sexuality (the act) and what it represents (feeling). The horrors, from which Margot is seeking protection, are also divorced from any usual associations, and they laugh harmlessly. "No one is safe," they say—not from external violence but from internal dislocation.

VI *"The Glass Mountain"*

One of his best-known stories, this consists of 100 numbered sentences that enumerate the artist's climb to the top of a glass mountain. (One should pause over the very image and enjoy its tactile and visual texture.)

Barthelme discards not only the conventional storytelling form, but he rejects as well the traditional explanations of the artist's final "discovery" (at least, his "sort" of artist's). What is of greatest interest—and this takes us back to "The Tolstoy Museum" and "The Balloon"—is Barthelme's proposition: one must function within the quotidian; the ascent is "traditional," for reality ("the mountain") is fixed, and the methods for climbing are "givens" (i.e., imagination or the nightingale). But once one ascends, he can reject all conventional accoutrements for totally personal satisfaction: "I threw the beautiful princess [the "beautiful enchanted symbol"] headfirst down the mountain to my acquaintances . . . who could be relied upon to deal with her." His acquaintances, scornful, jealous, and hostile toward his ascent, can well absorb and appreciate what he discards (traditional fiction). But for Barthelme's knight, who may or may not need an audience, traditional symbols and "endings" are not "plausible, not at all, not for a moment"—which Barthelme concretizes in the story.

A few of the numbered sentences describe the creative process. As the knight ascends, he notes not only the mountain but every detail of the world below—the known and unknown—each a potential ingredient for art: "16. Touching the side of the mountain, one feels coolness"; "19. The top . . . vanishes into the clouds"; "28. In the streets were hundreds of young people shooting up in doorways"; "30. The sidewalks were full of dogshit in brilliant colors: ocher, umber, Mars yellow, sienna. . . ."

He mocks the grandeur of the traditional questing knights who, now fallen to the mob, have become a part of the conventional world of ordinary consciousness. The voraciousness of the public is concretized in its grotesquely familiar vandalism "prising the gold teeth of not-yet-dead knights." Indeed, one requires a "good reason" to climb, but not "on behalf of science, or in search of celebrity, or because the mountain was a challenge." His reason, which can only be articulated in the jargon of ordinary speech, ends in the ellipses of his anticipated discovery: "At the top of the mountain there is a castle of pure gold, and in a room in the castle sits. . . ." And making his goal a symbol of symbols, he completes the sentence with the dependable terminology of fairy tale: "a beautiful enchanted symbol."

One climbs the mountain, in fact, "to disenchant a symbol," and this he proceeds to do. Although he explains (71) that "the conventional symbol [like "the nightingale," which symbolizes "melancholy"] . . . is *not* a sign [which is concrete] like the traffic light," he then treats the symbol as sign (and disenchants it): "72. A number of nightingales with traffic lights tied to their legs flew past me." This is as precise a definition of Barthelme's methodology—the concretization or literalization of metaphor—as we could hope for.

Then, reviewing the conventional means of ascent (i.e., Keatsian suffering and victory or Promethean struggle), he brings concrete reality to the fore: he has no "Bandaids" for this quest. Yet, because the route upward is fixed and he must follow the same path, the eagle cuts his flesh; like the traditional knight, he cuts off its feet. It is only when he arrives to meet "*only* a beautiful princess," that he can choose to discard her to the masses, his unique and totally personal response.

Barthelme has written another story about writing, metafiction. Although his format is new, and he may think he has destroyed the beautiful princess, he has expressed his experience in the only means available, traditional language. At the end, he would ironically erase everything he has written, and we see the entire story as a concrete example of his disenchanting a symbol: "Nor are eagles plausible, not at all, not for a moment." The story, until now, has seemed complete, but its author (who has again manipulated the new in terms of the old, and who has used words to define the indefinable) now retracts it all. "The Glass Mountain" retains both an open-ended, continuously evolving quality, as it simultaneously denies its own reality. Once again, Barthelme has completely disappeared from his work, and he stands distant, paring his fingernails.

VII   *"Kierkegaard Unfair to Schlegel" and "The Explanation"*

Both stories can be read together, since each is a comment upon the other, and in each Barthelme stretches the forms of fiction to incorporate black boxes and an unusually diverse mixture of tones and levels of irony. Both are written as a debate, in a Q/A (question/answer) format. This form, he explains in the first story, permits the omission of what one feels; one also associates it with both the Socratic method and the dialectical structuring of the short-story genre. In both stories "Q" is *presumably* the adversary—the black box, the computerized, mechanical mentality, the technologist who believes machines can handle all human needs, from sex to the government. "A" *appears* as the protagonist, the narrator of flesh, blood, and imagination.

To many readers the stories seem to portray the sterile, mechanical life versus the rich, intellectual one, with the victory of imagination (wit and irony) over dry fact. (However, Barthelme's brief but provocative comment, in a conversation with this author—"Irony is like masturbation"—may be helpful in reading the story.) Beneath the several levels of irony in "Kierkegaard," if there is any "victory," it is Q's, in his awareness of legitimate human relationships. In fact, it is A who remains removed (indeed solipsistic) from life in his dependence upon both irony and masturbatory fantasies, which function—like his irony—as only a poor substitute. As Jane puts it in *Snow White*, irony allows one victory over an empty plenum (a canceled space). What is wanted, as Kierkegaard is quoted in the story, is a reconciliation with the world. One might be able to overcome the disturbing aspects of reality through imagination, but at best, like masturbation, solipsism is a limited pleasure, a poor second for the real thing.

A is imprisoned in his mind. The story begins with his sexual fantasy of meeting a naive, young, blonde, braless girl, sitting and reading on a train in romantic France. She is moving about suggestively: "I use the girl on the train a lot," he admits. "Her legs are fairly wide apart. . . ." But even in his fantasy he is fearful and detached, and he avoids connecting with her: "I am carefully looking out of the window." Q, who (to our amusement) sounds like a psychiatrist, says: "That's a very common fantasy. . . . Does it give you pleasure?" A replies: "A poor . . . A rather unsatisfactory . . . ," unable to complete the sentence and admit, "a poor *substitute*." Q, again as though asking him of his masturbatory habits, continues: "What is the frequency?" A admits a great deal in his demuring: "Oh God who knows. Once in a while. Sometimes."

Q asks if A is involved in the world and is "political." A replies that he is, *through* his irony: "[I] turn my irony against the others," but, he concedes, his irony accomplishes "nothing." His real interest in life, it would appear, is the "girls," "running . . . laughing."

Q, who has, after all, just learned about the uselessness of A's irony, asks (ironically): "Do you think your irony could be helpful in changing the government?" A responds with another example of useless irony: the government, in fact, ironically undermines its own credibility through peddling "surplus uniforms." The result is a "splendid clown Army" of kids prancing about in costume.

Then, as if Q's programming suddenly went awry, in staccato fashion he babbles a series of funny and nonsequiturial questions: "How is my car?" "How is my nail?" "How is the taste of my potato?" "How is the cook of my potato?" and he finally states the understated: "You are an ironist," to which A replies: "It's useful." He then proceeds to further exemplify. Once he rented a ski instructor's house that was overflowing with toys and games, which he found very disturbing (ironically, *we* must observe; after all, if games are a substitute for life, why should *he*, the great escapist, be contemptuous of game playing?)

Then he says, "*Suppose* I had been of an ironical turn of mind [italics mine]," I might have canceled these out by merely affecting an ironic attitude. (Note: he is now fantasizing about his irony.) Then, continuing his *speculations* about irony, he says: "Suppose that I am suddenly curious about this amazing magical power . . . how my irony actually works." (Of course his speculation

becomes his reality, and he becomes more and more solipsistic
as he spells out his "Supposing.")

He proceeds to an elaborate discussion of Kierkegaard's *The
Concept of Irony* and explains how, unfortunately, to Kierkegaard
irony is ultimately destructive. It "has nothing to put in the
place of what it has destroyed," and he cites as an example
Kierkegaard's criticism of Schlegel's *Lucinde*. Canceling out the
world through irony leaves one, to the more religious Kierkegaard
(and to Jane in *Snow White*), with only a distancing toward the
world, an animosity rather than a reconciliation.

Then—and one must slow down his pace of reading here—A
makes the judgment that although he has been critical of Kierkegaard and his concept of irony, this is *not* what he believes. In
fact, he knows Kierkegaard's position to be correct about the
solipsism of irony (and about *Lucinde*). A has merely adopted
Kierkegaard's irony (as a canceling out) and applied it to Kierkegaard himself, to justify his own solipsism—both in his irony and
sexual (fantasy) life. "We have to do here with my own irony,"
he admits, "because of course Kierkegaard was 'fair' to Schlegel."

Having disposed of Kierkegaard (or has he?), he then feels
free to return to his sexual fantasies. The girl seems to be pleasur-
ing herself:

Q: What is she doing now?
A: She appears to be—
Q: How does she look?
A: Self-absorbed.

Q wants A to say the words—"You have to give more"—but A's
response is silence. After a bit, he admits: "She's caressing her
breasts."

Having come this far, in terms of articulating his experience
(indeed, A is as much a black box as Q), he recalls a concrete
emotional experience (whose details are personal), involving
frustration on several levels—personal and professional. The
recollection is this: after returning from Central Park alone with
his daughter, he was carried away with a sexual fantasy as he
read a critical book about a movie. (Note how many levels he,

the book, and film are removed from life.) He had dinner with a divorced man, drank a lot, and became depressed. This very personal experience, and his pain, may be the key to the entire story (cf. "The Balloon") and its very subject ("Indian Uprising").

Q can help him only by offering him other intellectual distractions, the complicated technology of the machine: "You could interest yourself in these interesting machines" (note Barthelme's sardonic repetition of "interest"), perhaps the next step after sexual fantasizing, irony, and drinking. At the end, A bitterly hears Q's last comment, a rather touching story concerning Louis Pasteur, implying connection, commitment, and generosity, a "reconciliation with the world": "Pasteur, distracted, ashamed, calls upon Mme. Boucicault . . . [for] money for his Institute. . . . They both burst into tears." The final blow, of course, is that the "machine" should know this story.

In "The Explanation," which anticipates "Kierkegaard" (not only in its complex themes but even in the repetition of certain phrases), it is difficult to ascertain whether Q or A is more removed from life. Q, who would again seem to represent the machine, asks: "Do you believe that, at some time in the future, one will be able to achieve sexual satisfaction, 'complete' sexual satisfaction, for instance by taking a pill?" But it is he (whose daughter is a black box) who provokes A into pursuing his sexual fantasies. (Q fantasizes through A's fantasies.) On the other hand, A is almost as dry and "emotionless," and as removed from life as the black box. He fantasizes an "extraordinarily handsome girl" in jeans, blue blouse, and sunglasses, crossing the street (whom he also looks away from). There is even less overt sexuality—in the fantasy—here than in "Kierkegaard." Nevertheless, through Q's prompting, he returns to the girl in the street, and finally he pictures her—undressing herself. The story ends on the mockingly climactic: "There is a bruise on her thigh. The right."

VIII   *"The Phantom of the Opera's Friend"*

Barthelme has revised *The Phantom of the Opera* with resonances from *Notes from Underground*. (Perhaps one should not assume that one is more "authentic" than the others.) The speaker is a friend (lover?) of the phantom, whose dilemma concerns whether or not to retain his elegant, underground quarters (with "rich divans, exquisitely carved tables, [and] amazing silk and satin draperies") and thereby retain his magical and mysterious identity—the formidable work of art. Should the Phantom come out of hiding, have plastic surgery, and then live the normal life: "One is never too old . . . a home . . . children." What should be done with the princess atop the Glass Mountain; should she be embraced or hurled down to the masses?

In Barthelme's very "campy" treatment of him, reminiscent of the Batman story, the Phantom, for mysterious reasons, opts to remain below. His friend (ambivalent about this) reacts in phrases, with melodramatic melody and kinky language (his slangy metaphor literalized and extended): "I will wait . . . a hundred years. Or until the hot meat of romance is cooled by the dull gravy of common sense once more." Barthelme draws a charming and rather magical story about the relationship between the individual and art, always rich, intimate, and elusive.

IX *"Sentence"*

That it is an act of supreme affirmation to mold and fashion words is given vivid expression in "Sentence" where, in a fragment of about 250 lines, Barthelme decorates the void and celebrates the wonders of life in the very movement of his sentence. In much of his work Barthelme attacks the trash phenomenon of language. In other work he dramatizes how words remain tied to the quotidian. But he always affirms the fresh use of language as an emblem of the life force, as our only means of connecting with the world of phenomena, of defining, through arbitrary structures, the nothingness around us.

Lacking a beginning or end, Barthelme's "Sentence" simply *is*. As it unravels, it asks and answers questions about meaning, origin, and authority; its lush, expansive, nontraditional grammar is a microcosm of Barthelme's rich universe; its profusion of details reflects the physical universe.

Joyous in its abundance, it is both a tribute to and a product of the imagination. Barthelme punctuates the ultimate silence, and his words—limited as they are—stand firm against life's finality, against what at the end he calls "the strength of stones": "the sentence itself is a man-made object, not the one we wanted of course but still a construction of man, a structure to be treasured for its weaknesses, as opposed to the strength of stones." One is reminded of a former poet's (Lucky's) speech in *Waiting for Godot*, a lamentation on how all human activity ends in death, the "earth abode of stones." In "Sentence," words chant into the void, worthy adversaries to the strength of stones.

X   *"Bone Bubbles"*

Fifteen sixteen-line fragments again illustrate the author's effort to punctuate the void. Unlike "Sentence," however, the fragments neither comment on and reflect "coherent meaning," nor do they fall into any traditional structural and grammatical units. Instead, each juxtaposes unlikely combinations of words (i.e., the title) which, through a variety of sensory associations (as well as the usual denotative and connotative ones), connect and re-form into new imaginative constructs. In this word collage reflective of raw reality, each unit *appears* to have its own autonomy within the flux, perceived and sustained through the artifice of form, but content is almost impossible to verbalize in traditional language.

The reader, touching and experiencing language in time and space, must make the creative effort to write his own text, to design his own organization within the world, the verbal flux, before him. It begins: "bins black and green seventh eighth rehearsal pings a bit/fussy at times fair scattering grand and exciting world of his/fabrication topple out against surface irregularities fragiliza-/tion of the gut constitutive misrecognitions of the ego most. . . ."

XI   *"On Angels"*

"It is curiosity of writing about angels that, very often, one turns out to be writing about men."

Barthelme has been posing questions about the function of words in a universe without absolute referents, if indeed we can "know the dancer from the dance." He has also questioned the mechanics of irony and how (to quote Kierkegaard from Barthelme's citation of him earlier) "irony deprives the object of its reality." "On Angels," one of his most ingenious stories, plays with an analogous problem: what is an angel without God? How does it function and sing its hallelujahs in a world of silence? What Barthelme is doing, of course, is literalizing the dilemma raised by the "God is dead" declaration and dramatizing the hence *ironic* existence of angels. (One might well compare this with "Shower of Gold" and Barthelme's play with "the absurd" there.) John Milton himself would howl at Barthelme's mini-*Paradise Lost*: "The death of God left the angels in a strange position. . . . New to questioning, unaccustomed to terror, unskilled in aloneness, the angels (we assume) fell into despair."

Citing former angel "authorities," Barthelme's researches reveal some interesting information. Traditionally, (1) angels look like human beings, (2) intelligence correlates with luminescence, (3) they know everything, never ask questions, and lack curiosity. After this (with some parody of LeMan and Baudelaire and even some self-parody), Barthelme focuses on the immediate problem, the authenticity of the angels. If "an angel is what he does," there is possibly a solution. "An angel proposed that lamentation be the function of angels eternally, as adoration was formerly. The mode of lamentation would be silence, in contrast to the unceasing chanting of Glorias that had been their former employment." But since it is "not in the nature of angels to be silent," with their newly created curiosity, they might study "the five great proofs of the existence of chaos" in order "to affirm chaos." Pushing logic to its absurd limits, he writes: "There were to be five great proofs . . . of which the first was the absence of God. The other four could surely be located." This might occupy them forever as "the contrary work has occupied human theologians."

Finally, one angel, in a television appearance, explained that angels, like men, have the "central" problem of "adoration." Like men, they too had tried "adoring each other," but it was "not enough." It would appear that angels, like the dwarfs in *Snow White*, remain in search of "a new principle" (a new script to give them identity) to regain their original equanimity. In the meantime, like other living creatures rejecting the extremes of suicide and adoration, they will simply survive in a purposeless, benignly indifferent universe.

XII   *"Brain Damage"*

"This is quite a nice University. . . . A University constructed entirely of three mile-high sponges! . . . That is the tenured faculty . . . the Department of Romantic Poultry . . . the Department of Great Expectations. . . ."

"Brain Damage" is a whimsical conglomeration of the excesses of the hypereducated, supersophisticated, insane society. Barthelme juxtaposes a series of vignettes, etchings (sometimes superimposing two from totally different sources), headlines, bizarre word combinations, and the refrain "WHAT RECOURSE?" to illustrate a brain-damaged world overwhelmed by "spirit teachers," technology, hollow ritual, texts, media, and art. With echoes of Eliot's final lines in "The Hollow Men," he concludes: *"This is the country of brain damage, this is the map of brain damage, these are the rivers of brain damage. . . ."* Of the damage caused by art, he writes: *"I should describe it better if I weren't afflicted with it."* Parodying Joyce's "snow" passage, in "The Dead" (which also treats the "hyper-educated" new generation living a death-in-life existence), Barthelme concludes his reading of brain-damage's *"unbreakable lease"*: *"Oh there's brain damage in the east, and brain damage in the west, and upstairs there's brain damage, and downstairs there's brain damage, and in my lady's parlor—brain damage. Brain damage is widespread. . . . And you can hide under the bed but brain damage is under the bed, and you can hide in the universities but they are the very seat and soul of brain damage— . . . and there is brain damage in Arizona, and brain damage in Maine, and little towns in Idaho are in the grip of it, and my blue heaven is black with it, brain damage covering everything like an unbreakable lease—."* His last line is terrifying: *"Skiing along on the soft surface of brain damage, never to sink, because we don't understand the danger—."*

XIII   *"City Life"*

"The problem today is not angst but lack of angst."

This title story sketches the humdrum existence of Ramona and Elsa, who have just moved into an apartment. Once again, everything in their world is equally significant—career, sexual partner, where to hang curtains and place the phone book. That life has lost its priorities is epitomized in Ramona's explanation of her immaculate conception pregnancy—a result, it would appear, of the subhuman isolation of urban life, if not the existential condition. The Virgin Ramona has been impregnated by the indifference, absurdity, and sludge of modern life: "Upon me, their glance has fallen. The engendering force was, perhaps, the fused glance of all of them. From the millions of units crawling about on the surface of the city, their wavering desirous eye selected me. . . . I accepted." Given such a world, she asks the bitterly rhetorical: "What was the alternative?"

In keeping with his image of words as emblems of the trash phenomenon, Barthelme portrays Ramona as pregnant with words. She says of her condition, both internal and external: "—I have to admit we are locked in the most exquisite mysterious muck. This muck heaves and palpitates. It is multi-directional and has a mayor. To describe it takes many hundreds of thousands of words. Our muck is only a part of a much greater muck —the nation-state—which is itself the creation of that muck of mucks, human consciousness. Of course all these things also have a touch of sublimity."

CHAPTER 7

Sadness

AS the title suggests, sadness is the predominant mood of this
volume. Despite "Flight of Pigeons," one of Barthelme's most
fanciful stories, one senses an underlying conviction that the
human condition is one of unfulfillment and failure. One's acts
and dreams frustrate: "the actualization fails to meet, equal, the
intuition. There is something 'out there' which cannot be brought
'here.'" Nevertheless, in "Daumier," the last and best story, Barthelme suggests that if one pursues, "there are always openings."
One can gain some "satisfaction" if he fights against habit and
"gets out of things what inheres in them."

Hence, we have male loneliness ("Critique") and the sheer
desolation of unfulfilled marriage and fatherhood without the
limited solace of either irony or creative activity. Nothing has
been learned from the failure of marriage, and one wearily re-
sumes the old humdrum, single life ("Perpetua"). In a world
that lacks priorities ("Party"), where people are anesthetized
by the media ("Critique")—like movies, which ape every emotion and lack any "truth" ("Film")—and morality is dictated by
mod culture ("Perpetua"), one fears the "risk" of living ("Subpoena").

The conforming society, in earlier works, concretized through
technology ("Paraguay") or contemporary philosophy ("Shower
of Gold"), is once again portrayed as repressed and repressive
("City of Churches," "Sandman"). A world of "emotional-cost-
control," boredom ("Rise of Capitalism") is the universal condition. Only on rare occasions do *Sadness*'s people express any
awareness: "Is this the best we can do?" asks one wearily ("The
Party"), reminiscent of "Do you think this is a good life?" ("Indian Uprising").

122

In certain ways these stories dramatize the dilemma raised in Jane's letter (*Snow White*) and "Kierkegaard"—that fantasy or irony separates one from life. That is, it allows only for an intellectual and solipsistic victory. While this may be a question Barthelme raises in theory (and concretizes in some of the stories—i.e., "The Catechist"), in practice one senses, once again, more than a pyrrhic victory. That is, behind his multiple levels of irony is a dazzling poetic energy whose linguistic evocations of reality reflect and provoke a continuously generative process. And lest we fail to mention it, his humor is always instructive.

"There are always openings" is the key phrase, for with words alone defining us (regardless of their distortions), each person in Barthelme's vision—even his priest—is a potential poet or architect, sculpting reality, creating balloons, climbing glass mountains, and parenting surrogate selves. Those with the greatest success locate the "openings" everywhere, aware, as Heidegger said, that "the ordinary is basically not ordinary; it is extra-ordinary."

Two different voices, then, characterize the volume, one regarding the "artist's" frustrations and failure ("Sandman," "Genius," "Pigeons"), the other concerning his victory. Indeed, there are times when, even if only temporarily, the artist may alter reality ("Klee," "Daumier") and transform it—not just for himself but for the world around him.

I *"Critique de la Vie Quotidienne"*

Barthelme returns to the theme of male loneliness, but where previously wit or the sublimating act of writing provided some consolation ("The Balloon"), now the sheer desolation of everyday life, both with and without a woman, is his focus. The balloon has forever been buried; there are no old or new costumes to adorn ("Broadcast"), no Hollywood scripts to mimic, no popular games or ironic poses to play out—even for temporary relief. These people have been so utterly consumed by public information that their emotional lives have atrophied. A profound sense of helplessness characterizes the narrator who, despite his efforts at wit, communicates a terrifying loneliness: "Our evenings lacked promise. The world in the evening seems fraught

with the absence of promise, if you are a married man. There is
nothing to do but go home and drink your nine drinks and forget about it."

He and his wife (and even their child, referred to as *"the
child"*) are all products of sophisticated contemporary culture.
In the evenings, they read the magazines that verbalize their
identities: "While I read the *Journal of Sensory Deprivation*,
Wanda, my former wife, read *Elle.*" "The child," smart, spoiled,
and provocative, demanded whatever "its" friends acquired (i.e.,
a horse in Manhattan), and with full awareness, drove his father
first into rage, and then guilt. Husband, wife, and child hated
one another.

At the end of the story, after their separation, the couple meet
for a drink and hurl ridiculous accusations at each other, as
though one could pinpoint a single event as cause for a lifetime's
misery: "And when I needed a new frock . . . you hid the Uni-
card." The happy ending is grotesque, as much in its details as its
predictability. It is not enough that Wanda became the manne-
quin *Elle* prescribed; she has now run off to study Marxist
sociology with the author of her beloved *Critique*; the child will
be cared for at an experimental nursery school by Piagetian experts, and the speaker takes heart in the eternal manufacture of
J & B Scotch. (The quotidian, of course, remains.)

II   *"The Genius"*

In thirty separate sections, Barthelme constructs an occasionally
serious but predominantly comic definition of the artist (although
he says the story is about a scientist) in his (1) moodiness, vanity,
insecurity, guilt, and sense of frustrated social purpose, (2) in
his peculiar relationship to his work—its occasional mystery or
even total autonomy from him, and (3) in his ultimately ludi-
crous relationship to the world—with its gifts and appointments—
the celebration of genius through all its ranks. All of this is
presented with great irony and self-mockery:

1. On the subject of form (Is Barthelme mocking himself or
his critics, who describe him as a pasticheur?):

Q: What do you consider the most important tool of the genius of
today?

A: Rubber cement. ["The genius carries his most important papers about with him in a green Sears, Roebuck toolbox."]

2. On the artist's political opinions: "He has urged that America should be divided into four smaller countries. America . . . is too big [and] . . . 'does not look where it puts its foot.'" (This comment elicits from the Chamber of Commerce four cases of Scotch.)

3. On the work of art's autonomy which may define or defy its creator ("the worker"), who may really be quite indifferent to it: "The work possesses a consciousness which shapes that of the worker. . . . The worker pays slight regard to the work, . . . is *unfaithful* to the work. The work is insulted. . . . The work becomes slow, sulky."

4. On when the university writes the genius to request his posthumous papers: "He takes a pair of scissors, cuts the letter into long thin strips, and mails it back to the Director of Libraries."

5. On the politics of awards: since neither he, nor his country, nor his discipline, won the Nobel Prize again, "to console him, the National Foundation gives him a new house."

6. On the students who accuse him of social inequality, the "tyranny of the gifted", "the genius smokes thoughtfully."

7. On his wish to change his life: "the genius tears out" advertisements on becoming an "interior decorator."

8. On the benefits society awards geniuses: "the License Bureau sends him a new license [the old one expired], by return mail."

9. On his ability and interest in effecting true social change—in "the sewer systems of cities."

10. On the critical mumbo jumbo and ego trips of his devotees and groupies, as well as the scholarly journals dedicated to "causes" like Structuralism: "An organization has been formed to appreciate his thought: the Blaufox Gesellschaft. Meetings are held once a month, in a room over a cafeteria in Buffalo, New York." Its *Proceedings* read: "'The imbuement of all reaches of the scholarly community with Blaufox's views must, *ab ovo*, be our. . . . He falls into hysteria."

The final detail is wonderful, as Barthelme focuses on the public and critical acclaim the hometown affords its prodigy—gifts which naturally reflect its taste: "A green Railway Express truck arrives at his door. It contains a field of stainless-steel tulips, courtesy of the Mayor and City Council of Houston, Texas." The genius understands his own irony, however, and never malicious, "[He] signs the receipt, smiling. . . ."

III   *"Perpetua"*

Early stories centered on ghostly "singles" groups (i.e., "Viennese Opera Ball") or "marrieds" ("To London and Rome"). At last these dreary people have separated from each other, but they have learned absolutely nothing. They retreat to the dull, emotionless ways of their previous lives.

Perpetua, now living alone, equates, like Ramona and Elsa in "City Life," oiling her trumpet with finding a lover. A consumer who has bought the sell that variety is the spice of life—i.e., one must have a postdivorce fling—she says: "Now I must obtain a lover. . . . Perhaps more than one. One for Monday, one for Tuesday, one for Wednesday."

Although to the reader her life is not what one would call uneventful, to Perpetua nothing has the least consequence: she plays the trumpet with the New World Symphony, smokes dope with a bassoon player, discusses art and revolution, and sleeps with a variety of men, after "cruising around" to find them. She remains isolated from her son, who calls her only for money and really prefers the company of his snake collection. At Christmas she visits her mother, who this year will be cooking "the eighty-seventh turkey of her life." Harold, her ex-husband, watches television, visits his son in boarding school, and devotes himself to tracking down some model (in fact, a friend of Perpetua's) who posed nude for a girlie magazine. The bleakness of their prospects is reminiscent of "Critique," underscored by the muted dialogue at the conclusion when they meet once again: "'I just want to ask you one question,' Harold said. 'Are you happier now than you were before?' 'Sure,' Perpetua said."

IV   *"A City of Churches"*

Reminiscent of "Paraguay" (and "Shower of Gold"), this is

another portrait of the totally homogeneous and presumably "perfect city." In Prester, every building is a church, although some do "double duty"; the Antioch Pentecostal, for example, is also a barbershop.

Cecelia, who has come to Prester to open a car rental office, has misgivings. She finds a world of churches and church people "a little creepy." In addition, if this is a perfect society, there would seem to be no need for a car rental, since that "implies that you want to go somewhere." Nevertheless, a real-estate broker takes her apartment hunting; once again, Cecelia runs into problems. She would like to live by herself—something "not usual here."

Defiant when asked to define her (religious) belief, she replies: "I can will my dreams. . . . Mostly sexual things." Although she is greeted by a howling resident and told to go home and that everyone in the town already has a car, the townsman traipsing about with her urges that she stay, that her office has in fact already been set up to "make the town complete." Though obviously there is no use for her business, the town must be like all others and have its car rental—the ultimate conformity.

When she threatens to "dream the life you are most afraid of," she is informed: "You are ours. . . . There is nothing you can do." At the end, like Peterson in "Shower of Gold," she defiantly proclaims the power of imagination which, as we saw in "Paraguay," can always dance in the red snow: "Wait and see."

V *"The Party"*

"When one has spoken a lot one has already used up all the ideas one has. You must change the people you are speaking to so that you appear, to yourself, to be still alive."

So utterly bored are the party guests that nothing moves them. Noise and silence are the perimeters of their consciousness, and canned language is their sole reality. If strange noises intrude from outside—"drums, whistles, howls, rattles, alphorns"—a label will surely be found: "probably it is . . . the new music."

The story begins: "I went to a party and corrected a pronunciation," as the narrator establishes the verbal level on which these people relate. He continues: "The man whose voice I had adjusted [as one would a tie] fell back [he feels assaulted] into the kitchen." He admits his own vacuousness: "I praised a Bonnard. It was not a Bonnard. . . . Significant variations elude me." Barthelme takes us back to the people of "The Viennese Opera Ball" in this portrait of zombies who are literally composites of public and literary information and opinion. Now, any vestige of residual vitality has burned out.

They are so exhausted that even the arrival of King Kong (a campy superhero, especially among the educated) is greeted by "loud exclamations of fatigue and disgust." Indeed, everyone reacts to his "giant hands, black, thick with fur, reaching in through the windows" (Kong's gesture "to make himself interesting") in his own myopic way, some even hoping for "other excitements."

Almost as buried as the guests is the narrator, whose real story is private—concerning the woman he has escorted (Francesca). Once more the details of their relationship are unclear, although it would seem that he is reluctant to be at the party, and he would have her understand the emotional cost of her life-style. He is one of Barthelme's few narrators who betrays any awareness of his "emotional cost-control" life: "Wouldn't it be better to openly acknowledge your utter reliance on work, . . . on carefully formulated directions, agreeing that, yes, a certain amount of anesthesia is derived from what other people would probably think of as some kind of a career?" Francesca has apparently been accepted by the academic community—ever since her recent compliance with accepted opinion about Kafka and Kleist. The "older faculty," he says, would "promote" or even "marry" her. But he, who has always held to that very same opinion, has been rejected: "I will never be elected to the Academy, Richelieu is against me and d'Alembert is lukewarm." Indeed, it may be Francesca who has the power to sway them.

He is ambivalent not only toward this group but toward what they represent. Although he speaks out against "anesthetization," his verbosity and chic jargon undermine his sincerity. He may say, "Can the life of the time be caught in an advertisement?" but when he comments on his world, his thoughts are trapped in clichés: "Is it some kind of a revolution . . . as when Mannerism was overthrown by the Baroque?" Similarly, when he says, "Carrying over into private life attitudes that have been successful in the field of public administration is not, perhaps, a good idea," his "perhaps" is the death blow. Finally, he asks, "Is this the best we can do?" but his answer lacks conviction, irony, or even clarity: "Of course we did everything right. . . . Is it really important to know that this movie is fine . . . to talk intelligently . . .? . . . Wonderful elegance! No good at all!"

The story is wonderfully imaginative with its dozens of mixtures of the trivial and presumably serious, the banal and the bizarre. Its details are unforgettable. King Kong, for example, no longer the great Hollywood star, is now an adjunct professor of art history at Rutgers, the coauthor of a text on tomb sculpture. As the guests drink "khaki-colored punch," two sisters (who may in fact be the most important people at the party) watch a bizarre T.V. game—the *Osservatore Romano* team versus the Diet of Worms—and then take interminable showers, after which "people are clustered in front of the bathrooms holding fine deep-piled towels, vying to dry the beautiful sisters" (a fair enough way to curry favor with one's hostesses). King Kong, who, unlike the Phantom of the Opera, has opted for the ordinary life, speculates on whether he would prefer sleeping with one woman or another. The overall effect of the story—in the reading of it—is similar to that of "Florence Green." Life and suicide, Bonnard and papier-mâché: "significant variations elude me."

Finally, the story is especially rich in its play with language and extended literalizations of metaphor. Speaking about the amount of deviation acceptable in today's society, Barthelme writes: "Small collective manifestations [of change] are O.K. insofar as they show 'stretch marks'—traces of strain which tend to establish that public policy is not a smooth, seamless achievement, like an egg, but has rather been hammered out at some cost to the policymakers."

VI *"Engineer-Private Paul Klee Misplaces an Aircraft between Milbertshofen and Cambrai, March 1916."*

Paul Klee, recently transferred to the German Air Corps, is assigned to escort three aircraft on their transport between Milbertshofen and Cambrai. "It is not a bad life," says Klee who, when he reaches "a notable town," tries to see "the notable paintings," enjoy the local Bavarian bread, wurst and beer, and when he can, see his lover, Lily, whom he meets in hotel rooms. But one day, while having lunch, an aircraft disappears.

The Secret Police, who remind us of the air force officers in "Game," and who watch Klee's actions, "yearn to be known, acknowledged, admired." Their problem, of course, is that by their very identity as *secret* police, they must remain anonymous. Nevertheless, once the aircraft disappears (because they too are lunching), they must deal with possible censure after filing their report. Klee, only slightly concerned about the aircraft, has, in the meantime, been mesmerized by the "shape of the collapsed canvas ... forming hills and valleys, seductive folds, the ropes the very essence of looseness..." He draws a picture, for "it is irresistible."

Fortunately for Klee, "Reason dictates the solution": "I will diddle the manifest. With my painter's skill which is after all not so different from a forger's. I will change the manifest to reflect conveyance of *two* aircraft."

The Secret Police applaud Klee's action, which allows them to maintain their normal omniscience; Klee goes off to buy some chocolate. The altered manifest is unchallenged, and the story concludes: "The drawing I did of the collapsed canvas and ropes is really very good. I eat a piece of chocolate. I am sorry about the lost aircraft but not overmuch. The war is temporary. But drawings and chocolate go on forever."

From this absolutely wonderful story, one could discuss at length a number of ideas—i.e., from the life (war) is short/art long thesis to the artist's ironic/nonironic "diddling" of reality. Primarily, Barthelme is playing with a number of situations that involve reality and appearance, signs and interpretations. The Secret Police, "defined" by their omniscience and omnipresence, must nevertheless remain invisible; although they represent the status quo, maintaining structure, order, and law, they must also embrace the painter's alteration of what they know is reality (his diddling the manifest), so that what is really a lie (Klee's report) becomes their reality.

The artist's reality—at least, his painting—is determined en-

tirely by an eccentric vision and private and unfathomable
process of selectivity. Klee, for example, is taken with the form
of the canvas and ropes, rather than the "total experience." In
addition, the artist can alter so-called reality (the manifest)
not only for the fact finders, the scientists, or the orderly masses
who need structure and facts in their lives (the Secret Police), but
he can also create the so-called facts history presents as truth.
Future generations will struggle to define whether this event in
1916 was "reported" correctly by the manifest, the painting, or
neither.

Of even greater interest (and, of course, fun) is Barthelme's
focus on the artist, who takes a totally *personal* pleasure in the
reality about him. Klee is more concerned with drawing than
the aircraft, as he cares more for his lover and museums than
the war. If, in addition, he has done something amiss in enjoying
his life (i.e., losing an aircraft as he lunches on wurst and beer),
he feels free to create a satisfactory "explanation" of his acts.
What this means, in effect, is that the artistic imagination can
alter a formidable or threatening reality (loss of the plane) and
make it perfectly palatable (or the opposite) for the scientists,
the citizens, his audience—whoever measures and watches his
behavior. In fact, the artist makes reality—in this case—more
comfortable. But once again, what he cares most about is his
own pleasure, especially in the moment of discovering a new
form within reality. The specific "morality" attached to the flux,
from which he draws his reality—did someone steal the aircraft? will a battle be lost?—is of no concern to him. Furthermore, because he knows the world, with its rage for order and
"meaning," may not accept his private pleasure (his balloon),
he forges another reality (the manifest) for others to enjoy.

Finally, the artist's world remains private, although his creation, like the sensuous pleasures in life (chocolate), remains the
fundamental eternal in human experience, long after war is
played out. The story celebrates the joy and freedom of creativity.

VII *"A Film"*

Barthelme parodies Hollywood's idea of creative art: "The idea
of the film is that it not be like other films." Indeed, every emotion is represented, with only one thing missing—truth.

During the production a real life drama occurs: a sick child is kidnapped by some vandals. By the end of the story, with the vandals now become actors, and the directors and script-writers using this life material for their "art," all distinctions between art and reality, real or simulated emotion, and evil and innocence, are blurred. The vandals, heroes in the film, "hit the trail, confused as to whether they should place themselves under our protection, or fight."

Isolated sections of the story reflect Barthelme's anger; once again his figures juxtapose the significant and insignificant and deal with experience with textbook expertise, rather than emotion. The story begins: "Things have never been better, except that the child, one of the stars of our film, has just been stolen. . . . But might not this incident . . . be made part of the story line?"

The "plot" is reported. "Today we filmed fear, a distressing emotion aroused by impending danger, real or imagined," and "hope," "fame," "wealth information," and "civilization." The story is not without its immodest wit, however, as Barthelme extends this into wildly extravagant analogies: "Today we filmed the moon rocks. . . . They were as good as a war . . . better than a presentation copy of the *Random House Dictionary* signed by Geoffrey Chaucer . . . better than a good cup of coffee from an urn decorated with the change of Philomel, by the barbarous king . . . better than a ¡huelga! led by Mongo Santamaria, with additional dialogue by St. John of the Cross and special effects by Melmoth the Wanderer."

The ultimate immorality of film is that it uses genuine human emotions for exploitative purposes, and these distortions are then presented to the public for emulation. "The rehabilitation of the filmgoing public through 'good design,' through 'softness,' is our secret aim."

A final and bitter irony remains. There never was any feeling or interest in the child—even *before* his kidnapping. "Whose child is it? We forgot to ask, when we sent out the casting call. . . . Its paychecks are made out to it, rather than a nominee."

VIII *"The Sandman"*

"What an artist does, is fail. . . . The actualization fails to meet, equal, the intuition. There is something 'out there' which cannot be brought 'here.' . . . What do you do with a patient who finds the world unsatisfactory? The world *is* unsatisfactory; only a fool would deny it."

Barthelme parodied Snow White's relationship with her psychiatrist; now in a letter to his "girl friend's [Susan's] shrink," his narrator pleads that the doctor stop being the "sandman," who "dusts the children's eyes with sand / And steals their dreams away." If Barthelme has attacked the conformity imposed upon contemporary society by technology ("Paraguay"), religion ("City of Churches"), and modern philosophy ("Shower of Gold"), here he lampoons psychiatry's efforts to both steal our dreams and make us believe that happiness is the norm.

Aware of the traditional ploys used to dissuade a patient from terminating therapy, the narrator says, mockingly: "I fully understand that Susan's wish to terminate with you and buy a piano instead has disturbed you. You have every right to be disturbed and to say that she is not electing the proper course, that what she says conceals something else, that she is evading reality, etc. etc. Go ahead. But there is one possibility here that you might be, just might be, missing. This is that she means it."

Barthelme's sense of humor is unfailing: "As a shrink rather than a piano salesman you would naturally tend to opt for the analysis. But there are differences. The piano salesman can stand behind his product; you, unfortunately, cannot." Of psychiatry's efforts to "normalize" or "stabilize" Susan's life—i.e., convince her she *should* marry—he brilliantly reasons: "In order to validate her nonacceptance of this norm, she defines herself as shrink-needing." The psychiatrist's efforts at having her conform, in fact, "are actually certifying the behavior which you seek to change." Therefore, "when she says to you that she's not shrinkable, you should listen."

IX *"Subpoena"*

"Subpoena" is both humorous and grotesque in its image of the proper and conforming American named, in fact, Citizen Bergman, who receives a subpoena from the Bureau of Compliance. Apparently he has failed to pay the proper taxes (even in a totally uniform society, part of its conformity consists of tax evasion) on his robot-monster-friend, Charles Evans Hughes (which he has built himself, and to whom he gives taxable pocket money). When an absurd fine is levied, and his "valium in the morning and whiskey beginning at two o'clock in the afternoon" fail to help, he calmly approaches his buddy, who agrees that he should be de-constructed; after all, as the robot puts it, the fine is "a pretty penny."

Barthelme's vision is acrid—not only in its implication that some day we will, with total equanimity, both build and destroy our intimates, and this for the same purpose, to achieve "complacency," but for other reasons: (1) the speaker's final timidity that without his mechanized alter ego he would "run the risk of acting," "the risk of risk," the risk of feeling, and (2) the implication that if one entered the benignly indifferent world, he would be completely alienated. "See, it is possible," he writes, "to live in the world and not change the world."

X *"The Catechist"*

This can be read as a literalization of language's diachronic and synchronic functioning. In other terms, it would seem to return to the Q/A debates of *City Life*: a priest is torn between his religious vows and sexual fantasies. The story is this: a a catechist, ordained years before, repeats (daily) the same ritual to a priest; he also remains tempted (daily) by a married woman in the park. From the text he reads, *"How to deal with the educated. Temptation and scandals to be faced by the candidate during his catechumenate,"* and he adds: "There is never a day" on which "we do not have this conversation."

Both funny and bitter, Barthelme obviously attacks unnatural church law with its rationalizing rituals. Once again he indicts the conforming society held in check through emotional and sexual repression. But nothing is ever this simple in these stories. Like Barthelme's St. Anthony, this priest is tempted by ordinary life, but unlike his supposedly more proligate spiritual father, he must settle for innocuous fantasy. ("She will press against me with her hands in the back pockets of her trousers.") This necessitates his daily penance, for fantasy (like irony) transgresses against the life force.

Barthelme's parody is wonderful. He parallels marriage and celibacy with the ritual use of peanut, rather than olive oil (as the sacrifical ointment). The priests question the sinfulness of adultery, since on an average Saturday they hear 49,140 confessions of it (one per person, it would seem, including perhaps the priest?). One of Barthelme's funniest sequences concerns the church's inspirational function each Sunday around the world: "Sunday the day of rest and worship is hated by all classes of men in every country to which the Word has been carried. Hatred of Sunday in London approaches one hundred percent. Hatred of Sunday in Rio produces suicides. Hatred of Sunday in Madrid is only appeased by the ritual slaughter of large black animals, in rings. Hatred of Sunday in Munich is the stuff of legend. Hatred of Sunday in Sydney is considered by the knowledgable to be hatred of Sunday at its most exquisite."

XI   *"The Flight of Pigeons from the Palace"*

In a spirit of total whimsy, Barthelme amplifies "It is difficult to keep the public interested" by juxtaposing a series of etchings—some of which he alters with superimpositions or the addition of perspective marks—along with a series of near-lunatic statements about the sorts of things "artists" must do to gain an audience. It is impossible to do justice to the spirit of this story, apart from making comparisons with the circus. Occasionally there is a straight comment, but this is immediately sidetracked by a barrage of dazzling and incredible visual and verbal materials which create a real three-ring atmosphere. If any "meaning" emerges, it is through the reader's creation of a text from these various stimuli, perhaps Barthelme's secondary point—to parody the machinery of the "readerly" text.

Listing the incredible possibilities for the artist, he writes, "the trapeze artist ... failed to catch me"; we auditioned "an explosion"; the "lineup for opening night" included: "a Grand Cham / A tulip craze / The Prime Rate." Nevertheless, such art works its moral lessons: "We did Theological Novelties and we did Cereal Music (with its raisins of beauty).... The people counted their sins."

At the end, one wonders if Barthelme is slyly attacking pop artists like Andy Warhol and his soup cans, but even this drifts into high wire lunacy: "The development of new wonders is not like the production of canned goods. Some things appear to be wonders in the beginning, but when you become familiar with them, are not wonderful at all. Sometimes a seventy-five-foot highly paid cacodemon will raise only the tiniest *frisson.*"

Though the speaker admits that at times some artists think of "folding the show," his spirit remains, as he both confirms and mocks "the new volcano we have just placed under contract [which] seems very promising." A print of same follows.

XII   *"The Temptation of St. Anthony"*

In this, one of his cleverest pieces, Barthelme once again concretizes the idea that only in the ordinary is there the extraordinary. He envisions the miracle of St. Anthony living an ordinary life among ordinary people: "In the world of mundanity... he *shone.*" Very much like "The Balloon," the story focuses upon everyone's reactions to the saint: "Yes, the saint was underrated quite a bit... mostly by people who didn't like things that were ineffable." Most found him "infuriating" and "irritating" and thought he should "go out and get a job." He is difficult to deal with, simply because he is different; his identity is not "tangible and clear," like everything else in their clean, utilitarian world.

Nevertheless, as the townsfolk seek out his apartment—for its "strangeness" and the "fabulous naked beauties" he is supposed to be "tempted with"—all they discover is the "ordinary beige wall-to-wall carpeting from Kaufman's" and his cooking style, "a little heavy on the fried foods." The saint's life is absolutely ordinary (he was even mugged), and everyone tries "to get something on him."

Although he is spied on and much envied, and is offered an enormous salary for endorsing a product, he is still tempted—by this "ordinary life." Hence he goes out to the desert to live in a more ascetic way. There, the narrator, "a sort of friend," visits him and hears strange noises within his ant- and vermin-covered hut. Apparently the saint has made advances to an attractive woman who "studied some kind of philosophy called 'structure' with somebody named Levy." This drives the townsfolk to rage, self-righteousness, and final rationalizations.

At the end, the narrator tries to rationalize his behavior: "Sexuality is as important as saintness, and maybe as beautiful... or else why was it part of the Divine plan?" In the last lines of the story, the saint is said to explain that he "regarded the temptations as 'entertainment.'" The distinction between temptation and entertainment is all-important. To the saint, sensuality was divinely ordained, a part of his (extraordinary) "ordinary" experience, his everyday "entertainment"; his prodigious sexual energy was his "ineffability." His true temptation was to renounce this for the life of greasy foods and beige carpeting.

XIII   *"Daumier"*

"It is easy to be satisfied if you get out of things what inheres in them, but you must look closely, take nothing for granted, let nothing become routine. You must fight against the cocoon of habituation which covers everything, if you let it. There are always openings, if you can find them. There is always something to do."

One of Barthelme's most inventive and complex stories, "Daumier" plays with a number of diverse styles—from Hollywood Western and melodrama to Dumas-style romance and Wallace Stevens elegance. These function in a number of stories within stories. The one closest to the reader focuses on the narrator, Daumier, who explains that if one is to be reconciled with life, it will be through his creation of fictional personae or "surrogate selves." Since the "authentic self," like a voracious author, is an "insatiable" "mouth" always hankering for the whole of experience, "rapacious to a fault," the inauthentic surrogate is "designed" for "satiability." Fictive selves act in a protective, if not corrective, fashion: "the false selves in their clatter and boister and youthful brio will slay and bother and push out and put to all types of trouble the original, authentic self, which is a dirty great villain."

Daumier illustrates this "thesis" in his "fictions" that follow

with Barthelme providing a clever twist in having this narrator-
"writer" ultimately become involved with, indeed inseparable
from, his fictional creations, which then alter his so-called reality
and hence provide him with at least temporary satiety.

The story also dramatizes how one's fictional characters ultimately have a life of their own. Once on the page, they take on
an identity and autonomy; they dictate their own plot. It is with
such characters that the individual-as-artist falls in love, and it is
they who alter his "reality."

The most difficult problem here involves unraveling and following the plots within the plots, and distinguishing the various
Daumier surrogates. Initially, the narrator-writer (let us call
him D_1) defends his position about surrogates to Amelia (in
other stories the lover is Sylvia or Candace). He declares that the
"miracle of surrogation" will now take place. But his mock-
solemn pronouncement serves to *separate* him from both his
creator (Barthelme) and his creation (the surrogates who will
follow):

A LONG SENTENCE
IN WHICH THE
MIRACLE OF SURROGATION
IS PERFORMED
BEFORE YOUR EYES

Daumier then begins the "miracle." (Note: the ritual is performed
by the artist, rather than by the Jesuits who will shortly be introduced into the drama.) His "monocle" in place, his subject is
not so much the variety of ways of looking at a blackbird but the
variety of ways of satisfying desire. Specifically, his tale involves
the rescue of girls and has to do with honor, responsibility,
sexuality, and repression; with knights or musketeers, thieves and
jewels; with royalty, romance, the Catholic Church, and the vast
thematic resources pertinent to these subjects tapped by literary
and film history, among other modes. (It is interesting to observe
that for many of Barthelme's narrators, writing is a surrogate
activity to lovemaking. In "The Balloon" and "Indian Uprising,"
among others, the narrators link insatiable sexuality with their
lust for living and writing. "There never seems to be enough

sex in a person's life," we read in "St. Anthony"; "that is a curiosity, that God made us that way." Here, the surrogate accepts his limitations: he "knows his limits. Desire has been reduced in him to a minimum.")

The plot begins: two hired hands (Bellows and Hawkins) and a scout (also named Daumier; let us call him D_2) are to make sure a "herd" of *au-pair* girls arrives safely, "intact in both mind and body," at the railway station. Although one is uncertain if the men themselves are rustlers or rescuers, D_1 introduces them as though they were subjects in a painting, specifically in pictorial and sculptural terms. He even interprets the landscape. Since one wants a world which is "satiable" (thereby, limited or enclosed), we get the "setting" of the story as if it were within the boundaries of a canvas: "The plain presented in its foreground a heavy yellow oblong salt lick rendered sculptural by the attentions over a period of time of sheep or other salt-loving animals. Two horses in the situation's upper-left-corner watched the men." But Bellows, who, after all, has a scenario (or "rules") to follow (he "knows the limits"), steps out of the frame, so to speak. He would bestow bluebonnets upon one of the girls. D_2 has also been distracted from his "script" by a message from the queen regarding her stolen jewels.

One may wonder how D_2 can be involved in a totally different story, one perhaps even out of Alexander Dumas (whose title is provided in the text—*The Queen's Necklace*). Indeed, as the narrator's surrogate, D_2 can have several roles and can function in several stories. As a fictional character he is, after all, totally amoral, let alone fixed on a diachronic level. Thus, he can simultaneously act as both the queen's protector and *perhaps* a kidnapper, here in the business of white slave trade. Too, D_2 may exist in Dumas's fiction if the author destroys all time and space distinctions, erasing any line between art and experience, the inauthentic (fictional) and the real (the authorial) self.

Returning to the "plot": "a band of hard-riding fanatical Jesuits" race toward the scene, their purpose to "release the girls from the toils so-called of the Traffic" for a life, instead, in the convent. In the midst of this, D_1 (who is, after all, Barthelme's fictionalized, inauthentic self), much like the artist climbing the Glass Mountain (although here in purple prose), describes the intense flux of reality about him. He also enumerates a long list of books to consult, in research for his fiction, with titles like *Self-Abuse, The Effaced Self, The Sordid Self*—appropriate materials (texts), we are told, to feed the voracious mouth of the authentic self: "transplantation of neutral or partially inert materials into the cavity." With proper digestion of such materials, perhaps one can produce a literature that is an appealing hodgepodge of styles (i.e., this story). Once again, D_1 explains the need for surrogates—because the authentic self is "a dirty great villain," "a mouth, a maw."

As we return to the *au-pair* story, the narrator plots his subject: he literally moves inert words around the page. Speaking of the girls he says, "NEUTRAL OR PARTIALLY / INERT MATERIALS / CROSS A RIVER"; we are then introduced to one of these "materials," Celeste. But Celeste acts as though she had a life of her own, independent of her creator. Much like Bellows, who would pick bluebonnets, which is not in D_1's script, she expresses her fear of "Poisonmouths" in the river.

D_2 contrives a scheme to distract the Jesuits, but the plan falls apart, and most of the girls are kidnapped when, taken by Celeste's beauty, D_2 sinks "into a swoon." From this point on, their fate is ignored. What is important, however, is that D_2's life (itself a fictional surrogate for D_1) has been altered by his own fantasy, his own linguistic ecstasy over Celeste's body, which is not the scenario D_1 (or even D_2) had anticipated. That is, through the poetry of D_2's utterance, he creates his own transcending reality over the issue of kidnapping: "Then Daumier looked at Celeste and saw that the legs on her were as long and slim as his hope of Heaven and the thighs on her were as strong and sweet-shaped as ampersands and the buttocks on her were as pretty as two pictures and the waist on her was as neat and incurved as the waist of a fiddle and the shoulders on her were as tempting as sex crimes and the hair on her was as long and black as Lent and the movement of the whole was honey, and he sank into a swoon." His role—his reality as scout—gives way to a new identity. His verbal ravishment satiates him, an amoral, artistic creation, free of any responsibility to the plot (to protect the girls).

Another "character" enters, as the narrator, D_1, debates with

Gibbon over the latter's position that art is the reaction to one's lifelong sense of personal worthlessness, inculcated in him through years of parental irony. Although D_1 disagrees (although most of the research texts he cited earlier suggest otherwise), he replies that rather than think about himself personally, he would rather think about his surrogates, which obviously distract him from his problems.

At that point, with another character newly arrived (a musketeer), the queen-necklace-problem is resolved; the narrator presents a series of notes (presumably either for future reference on the history of the Society of Jesus, or perhaps as background material for this *au-pair*-Jesuit story). His stories complete, D_1 admits his fondness for his surrogate Celeste, and his wish to alter his own reality through his fiction: "I began to wonder how I could get her out of his life and into my own." He abandons Amelia, aware that he would really need two Celeste-like surrogates to make him 100 percent happy. His solution is to give "a trial run" to another surrogate (D_3). Until now, we learn, D_3 has "failed" at having a lasting emotional experience; he might yet succeed, however, as he might also succeed as an artist, in the field of "light entertainment." D_3, who now functions in the second person (as opposed to the scout, D_2, who functioned in the third) is either told by D_1, or he says to himself, "There are always openings," the lines quoted above.

The story reaches its climax as Celeste suddenly appears in D_1's sphere. Obviously, she has "run away" from the other plot to join him. Either the trial run of D_3 was unsatisfactory, or it was so satisfactory that the surrogate (D_3) and the self have merged (although Celeste *remains* entirely fictional). The narrator celebrates his victory by preparing a "spiritual" meal for Celeste. Although it consists of ordinary items, he prepares it with such linguistic élan and finesse that it *seems* to him a feast (although to the reader it may be less so): ". . . cheese products from Wisconsin wrapped in gold foil in exquisite tints with interesting printings. . . ."

Happy at last with his creation (i.e., Celeste, the feast, the story itself—indeed with his life), the narrator wraps up in tissue paper his fictional characters, Hawkins and Bellows, as well as his Daumier surrogates (much as the narrator folded his

"Balloon"), and puts them all away in a drawer for another time. Celeste is preparing a *daube* in his kitchen, much as Amelia had, and he concludes: "The self cannot be escaped but it can be, with ingenuity and hard work, distracted." And then, in the identical language (yet different punctuation) with which he created D_3: "There are always openings, if you can find them, there is always something to do."

"Daumier" focuses on the totally private meaning of art, on the creator who is nourished through his surrogates. Like "Shower of Gold" it affirms the plenty afforded by the children of one's imagination, the words themselves (which takes us back to "Sentence" and "Bone Bubbles"). The artist may, indeed, even if only temporarily (and even if he is removed from the real, phenomenal world), feast on the nourishment of his fiction.

On a final and whimsical note, one ought not to worry about how D_1, merged with D_3, can enjoy Celeste, a fiction. He can for the simple and all-important reason that Barthelme wishes him to. D_1 is no more real than the bluebonnets or musketeers. Our final box, outside all the other boxes, is, of course, Barthelme.

CHAPTER 8

Guilty Pleasures

ONE would do well, in his first reading of Barthelme, to begin with *Guilty Pleasures*. Utterly flamboyant in its parody of both written and spoken English, this is Barthelme's funniest book—a wild escapade through the bizarre and sometimes corroded soul of contemporary America. Too, if one sometimes despairs over the solemnity of modern literature, he would do well to savor the wit here, for this is surely one of the funniest books in contemporary fiction.

In the preface, the author himself explains his structure. Part 1 is "parody"; part 2, "political satire directed against a particular [Nixon] Administration"; and part 3, "Fable," "bastard reportage," and "pretexts . . . for cutting up and pasting together pictures, a secret vice gone public." One might add that section 1 focuses upon the media sources responsible for our conformity —in mock versions of their styles—film, the critics, magazines, fiction, advertising. Section 2 hones in on Nixon, but strikes as well at the corruption of our other "fathers," like George Washington. The final story, in part 3, is completely different, Barthelme's most lush evocation of the richness of life.

The dust jacket calls this his "first book of non-fiction," but here, as always, Barthelme challenges traditional definitions of form, of so-called "fiction" and "reality." If anything distinguishes this volume, it is that the personal element is less prominent. Once again, he portrays the artist, but no longer in his loneliness and private exultations; the terror or insulated vapidity of marriage is now painted in its utter silliness. Barthelme's humor seems to militate against his pain. The problem of the ironic pose is clarified, as Barthelme's personae accept the paradoxical need for language to serve uniquely within its limiting structures, paral-

143

leling again existential "role playing" or "authenticity" in a universe lacking freedom. Yet these more serious elements are really parenthetical. *Guilty Pleasures* is, first and foremost, a lampoon on the American Way.

As to the title, Barthelme plays theme and variations upon it in one story, "The Photographs." Two very proper British scientists formally discuss the significance of capturing photographs of the human soul—evidence, at last, of the soul's existence. The only problem is that the soul looks like an ugly frying pan, the sort that gets corroded from overcooking kidneys. They decide (among other things) that it is best to destroy their evidence, so that with the continuing uncertainty regarding these matters (and hence guilt), humanity can pursue its pleasures. "Guilty Pleasures" are, they imply, after all, "the best." Indeed, Barthelme does anything but destroy his evidence, and the pleasures one takes in reading his photographs are anything but guilty.

I *"Down the Line with the Annual"*

This story portrays a society whose every aspect is molded by *Consumer Bulletin* language standards: "The world is sagging, snagging, scaling, spalling, pilling, pinging, warping, checking, fading, chipping, cracking, yellowing, leaking, staling, shrinking. . . ." Charles, the speaker, attributes his failure to be an "intelligent and informed buyer of goods and services" to his having "yoyoed away" his time in school reading the wrong things, "Herodotus, Saint-Simon, Rilke, and Owen Wister," seeking "answers to the mystery of personality and the riddle of history." He would now rescue his girl friend (stylishly named Candace) away from this "tense and joyless world." Candace busies herself with activities like testing out whether in fact she can wash and dry her Swedish tennis balls "without deleterious effect."

To be sure, the *CB* has tried to be a fortress against inferior products and false advertising, the anarchy loosed upon the world. ("O brave *Consumer Bulletin Annual*, holding the line in a world where the best lack all conviction. . . .") But the products continue to fail: "I check [a bedside clock] for loudness of tick. . . .

Tick seemed decorous. Once installed at home, it boomed like a B-58." Charles would first release from his wrist Hugo, his personal falcon, his killer hawk, and send it off to Iowa, where certain "worthless devices are manufactured." Then, good literature major that he has been (and constructing his life completely out of his books), he would coax Candace out of her Cumean bell jar and carry her off, with Hugo, to the Australian archipelago. Vexed to nightmare by a society of schlock merchandising and sales, Charles is himself a personal Second Coming. The only problem is that his very way of perceiving the world—of speaking—is not only out of his college texts but also the *Annual*: the only "appliance" he will take with him "is Hugo."

II *"Letters to the Editore"*

"How come you have ignored Elaine Grasso, whose work of now many years in the field of parentheses is entirely propos?"

In their "Letters to the Editor of *Shock Art*," art critics from "both sides of the Atlantic" debate the originality of the new art—five (or six) pointed asterisks. Parodying the critics and our whole value system, Barthelme stands close to Pope in heralding the sponsors and authors of dullness.

III *"That Cosmopolitan Girl"*

This is written apparently in answer, detail for detail, to an ad for *Cosmopolitan* magazine, promoting the independent, liberated "Cosmo woman." Published like a typed manuscript one might send to a popular magazine, the story contains a full-page photo of a Renaissance girl, whose style and looks are hardly the sort one would find in *Cosmo*. In the story, an appropriately nameless girl, the successful product of the *Cosmo* "sell," lives in a world of Louis Vuitton products; she speaks in *Cosmo* language (with similar cadences and emphases, marked by underlinings), and she acts liberated in the *Cosmo* style. She has no ideas of her own. "When *Stephen* picked me up for dinner at Vuitton, looking *hysterically* handsome in his Vuitton coveralls, I was a shade taken aback when he literally *demanded* that I pay for the cab."

(Though exaggerated, Stephen's demand is ironically consonant with the magazine's stance that a woman be financially independent.)

Stephen orders her to carry his Vuitton steamer trunk on her back into the restaurant (named Vuitton), and when she complains of a *"ruined"* back, he (ordinarily "really *sweet"*) criticizes her for reading *Cosmo* and being fragile: "I'm going to get you a *washtub* and *washboard* for your birthday." Already having paid for the cab, she now pays for their "N & S" (nitroglycerin and soda), all of which she rationalizes with a fashionable psychology: men, "just like women," have "their little moods." At this point, the chauvinist Stephen—really an old-fashioned chap—opens the trunk and Elberta emerges, wearing a housedress. Trying to maintain her *Cosmo* cool, our girl looks, in vain, into the current *Cosmo* for advice. The next best thing, she asks Elberta "what magazine *defined* her . . . [her] *phony* wholesomeness." Elberta's reply: "'*Scientific American*, dearie.'"

IV *"Eugénie Grandet"*

After producing *The Thesaurus of Book Digest*'s summary of Balzac's novel, Barthelme takes the linear plot, which neatly ties together its threads of stock melodrama, and instead rewrites odd sequences—without linearity, cause and effect, or denouement. (He also adds unidentified prints and odd typographical arrangements.) Is Barthelme's fiction less "true" of Grandet than Balzac's—or the *Thesaurus*'s?

V *"Snap Snap"*

Clitterhouse, who has nothing to show for his twenty-three years in the Bureau of Hatcheries, decides "the difficulty is with my style": it is "pure, unadulterated mouse"; "what is wanted is mouse*trap* style." (Barthelme plays with both "claptrap" and the imprisoning connotations of "trap.") Clitterhouse's solution is to use chic words, to conform, to "snap to," in language. He goes through a variety of newsweeklies, and what he discovers (this is the bulk of the story, in list form) is that everyone either "snaps," "cries," "warns," or "urges." The ironic truth behind this very funny story is that while it may be true that people seek out fashionable language, it is the media which, in its own stylized fashion, reports (and thus creates) speech and popularizes verbal styles (which, when reimposed on the world, are later picked up and sometimes further stylized, according to the latest fashion, or editor, and so on). Thus, contemporary history (reality) is reported (or created) in words—always a distortion of experience, and yet, in another sense, experience itself.

VI *"The Angry Young Man"*

In the fifties, a group of English writers, including John Osborne, Kingsley Amis, and John Wain, came out of the Red Brick Universities—rather than the aristocratic Cambridge or Oxford—and wrote about the gulf that separated the bored and empty British upper class from the rest of society. But since "signs" can lie, Barthelme's "angry young man" is perhaps himself rather than the British writer. The recipient of thousands of pieces of mail with "literary forgeries," the writer takes a flying jump to hurl himself away: "he is aloft . . . up in the air." This is virtually the title of a story in *Caligari.*

Yet, moving to another "signification," Barthelme characterizes his "angry young man" like his own fictional characters. Like the "Genius," for example, he is a popular lecturer, yet he lacks answers. When asked "What is your opinion of the present situation?" he replies: "—Well, it's better than sleeping with a dead policeman." He is vain, and in the spirit of Jane in *Snow White,* he asks before his mirror: "Who's the most baddest angry young man of all?" He raises the same questions about art that many of Barthelme's surrogates do: "What can be learned by studies on the shelf life of the average volcano?" ("Pigeons"); "What is the place . . . [of] the cup of tea?" ("Don B."). His greatest fear is a "crazy mad passionate bibliography": the fifties writer would then be recognized by the very group he attacked; Barthelme's surrogate would be heralded for all the wrong reasons and ignored for his genuinely creative efforts; and Barthelme—?

VII   *"L'Lapse: A Scenario for Michelangelo Antonioni"*

Marcello, a "wealthy film critic," and Anna, a "lengthy, elegant beauty, blond, whose extreme nervousness is exteriorized in thumb-sucking," talk to each other in this mock-Antonioni film script. In the background "shabby-looking pigeons wheel about meaningfully but in slow motion; . . . water sounds viscid, hopeless."

Marcello and Anna not only speak to each other in mock-Antonioni style, but their subject is his: boredom and communication. Furthermore, they discuss this in the context of specific films and critics. How, they ask, can critical language accurately describe film? Their conclusion: criticism, like art (film), which molds life, must cultivate "brilliant boredom" and "empty anecdote."

To Anna's complaint about a boring film, Marcello says, "You can't just say you were *bored*"; it was "obscure and baffling"; it had "a certain slow beauty . . . visual rubato." Once again Barthelme parodies how the canned language of films—more precisely, the reviews—creates our lives. When Marcello reads a Crowther (the *Times*) review, which expresses the same trashy rationalization of a boring film, Anna's pleasure with Crowther's different style enrages him. His reaction is to take her for a walk, which she doesn't want, but which he insists upon, because it's a film "convention."

That life is dictated by film rhetoric is further exemplified by Marcello's pill-popping before reviewing "Lawrence or Arabia" or "Lawrence over Arabia," which he has heard is "swift-moving." (Thus he needs a tranquilizer.) Anna later prepares a steak and peanut butter dinner, a "decadent" meal—"a little . . . Fellini."

That we have come to a point where the human and inhuman, the real and fictionalized, are indistinguishable, is underscored in the hilarious background details where actor/person/thing are merged. "The camera begins by thoughtfully considering a nearby construction project (played by the Tishman Brothers)." At one point Anna says: "Why can't we be like other people? . . . [and] spend our time in mindless eroticism?" Although she thinks they may have communicated, Marcello informs her that her mastery of film jargon is incomplete. Anna, frustrated and longing for the fulfillment (i.e., emptiness) promised by consummate cinema jargon, concludes by wishing to merge her life with the images on and of the screen. Ironically, her language *is* totally and masterfully clichéd: "I want my life to be *really* meaningless. Like in that film. Such boredom! Such emptiness! Such febrile elegance! It was penetratingly different, a magnificent, ironic parable, one of the year's ten best."

The final shot of "cement bags" reminds one of "Paraguay," where silence is sold in cement bags.

VIII   *"The Teachings of Don B.: A Yankee Way of Knowledge"*

Though chiefly a Carlos Castenada parody, this story, with its title and certain details (like Don B.'s beard and Greenwich Village apartment) prompts one to read eagerly—to gather data about the author. But if this is a "How to Become a Writer" story, Barthelme mocks Don B. as much as his narrator-novice—the star-worshipper-groupie, the seeker of knowledge.

Xavier, the "apprentice," is apparently doing anthropological field work in New York. He approaches Don B. to learn about the "nonordinary reality" (i.e., the "secrets of certain hallucinogenic substances") "peculiar to Yankee culture." Parodying the trials of any *rite de passage*, Don B. instructs him on the "pain, elation, shock, terror and boredom" the "prepared" heart must "endure." Is he, for example, "ticklish"?

At the apartment, Xavier sits cross-legged with his guru; books are thrown into the fire, and from these the Don's *"brillos"* burn. The ritual, however (and this the reader, not Xavier, knows), provides his introduction only to the *forms* of meaning; most of what Don B. tells him lacks communicative content, his words meaningful only to himself. Hence the disciple accepts his master's mysterious explanations of his *"brillos"* and his "ally" named (Cold?) Turkey. He also accepts Don B.'s physical abandonment. (He goes off to a flick, as Xavier tries to seat himself as comfortably as possible near the master's light.) When he returns, he makes it clear that that so-called special "luminosity" is nothing more than lamplight, and he proclaims (and again only the reader picks this up) his nonmystical, ordinary identity. On the other hand, defying any definition whatsoever, he claims that his

sneeze can shake the earth (humorous shades of Glendower).
In fact, he is full of hot noise, if not air: "The man of knowledge
both *has a brillo* and *is a brillo*. That is why . . . when he sneezes,
the earth shakes. *Brillo* is noise, arms, legs, liver—the whole
shebang."

His fears at one time were "fear, sleep, sex and the Internal
Revenue Service," and he conquered all but the last ("those sum-
bitches never give up"). One can conquer fear if he "takes a frog
and sews it to one's shoe" (if, indeed, he creates an "object covered
with fur," a unique work of art). Finally, with the room suffused
with "wet irony" and an atmosphere of "awe" and "dread," Don
B. fills two communion vessels and chants "torn," "pony," and
"feather." He places a pile of chips (like *Snow White*'s buffalo
chips?) before Xavier, and smiling and blinking (with crossed
eyes), he performs the final ritual. Xavier (whose name we
laughingly associate with Christ, the son), totally obeisant and
completely brainwashed—created anew—is ready to receive communion. Don B., creator and magician, pulls out of his imaginary
hat, "a colossal Publisher," "half-human, half-animal . . . a truly
monstrous thing!" What more could the diligent "apprentice" ask
for? The two go off to Lutèce, where, having been properly introduced to the world of "important emotions," they settle "on an
advance in the low fifties."

IX   "*Swallowing*"

"The American people have swallowed a lot," Barthelme begins,
"in the last four years": "electric bugs, laundered money . . . a
war more shameful than can be imagined." The history of swallowing, however, contains a lesson that will perhaps be instructive.
It appears that after the New York World's Fair, a jurisdictional
problem arose over a gigantic, 4,000-pound Wisconsin cheese on
display. No one wanted it.

The Wisconsin governor suggested that New York consider it a
gift: the people of New York could "eat it." After New York's refusal (who ever gives anything free to New York, anyway?), the
argument grew more formal and then vociferous. "Bull[s] covered
with seals and ribbons [sometimes] . . . delivered by a masked

motorcycle messenger" were in abundance. The cheese, maintained the Dairy State, was "not less than top-hole"; not only that, it might well cater to the densest rat population in America —New York.

In the meantime, with the governors adorning themselves in proper battle garb, the cheese developed "a certain fetor." But the problem was finally and quite miraculously solved. The cheese was given to an otherwise starving poet, after which both he and his art prospered. His best line, in fact, was: *"I can't believe I ate the whole thing."* Barthelme concludes with "The American people have swallowed a lot in the last four years, but as the poet cited goes on to say, there are remedies."

This is a wonderful example of Barthelme's method. First, he briefly suggests his subject (an attack on the Watergate fiasco and Vietnam war) by literalizing his metaphor ("swallowing," "electric bugs," "laundered money"). Then he parodies the bureaucracy, as the governors utilize the pompous language and exaggerated dress and drama that Hollywood and the comics have made synonymous with the political and historical big cheeses. (At one point the New York governor looks like George Washington about to cross the Delaware.) It is only near the end that he shifts into his anecdote—to displace our focus, and yet simultaneously underscore his satire on politics, art, and the public.

When the poor young artist enters in his "poetpuppyhood" ("subsisting on a daily input of one [1] pot of warm water over which one [1] chicken bone had been waved, once"), we expect the hero to save the day (and vice versa). Instead, Barthelme portrays him as Superrat, feeding on the same garbage—indeed, the ambrosia of mice—to get fat in brain as well as in spirit, to produce the same "dreck" and morality ("steel verses") upon which our lives are modeled. He is so successful, his words have become an immortal part of us, *"things* to be chiseled on tombstones." Barthelme continues: "He lives among us still and there is no tree from which a bird cannot be charmed by the sweet soft steel of his verse." A wonderful inversion, if at one time the bird, associated with the poet, charmed the ordinary man, now even the bird is programmed by the poet's "things."

Barthelme is ironic to the end. "There are remedies" (for all the swallowing), he concludes. But if our concern is the malaise of modern life, it would seem that the cure is indeed worse than the disease.

X   *"The Young Visitirs"*

In this parody of elite Washington society, another attack on presidential politics, the not-so-distant relative of *Caligari's* Baskerville, Basker, reappears. Visiting from Norman, Oklahoma, he and his wife, Letitia Filter, attend a White House party. There, surrounded by the President's guards ("tackles" and "ends"), they kneel and meet the Great Father, who greets them with "Peace, my children!" Basker explains that while the President is building the U.S. Interstate Bicentennial Teeter-Totter from Maine to California (obviously to bind the nation together), the "people down home are still hungry . . . *eatin'* chalk."

The President's response is increasingly hostile and moralistic: they can move to another country. With the same cruelty implicit in fairy-tale authority figures, the Big Daddy will punish his children: "In my view, eating chalk is a mistake" to be paid for. They will be forbidden "to ride on the Teeter-Totter," an image that well conveys the insidious ways the poor are punished for their poverty. But there is more; since Basker himself obviously has influence and resources—he is perhaps an aspiring politician—the President gives him a parting gift, a goodie bag with two lollipops, the trademark in recent years of another American hero, T.V.'s Kojak.

XI   *"The Palace"*

Still concerned with the poor, Barthelme's narrator had a fantasy one day in the bank. He saw a room of white and black Puerto Rican women, each holding a check for $84.06. After "running down" its purchasing power (i.e., $50 an hour for an analyst, $2.50 for panty hose, $350 for a purebred Rhodesian Ridgeback), he figured that "you get a prettty good tennis racquet for $84.06." In an instant, all the ladies were at Abercrombie and Fitch and then upon the royal tennis courts of an extraordinary palace, filled with magnificent, fashionable furniture and art, and "other high-class cultural grid coordinates." At the peak of his fantasy, he screamed, still in the bank: "Tennis, everyone" [not "anyone"], at which point all the women, bank tellers, and clerks set out for the palace. Possibly, one might say, at this point, that fantasy is the only revenge upon reality.

But the fancy does not cheat so well as it is famed to do. The narrator is brought back to reality, and he concludes, in a grim statement of fact: "The truth is that the palace does not exist but the serfs do." In addition to underscoring his real subject in the word "serfs," Barthelme illustrates once again that the artist, with all his resources, is ineffectual in initiating social or political change.

XII   *"The Dragon"*

A disconsolate dragon prances around New York, unnoticed by its unseeing inhabitants. He is told by the Colonel of Sanitation, a specialist in problem-solving and an existential psychoanalyst, that if he wants "a meaningful life role," he should identify himself as an "endangered species": "We love and cherish [them]"; the President even "has a list" of them. When he asks if "men" are on the list, the Colonel becomes enraged. Nevertheless, feeling victorious, and believing he has "at last gotten a message to the authorities," he gives up smoking (dangerous for both dragons and men) and, one assumes, his suicidal impulses.

Barthelme creates a fable of the mild though threatening dragon-social-observer, whose flame in fact still burns, but he mocks every aspect of his subject. He lampoons those authorities who embrace as "endangered" or "lovable" any exotic, as they ignore the human race, the most endangered specie of all. He also mocks the audience to whom the dragon speaks: the Colonel of garbage trucks, a subordinate to the Commander in Chief of the biggest dump of all. Finally, he mocks the dragon-as-critic who, in order to be taken seriously, has had to give up his uniqueness (and "eat the cheese"), who, in the exotic category of "the endangered," is himself now part of the growing sludge.

XIII   *"An Hesitation on the Bank of the Delaware"*

Barthelme takes one of our most common, anecdotal associations with George Washington—that he slept everywhere (as if he lacked a house)—and exposes Washington as compulsively collecting houses everywhere (Virginia, Fig Island, Georgia, Louisiana). Decorating these, moreover, was his sole purpose for going into battle: "No man," he pronounced, "can lead the patriots into battle without solid-silver wallpaper." Everything had to be attended to before he would "budge": landscaping, oriental rugs, and golf courses, where he set up games "with Cornwallis and the other soon-to-be-defeated Limey generals." It didn't matter that the cost to the Republic was four million pounds, that every citizen had to contribute, even if this meant selling his cow. Nothing was "too much" for the "Father of his country."

With the story written in parody of eighteenth-century typography (i.e., when the *s* looked like *f*), Barthelme achieves some wonderful visual and aural slapstick. Washington finally would not cross the Delaware in his boat's hand-carved rosewood seat ("An Hesitation") unless the Continental Congress provided a "houfe" for his "horfe." Sounding a bit like another American hero John Wayne, and interjecting a bit of Richard III's eloquence in his scurrilous blackmail, he demanded 2,000 pounds in advance: "No houfe for my poor horfe! Oh, vile! My horfe! houfeless [houseless and hooveless?].... It takes a heap of houfing to make a head at home."

XIV *"The Royal Treatment"*

Although Lily McNeil finds it hard to believe, she accepts and publicly proclaims—in rhyming legalese (*à la Cosmo*)—the extraordinary "malfeasance" of the entire Nixon crew. She begins:

> I would like to publicly proclaim that I, for one, do not think the President is guilty of base, low, or tiny-minded malfeasance.
> And that although the former Vice President has made me sad, at least he didn't do anything that could correctly be described as high treasance.

Focusing on the political dilemma, she continues: if this proves the American government "exhausted," she will just have to nominate herself "the first woman king"—fair enough, she says, in these times of consciousness-raising and equal opportunities.

Then (in more *Cosmo* terms), she could save "trillions and trillions" for the U.S.: "The Supreme Court judges could just wear ordinary clothes." Although her many propositions are, she admits, "anti-democratic, un-American, and anachronistic," "wouldn't it be better than the present megillah?" Even if she did something reprehensible, she alone would be responsible. "You wouldn't have to *convene* eighteen different investigatory bodies to figure out who to *guillotine*," she says. But this final (rhyming) statement is ambiguous. Would she use the same tactics as Nixon, or would she in fact submit herself to self-destruction?—"there'd only be me, walking in a stately manner in my best Halston toward the shredding *machine* [italics mine]." Would a Nixon by any other name smell the same?

XV *"Heliotrope"*

This begins: "It is April, and Heliotrope, the Open University of San Francisco, is once again turning toward the sun of felt needs and marigold-yellow fulfillments." "Come," invites our cavalier poet, "let us go, then, love," and "enlist ourselves" in Heliotrope. "Too long have we tarried in the dismal sunless cities of the East." He then enumerates the offerings, including "Hypnosis with Color" and "Two-Stroke Motorcycle Maintenance."

Away from "the Unreal city," they will "return to basics." Instead of "seeking answers," they will find beginnings. After all, he reasons in his corniest mock-Eliot style, "when an answer is found, it is not the end but only a beginning." As for their emotional life out at Heliotrope, "if we can't clarify our feelings, perhaps we can clarify our butter."

Taking potshots at both the lightheaded mysticism of the West and the pompous self-importance of the Eastern establishment, the narrator concludes: "You can teach a course in Paying the Telephone Bill, and I will teach one on Napping, and we will both, at long last, be avenged upon that fancy-Dan Lionel Trilling."

XVI *"And Now Let's Hear It for the Ed Sullivan Show!"*

In what functions as a deadpan verbal equivalent of the Ed

Sullivan style, Barthelme conveys the quick onslaught of variegated "dreck" that paraded as talent on a T.V. show, around
which American society was mesmerized for over twenty years.
In just a few pages, he races through the guests and their jokes,
their style, the audience, and all of Sullivan's mannered and predictable responses. Helen Hayes, the grand-dame of American
culture, is the special guest—to plug her book, titled, of all things,
On Reflection. Priestess of this "Church of the unchurched," she
repeats her faith in the American way, its "blague," the meaningless onslaught of words. "I have always been concerned with the
whole, not the fragments; the positive, not the negative; the
words, not the spaces between them."

In the midst of this continuous show—and Ed Ames's "sub-
memorable" song—the narrator's memory shifts to a bizarre T.V.
malfunctioning that Sunday morning (which he recalls in parentheses). For eight minutes the cameras captured a "pornographic
exhibition" of a naked man and woman "doing vile and unimagin-
able things to each other." (If Sullivan's show was an exercise in
mass anesthetization, the "exhibition" is one in living art.) The
couple then disappeared "into the history of electricity." The narrator remarks: "What we really want in this world, we can't have."

Sullivan returns with bullet-fast parting remarks, and Barthelme
lists all the credits and concludes: "The Ed Sullivan Show is over.
It has stopped." But one is left not with the Sullivan tidbits or
Hayes "fill-ins," but rather with the narrator's parenthetical material—the fragments, the spaces *behind* the words, the solitary,
guilty pleasures of that nasty couple.

XVII   *"Bunny Image, Loss of: The Case of Bitsy S."*

In an epigraph, Barthelme manipulates a *New York Times*
report that four bunnies, who were discharged by the "interna-
tional bunny mother" for losing their "bunny image," are suing
Playboy for "sexual and age discrimination" (somewhat late,
perhaps, for the first). " 'You look old,' " they were told; but they
maintain that they lack "crinkling eyelids, sagging breasts,
stretch marks, crepey necks and dropping derrières."

Barthelme then defines Staub's syndrome, or loss of bunny

image—in all the psychologese he can mockingly muster. His best "insights" are from the case history of Bitsy S., who at age twenty-eight was admitted to Bellevue complaining that after she was fired, she looked in the mirror and couldn't find her body.

If Barthelme parodies the bunny fever that afflicts a fair portion of our society, he proceeds to explode another American "myth." He actually revives, or reverses, an already dead dream—that a girl (especially an older one) can marry a rescuing prince. Bitsy in fact marries, of all the dreams-come-true, her therapist (whose "Teddy Bear Therapy" made her "mature" and "stable"). But Barthelme's conclusion is a real turnabout: "The life of man," he writes, as the great football father Vince Lombardi (and Hobbes) said, "is nasty, brutish, and short." Lombardi's comment on his (Green Bay) Packers, bunnies of another sort, recalls the harsh reality and brings us back to the story's beginning.

XVIII   *"The Expedition"*

A combination of over a dozen prints and photos with a sentence under each, this story appears to deal with the trials involved in some search trials of love, separation, battle, death, animosities among friends, mutiny, perseverence, victory, and loss. As in "Bone Bubbles," "Glass Mountain," and "Tolstoy," Barthelme stretches the fictional form to accommodate a totally private vision, always the subject of art. Hence, the "climax," marked by "We found it!" has two men (in one print) standing over a strange object (from a second print). The "thing," like the subject of art, is some mysterious animal, vegetable, or mineral.

XIX   *"A Nation of Wheels"*

In this word/print collage, Barthelme superimposes pictures of tires upon a variety of other images in order to once again redefine the fictional mode. Although his point is clear enough—we are a nation of wheels—his extensive literalizations and visualizations of it, along with his mixtures of mock-formal and slangy language, are uproarious. Wheels now literally have a mind of their own and are "calling the shots" for our "elastic consciousness."

The country has been taken over by hundreds of Welcome Wagons "directed by no human agency." This he conveys with a picture of a huge ice cream cone on wheels.

Our very own Frankensteins have effected such political, social, economic, and even romantic and artistic repercussions, history has had to be rewritten. Presidential statements have been issued that assert that America is, and has always been, based upon the wheel. Museums have been filled with artifacts to support the history books. What the wheels want, however, is "*lebensraum*," their own space.

In the meantime, the American public has retained its usual optimism—its happy-go-lucky indifference to what is going on. Though overrun by the wheel, "tight is right" has become the current motto. At the end of the story, as the wheels take over the world, "stretches of pavement" are heard talking to each other. "What do we need them for?" they ask, followed by: "A perfectly paved globe," an image of a world without people, perhaps without wheels (having outlived their usefulness). The next level of progress to anticipate is that of perfect concrete.

XX "*The Photographs*"

Pioneer 10's mission to Jupiter has been successful, and two photos have incidentally been taken of the human soul. Dr. Reginald Hobson, F.R.S.—in totally blasé fashion—discusses these with Dr. Winston Watnick-Mealie, F.R.S. They conclude that having subjected them to a variety of scientific tests—and other "continuous smearing grids"—the photos can only be the "soul on its way to Heaven."

The problem (and Barthelme includes prints) is that the soul looks ugly, like a "heavily corroded frying pan" with a handle or knuckle sort of thing on top, and with a "nipple-shaped business" in the middle. One would, after all, prefer to think of it as more ethereal, "like the stuff one puts on the Christmas tree."

Perhaps, Reggie suggests, it is ugly, because "there *is* sin and all that," at which point Winnie acknowledges his affair with Reggie's wife. But since business must come before "pleasure," they return to their more immediate concern: what to do with the photos. In a sort of "to be or not to be," in terms of the human soul, they discuss the advantages of acknowledging it; they compare themselves with "the chaps who made the atom bomb." The final question is: Is it better to know it "exists" and then to see how ugly it is? Winnie argues that uncertainty is best, and he gives as his example his affair with Dorothea. "Nonspecific anxiety," he explains, defeats "the humdrum." Without the zest this motivates, people would "all have to go around being good and all that." Reggie might well get the Nobel Prize for his discovery, but he would surely lose all his friends.

Barthelme is playing with the ironic disparity between the awesome godlike power of modern science and the ordinary human fallibility of the modern scientist. He is further examining the nature of human pleasure as well as its price. As we see from the Reggie-Winnie-Dorothea situation, the possibility of the soul (and hence "guilt") stimulates one's "best" pleasures. Yet morality stirs some "fallout," though not atomic—Reggie's and Winnie's disintegrated friendship. Reggie says to Winnie's confession: "I don't like you any more."

The final irony of the story is that for *both* traditional believers and atheists, pleasure is most intense in a world of uncertainty, whether the issue is the timing and finality of death, or the existence and shape of the soul.

XXI *"Nothing: A Preliminary Account"*

This is a richly lyrical piece, a prose poem of sorts, affirmative in tone. Its message is "Hurry on," Barthelme's *carpe diem*, the answer to his earlier question "WHAT RECOURSE?"

Life may mean nothing, and we may fail in understanding it, but it is the "nothing" that "keeps us waiting (forever)." If Beckett's Unnamable says, "I can't go on, I'll go on," Barthelme more jubilantly says, "How joyous the notion that, try as we may, we cannot do other than fail absolutely and that the task will remain always before us, like a meaning for our lives. Hurry. Quickly. Nothing is not a nail."

"Nothing is not a nail"—to hang (depend) upon, or to be hanged upon (sacrificed to). The contrarieties and dilemmas of human experience coalesce in existential terms and the concrete way one must live and communicate (in an absurd universe).

One seeks a new language, but the only one available is the given one. One seeks in his everyday commitments and roles to forget about death, the ultimate grim reality, yet this alone prompts one to live fully. The artist's plight is that of Everyman. While acknowledging inherent limitations, he must embrace language—experience—with a passion and inventiveness.

This is a beautiful story, reminiscent in its repeated affirmation—"Hurry on"—of Molly's soliloquy at the end of *Ulysses*. For a lengthy citation, see chapter 2.

CHAPTER 9

The Dead Father

"No tale ever happened in the way we tell it...but the moral is always correct" (46).
"Repetition is reality" (87).
"When he [the child] loved you, you didn't notice" (143).
"[Fatherhood] is a substructure of the war of all against all" (76).

*T*HE DEAD FATHER, Barthelme's second novel and most sustained metafiction, is difficult to discuss, since Barthelme creates characters, plot, drama, and denouement that only tentatively coalesce into concrete meaning, after which they dissolve and, with geometric progression, shift in and out of other levels of signification—psychological, anthropological, mythic, political, philosophical. As a result, the Dead Father "is dead only in a sense" (14), and his quest, seemingly for the Golden Fleece, is almost completed but never really begun, because its goal is in fact unattainable. His "journey," furthermore, with only *some* of the trials traditionally associated with "the quest," shifts forward and away from his son's (Thomas's), which also dissipates and intensifies alongside the quests of each of the other principals in the novel and finally even those of its nineteen minor figures. *The Dead Father* is a supreme example of the verbal collage, and its moods waver between the extremes of comedy and tragedy.

This montage of shifting textures lacks a concrete background of space and time. In addition, Barthelme omits the cultural detritus that formerly characterized his figures' social and mental worlds. The nature of detail given the Dead Father (hereafter referred to as the D.F.) is such that one comes to realize that Barthelme's subject is language—or any frame of reference or

161

creative activity—as a necessary and yet inadequate index of reality.

In his work thus far Barthelme focused on the difficulty of using language—in fact, an approximation or metaphor of reality, limited by linguistic (arbitrary) structures and totally separate from the experiential life of the senses. He literalized a variety of abstract problems—i.e., "signs" sometimes "lie" ("Me and Miss Mandible"); the dilemma of breaking free from scripts (*Snow White*); the artist's limitations within the quotidian ("The Glass Mountain"). Now he expands his emblem of the word—the D.F.—and has it include any particularized belief system (honor, law, truth, tradition, art) and any human experience (the parent) which creates and structures one's reality. The D.F. hence has the function of God, or any value-made absolute, which defines, governs, and then limits. But it also has the function (recall the Platonic/Aristotelian dualities) of any and all of its concrete manifestations. Indeed, what is the father without the child; what is God (or the Word) without one's realization (or articulation) of "Him"? Yeats's "How can we know the dancer from the dance?" is a convenient gloss on the novel and the functioning of its parts. It also explains the important and otherwise enigmatic statement: "[The D.F.] is not perfect."

Barthelme's planes shift and blend, but among the multiple and fragmented concretizations given the D.F. (any of which can be traced throughout), is his mythic dimension. He is Orpheus, Zeus, Prometheus, Anchises, Oedipus (and even Lear and the Fisher King)—essentially the ritualized, dismembered god who retains authority and creates morality, culture, and the functioning society. On an entirely different level, he is the novel, or any traditional art form or system of literary, social, or political history, from which Everyman-as-artist struggles in his efforts toward originality. On a more specific and psychological level, he is the Oedipal father, jealous of his son's youth while the target of his sexual envy. He is the father, the authority, in every structured context—anthropological, literary, psychological, philosophical, mythic, and so on. He is the archetypal father, the force of history, time, and experience, from which every child struggles in his weaning toward authenticity, originality, and identity.

At the same time he is the very flesh and blood of his offspring, the mind and spirit of his rebellious son, the words and spirit of his artistic creation, to which he stands in a most complicated relationship. For example, as artist, his creation (the child of his imagination) transports his unique vision, as at the same time it is limited by the medium of his art. Once complete, the work of art may be irrelevant to his life; once "read" by others, it may be transformed into something totally alien to his intention. With this divergence of intention and interpretation, the artist, publicly, may indeed reject the role of authorship, while on some personal level he may remain intimately involved with his creation, which alone may inspire his future work.

Although one could discuss the identity of the D.F. in virtually an endless number of different terms, the following will be limited to a focus on (the more generic) father/son relationship and the more general matter of existential "definition" in a universe lacking "essence." Needless to say, that Barthelme should humanize his D.F. and allow him to function in a concrete way in the ordinary world gives the book its extraordinary texture.

The father-son ambivalence exists throughout the generations, and Barthelme steps in and out of past and present, historic and mythic time, to portray this. The D.F. is the sexual progenitor, the biological father, whose child demands a name and context in which to grow, a morality and reality in which to gain an identity: "The key idea in fatherhood is 'responsibility.'" But once the child is conceived, the father withdraws from this responsibility, for its bonds are excessive. Like the artist, the father feels estranged from his offspring at the same time he feels most keenly its link.

The son, born out of his body and struggling for autonomy, mimes (or parodies) his father's words, actions, and morality. Yet in his rebelliousness and need for freedom, also like the father, the son is ambivalent in this most basic "relationship." The son is torn between rejecting and relying upon the givens of his world (moral and linguistic). Survival requires, as Barthelme's Thomas stutters, his admission of "inadequacy"—"he was wrong

and had always been wrong and would always be wrong"—and
his subsequent capitulation ("accommodation") through the
pangs of conscience (defined in linguistic terms: the "binary
code, yes no yes no" [144]).

As author-rulemaker, the father has created, limited, and punished his offspring for the very freedom he has given him. In
more concrete terms, the youth's efforts at fresh language and
sexual freedom—"the unique" on any level—are illusory, since
all acts—anything "unique"—are measured in the framework of
the old. The father, Barthelme writes, governs "your every . . .
movement, mental or physical. At which point do you become
yourself? Never, wholly, you are always partly him." In fact,
the father defines reality at the moment of consciousness; he
then becomes that very reality: "The fucked mother conceives,
Julie said. The whelping is, after agonies I shall not describe,
whelped. Then the dialogue begins. The father speaks to it. The
'it' in a paroxysm of not understanding. The 'it' whirling as in a
centrifuge. Looking for something to tie to" (77). As one wishes
(rather than acts out) "murderinging" the father, he incorporates
through guilt what he stands for: when a father dies, "you must
deal with the memory of a father . . . more potent than the living
presence . . . an inner voice commanding, haranguing" (144). One
becomes the Dead Father.

Ultimately, as this passage suggests, human experience is a
matter of linguistic survival and identity, the problem of definition once again in a contingent universe. The "it," whirling as in
a centrifuge, looking for something "to tie to," relates to both
the word (the creation of language, the sign looking for a signification) and to one's existential acting, his role playing
upon a stage without rules or essence. *The Dead Father* is indeed
about the existential plight, where in a contingent universe each
person is called upon to author or father his own life. One affects
his mask, whatever its specific coloration and believes he is
free; he mimes his script as though it were entirely original,
as though he could understand his "beginning," create a "middle," and fathom its "end." One acts with the ultimate illusion
that he could control his life. What in fact he comes to realize
is that his very words and his role options were limited all along
by the accepted rules of his language, ironically inherited from

other fathers, of other times. In addition, the larger stage against which all has been acted—the universe—is completely and mysteriously in control, separate, and beyond his illusory freedom. The very idea that he might choose his life, indeed, that any quest is possible, is the ultimate illusion.

The most dramatic rendering of this occurs at the end of the novel, where it becomes clear to all that the quest was illusory, indeed a fiction of the D.F.'s survival instinct: "I wasn't really fooled," says the D.F., to which Thomas replies: "We knew you knew" (176).

In a world whose only certainty is death, one embraces the role of "father" to create his life, as he simultaneously remains the child, ever dependent upon the mercy of a gratuitously benign or cruel universe. Although one knows his end, he lives as if he were immortal, on a variety of roads (quests). The only "heroism" is control and stoicism: to be "boss" of one's life is "one of the best pleasures. . . . Mostly we downplay the pleasure. Mostly we stress the anguish" (66). It is only at the very end, when one has no choice, that he must—and Barthelme's description is bluntly literal—lie down in the hole.

One is reminded of Samuel Beckett's world. Not only is the mood similar to *Endgame*, Beckett's play about "accursed" fathers and sons, but the tragicomic enactments of daily survival and the theme of growing old are especially reminiscent of *Waiting for Godot*. Here too is a world stripped down to its essentials. The D.F.'s final "vision" is "endshrouded in endigmas" (172), a Beckettian neologism that combines the womb/tomb image with a sense of final ignorance.

The D.F. lacks any final victory, such as one associates with Camus's Meursault, who gains that sense of final relief in meeting (and joining) the ultimate and inevitable benign indifference of the universe. For the D.F. this is an alien universe, which one leaves in as helpless a state as the one in which he entered it.

Finally, no quest—in terms of progressive enlightenment—is possible. At best there is only temporary relief—in removing the self from all traditional bonds, even the world, and in immersing oneself in the private world of personal language—the artist in a state of complete solipsism.

With this as a general introduction, we can focus upon Bar-

thelme's difficult text, its (1) "plot," very much in summary
form, (2) traditional quest elements (and look closely at the
opening), (3) "nonfictional" elements, (4) the "digressions" and
"fill-ins" from chapter to chapter, and (5) a few concluding remarks. Since the work as a whole is so complex, and since the
plot and digressions are so intertwined, section 4 will of necessity
allude to the way in which these seemingly disparate narrative
elements actually complement each other.

I *Plot*

The D.F., 3,200 cubits in size, is being hauled by a steel cable
across the countryside. Although he believes he is in quest of the
Golden Fleece—in fact a woman's pubic hair which will sexually
restore him ("When I wrap myself in its warm yellowness, then
I will be young again" [9])—he is being led to his final burial site.
(*"We want the Dead Father to be dead,"* say his children [5].)
Aware of this, he periodically says the journey is "for the general
good." Hence, he both gives and takes orders from his children,
the couples Thomas and Julie, Edmund and Emma. He is both
powerful and powerless. ("He is like a bubble you do not wish
to burst" [67].)

The D.F. is austere and punitive; he begs and weeps. His
greatest and incontrovertible grief is his age. No one desires him
any more: he is a dirty old "goat." As he looks at the many
sexual displays along the way (in porno films and comics, as well
as in young children and adults) and "tries" to "cop a feel whenever he can," both his despair and desire grow. "Come to bed
with me," he begs throughout, and after each rejection (at
least while he has his sword), he retaliates by killing any form
of life that runs in his way. Thus, while he is humiliated by his
children, he is the equally unsympathetic sensualist—self-righ-
teous and tyrannical, refusing to relinquish the slightest power.
(He forces his sons to wear dunce caps from age sixteen to
twenty-five.)

Eventually, after several "stops"—to eat, drink, and wend their
way through the "Wends" (a society that has discarded the
"father" function), where he allows his left (mechanical) leg to
be "whacked off"—he transfers to his children all the trappings

of his authority: belt buckle, sword, passport, keys. Arriving at the destination, though still desirous of life and the prohibited, illusory Golden Fleece, he sets himself down in the enormous excavation site prepared for him, and the bulldozers begin their work.

II *Traditional Quest Elements*

With this in mind, one can isolate Barthelme's parody of traditional quest elements and his innovations. His digressions, for example, are often more integral to the plot than his traditional materials; certain bizarre sequences communicate pure fun, perhaps the ultimate "quest." This makes the job of critic especially difficult, since it is the experiencing of Barthelme's words, as they defy and redefine convention, that is most compelling and most difficulty to verbalize. The opening, for example, suggests the traditional and unique qualities of the "quester":

The Dead Father's head. The main thing is, his eyes are open. Staring up into the sky. The eyes a two-valued blue, the blues of the Gitanes cigarette pack. The head never moves. Decades of staring. The brow is noble, good Christ, what else? Broad and noble. And serene, of course, he's dead, what else if not serene? From the tip of his finely shaped delicately nostriled nose to the ground, fall of five and one half meters. . . . The hair is gray but a young gray. Full, almost to the shoulder, it is possible to admire the hair for a long time, many do, on a Sunday or other holiday or in those sandwich hours neatly placed between fattish slices of work. Jawline compares favorably to a rock formation. Imposing, rugged, all that. The great jaw contains thirty-two teeth, twenty-eight of the whiteness of standard bathroom fixtures and four stained, the latter a consequence of addiction to tobacco, according to legend, . . . a bit of mackerel salad lodged between two of the stained four. (3)

Typically, this moves in and out of reality, from the concrete to the abstract, from moral characterization, the allegorical and mythic, to the most extreme manipulations of metaphor and description, and the creation of new grammar and words. The line "The main thing is, his eyes are open," should be taken more figuratively than literally: the D.F. knows what he is doing. His eyes are "a two-valued blue," an odd but original modifier, "the blues of the Gitanes cigarette pack," an even stranger modifier (though more descriptive than "sky blue"). We then move back to the head and the initially abstract "decades" of staring—followed by the mention of his "noble" brow and "good Christ, what else?" This last phrase functions both to suggest his identity as Christ and, at the other extreme, used in a slangy way, to invite us to attribute any and all clichéd details to a "noble" hero. Following are the grotesque, surreal details of the "finely shaped delicately nostriled nose," "five and one half meters" from the ground. The description of his "admirable" hair drifts off into an extended and literalized metaphor that refers only to a minor detail: "It is possible to admire the [young gray] hair for a long time; many do, on a Sunday or other holiday or in those sandwich hours neatly placed between fattish slices of work."

Barthelme again draws attention to his role as writer and the fact that what follows is commonplace; he provides a form of "etcetera" to the reader: "His jaw" is "imposing, rugged, all that." We then move back to the more bizarre analogues. His teeth have the "whiteness of standard bathroom fixtures," and then continuing to undercut any traditional associations we might have had with the noble hero, he attributes the four additional stained teeth ("a beige quartet") to the D.F.'s addiction to tobacco (as legend has it).

We are provoked by "He is not perfect, thank God for that." Is this referring to Christ and his relationship to God, to his smoking habit (although trusted legend provides this detail), or to his moral qualities generally? Or, as the next lines suggest, are we talking about his failure to brush his teeth, for the "sagas" now have it that the D.F. has mackerel salad between his teeth? (Is cleanliness next to godliness? Is this Barthelme's way of attributing the fish symbol to his "God," with "Avenue Pommard" the wine equivalent?)

As to his body, he is "positioned like a sleeper in troubled sleep," initially half-buried. His left leg is entirely mechanical, "the administrative center of his operations." We can be very traditional in our symbolic reading of his leg as the source of our morality, which then becomes our culture, for in the leg are "facilities for confessions," which then are recomposed "to appear as feature-length films every Friday." That we sit "doing amazing things with our hands," suggests the wonderfully ambivalent role of the D.F.'s children—who may be praying, applauding, or wringing their hands, let alone playing with each other or themselves, in the midst of the D.F.'s travail.

So much for the "noble," "imposing," "serene," and "imperfect" figure. Taking a broader view of the novel's additional quest elements, which are always parodied, we have the straight line journey for renewal—and Barthelme even draws a diagram for us. The quester, however, is not only the childish and tyrannical D.F. but also each of his equally domineering and passive children, and the nineteen men hauling him. (Interestingly, the *Manual* deals with nineteen of twenty-two kinds of fathers.) Everyone is at least ambivalent, if not miserable, about the trip. "Why do I feel so bad?" says Thomas, anticipating the complaints of the nineteen.

Each quester has an accomplice (a father or son) who must similarly undergo a trial, and each is dependent upon every other one. The so-called trials, which shall be discussed in the next section, are really the bulk of the book. They often appear in a casual or offhand way, and only some "educate" the questers. Basically they serve to entertain the reader, since most are feats of linguistic virtuosity. The D.F.'s recollections of his sexual adventures and his descent into the underworld, for example, are remarkable for their parody. He fathered everything from the kazoo to the Pool Table of Ballambangjang in his long liaison with "a raven-haired" beauty (36)" (after which she muttered "enough is enough Pappy," and died).

Finally, the traditional female figure, often at the end of the quest or its inspiration, materializes into two women, both indifferent to the D.F. The golden fleece has belonged all along to Julie; and "Mother," whoever she is, appears at the end, apparently the "mysterious horseman" who has followed them throughout their trip. Totally undefined, she is dispatched to perform the only thing even the legendary, though nonspecific woman, can do: buy groceries. At the end, after reluctantly making his will, the D.F. acknowledges his mythic role and his knowledge that things will end and he will die (the only real journey in human experience—and Barthelme's subject): "I wasn't really fooled. . . . I knew all along. . . . Did I do it well?" (176).

III   *The Departure from Quest Elements (Even in Parodic Form) and the Incorporation of the Other Arts*

Apart from the D.F., the novel's figures are flat. They lack much of a past, are difficult to distinguish, and they talk in cold, objective terms. Even the D.F. speaks of himself as though he were an actor in a play: "Did I do it well?" These people are drawn either as functions of language ("printed circuits recreating themselves"), or their experience is described in terms of the other arts. (Sex is an "aria of three notes.") Barthelme's extensive fragmentation of character and event undermines the traditional fictional element. It is as though action were taking place solely on a linguistic level or as the subject of other media —as though Barthelme were substituting the structures of painting, theater, cartoons, opera, film, and music, for the structures of traditional language and the traditional novel form—as an equally valid (yet artificial and distorting) way of viewing human experience. If language is a metaphor, an approximation of experience, so is art in all its various forms.

Isolated examples illustrate how Barthelme describes experience in the different art forms:

1. The troubled nineteen men en route "will be adequately recompensed by the red and blues . . . [of] the composition" (81).

2. Discussing the meaning of life:

> [D.F.:] Young men never understand the larger picture. . . .
> [Thomas:] . . . I do understand the frame. The limits.
> [D.F.:] Of course the frame is easier to understand.
> [Thomas:] Older people tend to overlook the frame. (32)

3. Assuming his responsibility for creation, the D.F. says: "I am the Father. All lines my lines. All figure and all ground mine, out of my head. All colors mine. You take my meaning" (19).

4. After the D.F.'s slaughter of the artists, Julie, an artist herself who shapes reality, retracts his actions and places every-

thing in the perspective of illusion: "Impressive [she says of the slaying]...had they not been pure cardboard" (12).

5. The D.F. does not want to be old, "stumbling from the stage" (78).

Barthelme literalizes the metaphor of experience as linguistic and of language as an approximation of experience:

1. "Processes," says Thomas to the D.F., speaking of the structures of language, "are killing you, not we." "Inexorable inapplicable in my case," answers the D.F., "hopefully." Thomas replies "'Hopefully' cannot be used in that way, gramatically" (158).

2. At birth "the dialogue begins. The father speaks to it [the child].... The 'it' whirling as in a centrifuge. Looking for something to tie to" (the sign looking for a signification).

3. The enormous D.F. is maneuvered "around bends in the road" as "he is articulated" (12).

4. Characters are sexually aroused by language (or they respond to sex verbally), i.e., the physical eroticism of the word "toe": "The D.F. continued to grasp the toe [Julie's]. Toe, he said, now there's an interesting word. Toe. Toe. Toe. Toe. Toe. A veiny toe. Red lines on toe. Succulent toe. Succulent succulent succulent—" (55).

6. Confessing that fatherhood was thrust upon him, the D.F. would just as soon outlive his most productive years as an ordinary restrike: "I wanted only...the feel of a fine Fabriano paper" (18).

This is epitomized in the *Manual* when, after Thomas is told the D.F. must be "deballocked" in order to continue the journey (a Skilsaw is offered), the linear narrative is interrupted. At this traditionally climactic point of the novel, three quarters through, Barthelme includes a thirty-one-page book within his book. A searing indictment (a verbal castration) against the father in the form of a compendium on how to deal with father-monsters, the text is as important to plot as anything preceding it. In fact, whatever has happened to the D.F. thus far is recapitulated and, though at points parodied, expanded. The *Manual* is a portrait of the father's unkindness to his children and their projection of rage upon him.

If, in fact, all journeys are epistemological—the search for knowledge of self, of meaning, of words—this seeming digression provides the definitive portrait of the D.F. and his children and is the heart of the book. A commentary (on another commentary) it is, in effect, no more distorted than the initial story itself, also a metaphor of experience. Only a few lines are quoted now, since this shall be more fully discussed in the next section: "We have seen that the key idea, in fatherhood, is 'responsibility.' ... The responsibility of the father is chiefly that his child not die"(143).

IV   *The Digressions and Fill-Ins*

With this in mind, the "digressions" often seem less digressive than variations on the artifice or linguistic core of experience. In order to round out the journey, it is useful to summarize each chapter and elaborate upon a few key sequences.

Chapter 1: Lunch (with diagram) of toasted prawns and fig newtons; Thomas's and Julie's sex play before the D.F., who then "slips his cable" to storm about and slay musicians; Julie retracts everything, the "cardboard figures." Typically, Barthelme jumbles anachronisms: the D.F.'s mechanical leg, his sword, mythic animals.

Chapter 2: An explanation that the D.F. acquired his mechanical leg to understand all experience; Hilda and Lars (mock–"Elvira Madigan" youths) appear; the D.F. witnesses their "gross physicality" and silly displays of modern education; they are taught through language (from which "there is no way to excape") the descriptive and declarative, the definitive and nonsensical: "We are invigorated with the sweet sensuality of language. We learn to make sentences. Come to me. ... Christmas comes but once a year. ... The light comes and goes. Success comes to those who strive. Tuesday comes after Monday. [Note the repetition of 'come']" (16). The D.F.'s confession: "[I] would have preferred remaining in my study. ... I never wanted [fatherhood] ... it was thrust upon me. I wanted to worry about the action of the sun fading what I valued most, strong browns turning to pale browns if not vacant yellows, how to protect against, against that sort of thing ..." (17).

Chapter 3: Typical abrupt shifts in style, rather than action,

emphasizing language as subject; written as an Antonioni parody:
"the cable relaxed in the road. . . . Bird stutter and the whisper
of grasses" (20)—Angry men complaining; a porno film forbidden the D.F.; a conversation between Emma and Julie, the first
of four which divide the book into a five-act drama—their communication in musical phrases on sexuality, pain, time, drugs,
the father.

Chapter 4: Diagram of cable line; sparse dramatic dialogue;
the bartender in the field; Thomas's and Julie's sex, as though
on stage, a communal rite, described as a painting, and aesthetic
experience: "Thomas began to write something with lipstick
on the stomach / Oh, you rascal! cried the crowd. Oh, you
rogue! / Julie rotated the stomach at the crowd / . . . / Our
stomach! they said. He's taking it away! / . . . The pink of you
against the green of the fields, said Thomas. Several of my
favorite colors" (31).

Chapter 5: The fabulous parody of the sexual exploits of great
legendary, mythic, biblical heroes, with overtones of Greek,
Norse, and Middle Eastern mythology; the D.F.'s account of
his "raven-haired maiden" whom he won by turning himself
into a haircut; his descent to the Underworld to reclaim her;
her preference for the eight thunders in hell; his return, after
purifying himself in the River Jelly, and fathering the deities
Poolus, Ripple, Gorno, and Libet, the last "who does not know
what to do and is thus an inspiration to us all," and the great
Pool Table of Ballambangjang, and a Savings and Loan Association, "six and three quarters percent compounded momentarily"
(36–38).

Chapter 6: The nonnarrative in what is called a "dramatic
narrative"; Thomas's explanation of his "tests"; kidnapped by
four men to learn he "was wrong and had always been wrong
and would always be wrong"; his "accommodation"; his initiation
into the inadequacies of language; forms of experience (epi-
sodes) reported without meaning (Thomas's confrontation with
disordered reality): "They sped me on horseback through the
gathering gloom up the side of a small mountain, . . . to an
even wilder place still farther from the city. There, they proceeded to lunch, . . . to a yet wilder place rank with the odor of
fish and the odor of dead grasses still farther from the city. Here

we watered the horses, against their will..." (40–42); Thomas
taken to the Great Father Serpent and his "greatest test," "the
great riddle": *What do you really feel?* (a parody of both
Freudianism and the Oedipus riddle asked by a monster). With
no answer in mind, but reading on a sheet of tin in the serpent's
mouth, Thomas's correct answer: "Like murderinging"; Thomas's
marveling: "What I had answered accorded with my feelings,
my lost feelings that I had never found before"; the serpent's
assurance: "You don't have to actually do it" (46); the guilt
such a confession evokes, a part of the *rite de passage*; Thomas's
lesson that literal patricide is unnecessary, since (1) it is illegal,
(2) it would prove true the father's judgment that the child was
"thoroughly bad," (3) it is unnecessary, since time will slay
the father (145); having understood the lesson, Thomas's demanding his father's first emblem of power, his special belt
buckle.

Chapter 7: Reversing the form of Lucky's speech in *Waiting
for Godot*, while expanding its language, the D.F.'s soliloquy
on survival in a contingent universe; his concerns with fatherhood stated initially: "In considering, he said, inconsidering
inconsidering inconsidering the additionally arriving human beings annually ... not provided for by anticipatory design hocus
or pocus and thus problematical, we must reliably extend a set
of ever-advancing speeding poised lingering or dwelling pattern
behaviors sufficient unto the day or adequate until the next
time" (49–50); Julie calling the D.F. old, filthy-mouthed; his
slaying of animals; the details of Thomas's earlier life; the usual
education, military service, bad marriage, futile searchings for
knowledge; his "failure" now, at thirty-nine.

Chapter 8: The men's grievances; Thomas's point by point
response (omitted in the text); Emma and Julie in dialogue.

Chapter 9: Stopping for a drink; Thomas and Julie, on the
decline of the D.F.'s authority and their relationship fighting
time and contradicting each other: "the two of us against the is"
(68).

Chapter 10: The Wends, seemingly aware of the "D.F.-myth"
warning that the fleece may not exist; the Wends, who father
themselves by marrying and impregnating their mothers ("that
which all men have wished to be, from the very beginning");

their abolition of the "flaming great fathers about to pick at and badger us"; to get by the Wends, Thomas told to "whack off" the D.F.'s left leg, emblem of his sexuality and instrument of his morality (73).

Chapter 11: Julie's reflecting on what is lacking in the Wends; the whelping-centrifuge speech (77) discussed above; overhearing this and the additional abuse about "old men," and again denied sexual expression, the D.F.'s third rampage, interrupted when told to surrender his sword.

Chapter 12: The D.F. recompensing the men with "colors" and imperiously discussing his acts of love and punishment in terms of "objet d'art" and "images."

Chapter 13: Stop at the cathedral; music, sketching, affection; Julie's and Emma's dialogue; shifts in language with Thomas's deepest descent on the quest: "Egg-shaped apertures like seats opening into the void. The drop . . . Thomas . . . slipping . . . toward the edge. . . . Erotic and religious experience. . . . Slipping" (84–85); Emma and Julie.

Chapter 14: "Complaint" of the men: "We that is to say us the men have a faint intustition that maybe the best is not to come in terms of the grand Father the moon-hanger the eye-in-the-sky the old meister the bey window, the bit chammer the gaekwarder the incaling the khando kid the neatzam . . ." (92).

Chapter 15: Flattering Emma's bosom, the D.F. reminded of another sexual conquest with a lawyer-become-judge, whose bosom "is still growing in wisdom and beauty"; Emma tells him he is too old.

Chapter 16: The D.F., keeping time with his restored left leg, observing the "Registration" and "Penetration" waltzes in the dance with the apes.

Chapter 17: Barred from another "outpost of civilization," the D.F. told he will have to be "deballocked"; a Skilsaw offered; the "dolt" Peter Scatterpatter's *Manual for Sons* substituted (originally printed on pumpernickel, a translation from English into English); the serious and mocking commentary—in a variety of styles and dialects—on all the action and dialogue thus far: fatherhood, jealousy, responsibility, the wish to murder (from aesthetic, philosophical, social, psychological, and sexual points of view) (111–45); fathers characterized as "teachers of

the true and not true," as "names," "choices," "colors," fearful
of responsibility and helpless in a role they did not choose; the
father as tyrant, the awareness of which is perhaps the ultimate
goal for the D.F.

Lines echoing and moving in and out of meaning, *almost* tying
together earlier strands; the surreal father-son connection (as
the Great Serpent, art, sexuality, and the lesson of "accommodation"): "Fathers are like blocks of marble, giant cubes,
highly polished, with veins and seams, placed squarely in your
path. They block your path. They cannot be climbed over,
neither can they be slithered past. They are the 'past,' and very
likely the slither, if the slither is thought of as that accommo-
dating maneuver you make to escape notice, or to get by un-
scathed" (129); summarizing the father's deepest cruelty and
the son's most bitter resentment: "[The son] is mad about being
small when you were big, but no, that's not it, he is mad about being helpless when you were powerful, but no, not that either, he
is mad about being contingent when you were necessary, not quite
it, he is insane because when he loved you, you didn't notice"
(143); The *Manual's* conclusion: when the child grows up he
must embrace a less severe and tyrannical (an "attentuated form
of") fatherhood and move toward the "golden age of decency."
"Fatherhood can be, if not conquered, at least 'turned down'"
(145); Julie's and Thomas's response: Is this *Manual* "too harsh"
or "not harsh enough?" Julie: "I hate relativists . . . and threw
the book into the fire" (146).

Chapter 18: Julie and Emma on the fading father.

Chapter 19: The D.F. chewing the earth, surrendering his passport, reading a porno comic; sex between Thomas and Julie,
again described in mechanical terms; the D.F. told "inexorable"
"processes" are killing him (158).

Chapter 20: The D.F.'s reluctantly written will; Thomas's "I
do not wish to profit from this transaction"; Edmund, the benefi-
ciate (166).

Chapter 21: The man on the hill, actually "Mother," appearing
and writing a shopping list.

Chapter 22: The D.F.'s dying speech, an extraordinary *tour
de force* (reminiscent of Beckett and Joyce, yet even fuller);
a progression through the different stages of youth, adolescence,

and maturity, to a statement of final purposes (to do his best as father); the D.F.'s lack of freedom ("AndI") and dependence upon the world for identity; his sense of powerlessness in this "endifarce" of life; his ultimate fear: Will it hurt?

AndI. EndI. Great endifarce teeterteeterteetertottering. Willit urt. I reiterate. Don't be cenacle. Conscientia mille testes. And having made them, where now? . . . I wanted to doitwell. . . . AndI a oneoh-sevenyearoldboy, just like the rest of them. Pitterpatter. . . . I the All-Father but I never figured out figured out wot sort of animal AndI was. Endshrouded in endigmas. Never knew wot's wot. I reguarded my decisions and dispositions but there wasn't timeto timeto timeto. Endmeshed in endtanglements. There were things I never knew what made the pavement gray and made the giant monuments move back and forth on the far horizon ceaselessly night and day. . . .

His resistance to death:

Enowenowenow don't want to undertake the OldPap yet. Let's have a party. Pap in on a few old friends. Pass the papcorn. Wield my papenheimer once again. Old Angurvadal! Companion of my finest hours!
Don't understand! Don't want it! Fallo fallere fefelli falsum! My broad domainasteries! Pitterpatter. The greatestgoodofthegreatestnumber was a Princeapple of mine. I was compassionate, insofarasitwaspossibleto-beso. Best I cud I did! Absolutely! No dubitatio about it! Don't like! Don't want! Pitterpatter of please pitterpatter. (173)

Chapter 23: The D.F.'s last gasp and grab for the Golden Fleece—"That's all. . . . That's the end? . . . No more after this?" (175–76).

V *A Final Comment*

Barthelme has accomplished something extraordinary here, because despite the density of the book, at the end one is genuinely moved by the Dead Father. When he says: "I wasn't really fooled. I knew all along," he is expressing an acceptance of his ultimate fate. He would live forever, and perhaps the ultimate illusion or quest is simply to never have to give in.

It is indeed a bitter reality to acknowledge that the vital functions, the generative organs (creative or sexual) in which one projects magical powers for renewal and immortality, do not rejuvenate their bearers.

Perhaps after all of our talk of authority figures, fathers, and linguistic constructs, the book's appeal is even more basic. Children, whatever their age, do project their parents as giant and eternal, as endlessly powerful and immortal. The process of growing up involves, paradoxically, both one's inevitable resentment of them as omnipotent authority figures, and one's bitter disillusion at coming to see that they are not in fact the giants we have made them. Barthelme writes a book that touches our deepest nostalgia for that time when we were secure in the world, when limits, though resented, were known, and when our God, or the father—or whatever our deepest dreams—raised in us the belief that life was more coherent and less contingent.

The Dead Father is Barthelme's masterpiece, certain to take its place among a handful of brilliant and imaginatively original modern works.

CHAPTER 10

Amateurs

*A*MATEURS brings back familiar motifs, such as weary marriage and sex ("110 West Sixty-first Street," "Captured Woman") and the hypereducated and technological society ("You Are As Brave," "End of the Mechanical Age"). Barthelme scrutinizes the military ("Sergeant"), and he parodies education ("Porcupines," "Educational Experience"), politics, and business life ("The Reference," "Our Work and Why We Do It"). The problems of language, the privacy of art ("What to Do Next," "Rebecca," "The Great Hug"), and the joy of creativity ("And Then") reappear. There is also the rare and poignant story about personal failure ("The Agreement"). "The Wound" and "At the End of the Mechanical Age" are among his finest satires.

Several stories, however, are different. Dealing more directly with metaphysical issues ("Colby," "New Member"), they are a variation of traditional (symbolic) fable. Issues of God and death, which earlier were buried in analogues with words and roles (and their relationship to authenticity and the absurd), are now explicit subject matter, and it is these that are now literalized.

I *"Our Work and Why We Do It"*

Bored sex, "extra vodka," and "bandages" nourish and bind the bourgeois publishing set. "Admirable volume after admidable volume," on every conceivable subject, comes out of this particular house—from "The Acts of the Apostles" to the "Fingerprints" of "Criminals." The house also publishes the reviewing press and thus controls public taste. Mechanical and

179

human elements are reversed: printing machines "sweat," while
managerial power is displayed in mechanical and overt sexuality. William and Rowena sit naked in bed, everything and everyone part and parcel of "the house's" furnishings.

Again, nothing is of moment to these people. One's concern
with a "weeping woman" sequestered in a car is aborted for the
more pragmatic concern that "today we are running the Moxxon
Travel Guide"; life will never be as appealing as books. William,
the apparent liberal intellectual, is diverted momentarily as he
dwells on the plight of the Sabrett hot dog peddlers. If only he
had a "workable revolutionary ideology and/or a viable myth
pattern," he rationalizes, he "would have rescued them." Such
is the "art" of publishing (and living): "It isn't our job, to
make sense of things."

II *"The Wound"*

In this wonderful literary parody, Barthelme takes the clichéd
elements of the Hemingway short-story form (plot movement,
characters, and sentence style) and fleshes them out with his
own linear but nonsequiturial adventure. He has the gored
bullfighter, his mother, the mistress with the beautiful breasts,
amateur afficionados, a bishop, a Queen of the gypsies, and, of
course, a bull. What is funny is that his parody of grand and
ritualistic event, piled upon further grand and ritualistic event,
lacks any motivating logic. Barthelme's torero, in the rhythms
of colloquial Spanish, "makes a wild grab for his mother's
hair. The hair of his mother!" But any explanatory details are
omitted. What follows are fast thrusts and counterthrusts—the
cadences of the bullfight itself—all written with the seriousness
in mood and attention to detail typical of this sort of fiction. The
mother tastes the roast beef; the torero tastes it as well (turn
and counterturn) with an eye on his mistress; the mistress reaches
for the sauce; the torero offers the afficionados roast beef with
his sword. Such heroic behavior, the model for a society, plays
before buzzing and clicking cameras (including T.V.).

At times the satire is outlandish. The Bishop of Valencia
enters, "a heavy man with his head cocked permanently to the
left—the result of years of hearing confessions in a confessional
whose right-hand box was said to be inhabited by vipers." He

discusses his psychoanalysis, and the torero opens some Chivas Regal, which his mother grabs. Again "the torero makes a sudden wild grab for her hair. The hair of his mother!" At the climax, the Queen of the Gypsies enters in search of the wound. If one has been struggling for meaning thus far, the following is disorienting: she whacks off a huge portion of the roast beef, and then prepares to ritually take away the torero. Is *this* the climax?

If until now we pondered a romantic, gypsy-torero conquest, or even a more bizarre relationship of incest and jealousy (focusing on the wound-beef symbolism), Barthelme leaves these to their own fictional conclusions and implies a sort of "Etc." about them. He introduces an unexpected development. (By now one realizes that his subject is language and form, not event.) The story concludes: "But the doorway is suddenly blocked by the figure of an immense black bull. The bull begins to ring, like a telephone." Until this sentence, like the characters in the story, we have been swept up by the form of action and the patterns or cadences of meaning. The bull, like an alarm clock, awakens us and the fictionalized characters to everyone's place within the artifice of the story. It also alerts everyone to the reality that exists outside fictionalized limits (now, ironically, brought into the story and thus a fiction itself). It is also perhaps Barthelme's way of saying: you know this is all bull.

III *"110 West Sixty-first Street"*

Focusing on the eternal and hollow bond that ties loveless married people together, Barthelme's details are grim. Their young son dead, Paul and Eugenie express no emotion; they go to erotic films that are nonerotic, plan a vacation or the refurbishing of their expensive house, have affairs, get job promotions and even more money, and eventually have another child.

IV *"Some of Us Had Been Threatening Our Friend Colby"*

If Camus dramatizes the gap between law and morality in *The Stranger*, Barthelme takes the same pattern but reverses his victim's plight. This is a strange tale about friends who justify hanging another friend because he has "gone too far." Then, with the sort of attention paid to weddings, they plan his execution—with music, cocktails, invitations, and limousine service and, of course, the "preferred wood" for the gibbet. The hangman, of greatest importance (like a minister?), must be a "professional," "not just some money-hungry amateur [the only reference to the volume's title] who might bungle the job and shame us all."

In focusing on the victim's calm throughout, Barthelme parodies the absurd confrontation with death (i.e., Meursault's). He also parodies the rituals with which our society performs its death ceremonies. His conclusion is disturbing. The narrator, after the event, can only recall peripheral details (as one remembers the food at a wedding). Furthermore, he concludes: "Nobody has ever gone too far again." This is actually a rather frightening story, as it concretizes the rage and murderous instincts that may exist among friends. This is the first of the volume's several surreal "fables."

V *"The School"*

Everything was dying at school—in this upbeat Kafkesque fable—the trees, pet snake, puppy, herb garden, tropical fish, Korean orphan, and two boys. Although the narrator, Edgar ("The Dolt"?), tried to provide an explanation—i.e., improper soil, insufficient food—and the parents sued for the poorly built structure that fell on their children, the students were genuinely moved. "They asked me, where did they go? . . . And I said, I don't know. . . . And they said, who knows? and I said, nobody knows. And they said, is death that which gives meaning to life? and I said, no, life is that which gives meaning to life. Then they said, but isn't death, considered as a fundamental datum, the means by which the taken-for-granted mundanity of the everyday may be transcended in the direction of—?"

Having heard that life, not death, gives meaning to life, they ask Edgar to make love with the assistant teacher, so "we can see how it is done. . . . We require an assertion of value." As Edgar and Helen embraced "there was a knock on the door. . . and the

new gerbil walked in. The children cheered wildly." With the
life-giving couple before them and the new gerbil, at last they
understood the concrete metaphor: Life gives meaning to life;
love, not philosophy, produces gerbils.

VI   *"The Great Hug"*

"[One day] they'll roll down the hill together. . . . Balloon Man's
arms will be wrapped around Pin Lady's pins and Pin Lady's em-
brangle will be wrapped around Balloon Man's balloons."

Barthelme takes the balloon and pin as metaphors, concretizes
them, and then works out an elaborate story. However, by the
end, one is unsure if puncturing a balloon is at all *un*desirable.
The story is typically antiteleological, in the ambiguity of its
ending and in its blurring of clear-cut distinctions.

At first, the balloon seems to be the created form (i.e., Barthelme's work of art) that stands in opposition to reality. Later
on, it appears to be the putative, the literary, or the historical—
set against basic emotional or instinctual truths. Ultimately,
however, the balloon (and pin) lack consistent opposing (binary) characterization. Those things that prick it complement
as well as contrast with it. In fact, the two merge at points.
The story is like a cartoon that describes without commentary
the variegated possibilities of experience—the Balloon Man and
Pin Lady ever ready to embrace.

What is fascinating is the story's structure. It begins with a
concrete situation: "At the last breakfast after I told her, we
had steak and eggs. Bloody Marys. Three pieces of toast. She
couldn't cry, she tried." In a sense, the speaker has punctuated
his lover's balloon by breaking up with her. But this is the extent
of the details of their relationship, as far as the rest of the story
is concerned.

The single recollection is necessary only as a trigger to what
follows—the making of the story (a balloon). The narrator
speaks with immodest parody and self-mockery: this is his
"Balloon of the Last Breakfast [not Supper] After I Told Her."
As in "The Balloon," one militates against dull or unpleasant
reality in his private constructs. But the balloon, which takes
on an autonomy of its own, may not always work for its creator;

the pin may indeed prick it. But then again, in its embrace,
the pin may complete it, and on, and on. Either way, it is ex-
perienced as a sublimating sexual act.

VII *"I Bought A Little City"*

The speaker bought "a little city" (Galveston, Texas) and
planted trees, rebuilt houses, gave everyone a piece of the
grand design, and, having exercised his "proprietorship," went
out to enjoy himself by shooting six thousand dogs. When a dog
owner complained, he warned him to beware, or he would end
up in jail. With all this behind him, "the thing is, I had fallen
in love with Sam Hong's wife." She, alas, was uninterested.

Several levels of traditional symbolism are obvious: Man/God/
the artist creates, and he may fall in love with his creation, but
he has no control over it. More precisely, and with echoes from
The Dead Father, man can play at being God—in his authenticity—but finally he is not God, for like the universe, God has the
"better imagination" and can cause him pain, like a constant
"toothache." On an entirely different level, this is a satire
of do-gooders, big business, and government, and its ending
is like *Candide's*, with the speaker returning to cultivate his
own garden.

VIII *"The Agreement"*

One of his rarely poignant pieces, consisting mostly of questions, this captures the speaker's sense of loss following divorce.
Juxtaposing his small and large fears—sometimes in funny and
surreal ways—he is primarily concerned with whether or not he
can essentially survive and then relate to the people in his
life. Identities merge as he describes himself in the language he
has used about the others, his pain concretized and then general-
ized, as in a dream: "What if the bell rings . . . an old woman
. . . begins spitting blood. . . . Instead . . . the bell rings . . . my
lover's lover is standing there? . . . I suddenly begin spitting
blood."

Barthelme, who has invited us repeatedly to enjoy the possibilities of life, here laments one's inability to locate himself,
to find himself, within the flux. Every question raised (i.e., "What

crucial error did I make?") applies to his every role. As father and husband, for example, he is innocent and detached, indeed divorced from the world.

Answers are, of course, connected to questions. His reality is not fixed long enough to be molded into a sustained question. Hence, the flow of his questions, and one's inability to fix upon any on the page. He understands his failure to comprehend his misery: "If I embrace the proposition that, after all, things are not so bad, which is not true, then have I not also embraced a hundred other propositions, kin to the first in that they are also not true? That the Lord is my shepherd, for example?"

Near the end he turns to declaratives and sets forth the only truth (facts) he knows, the divorce agreement: "the husband and wife each hereby, for himself or herself and for his or her legal representatives, forever releases and discharges the other . . . from the beginning of the world to the execution of this agreement." The last phrase (his interpolation) particularly evokes the unreality of divorce, the cutting away of one's past.

Despite the pain he feels, especially for his daughter, his final declaration reflects the sole reality of postdivorce (its language a moving evocation of the inner and outer reality): "The painters are here. . . . From the beginning of the world to the execution of this agreement. Where is my daughter? I am asking for a carrot to put in the stone soup. The villagers are hostile." (His only certainties lie in the disparate concrete, which is ultimately swallowed up by the incomprehensible, unreal reality: "Where is my daughter? . . . from the beginning of the world.")

IX   *"The Sergeant"*

Reminiscent of "Me and Miss Mandible," "The Sergeant" presents a forty-two-year-old narrator-veteran of the Korean "conflict" who finds himself back in the army with all the same "whitewashing" assignments. The story treats how, in reality or fantasy, one must always repeat the same patterns. At the end Barthelme evokes both the concrete and mythic dimensions of war's brutality. The captain threatens the speaker that if he doesn't harm the civilians with his M-16, he "can stuff olives

with little onions for the general's martinis." Barthelme writes:
"Four olives this time, sergeant," followed by the sergeant's
cry "Andromache!"

The most modest engagement in war reflects its eternal brutality, evoked in Hector's wife, who in war lost her parents,
brothers, husband, son, and at last, her own life.

X   *"What to Do Next"*

A parody of the confessional self-improvement texts, this
begins: "So. The situation is . . . desperate. . . . These instructions . . . will save your life." The speaker (as text) tells his
suffering reader the power of positive thought. It doesn't matter,
for example, if one's dog dies; there are other dogs in the sea.
He also parodies the excessive reverence paid the dead. If one
scatters dog pictures around the house, eventually he will notice
"the other" dogs and realize that life should go on. One can
always start life afresh—by breaking off with his current romantic
liaison, taking a trip, getting a new job, or changing his identity.
Barthelme advises: "Starting fresh, as it is called, requires that
you know the appropriate corn and rain dances, but also that
you can stand the terrific wrenches of the spirit that accompany
frontier-busting, as it is called."

The happy conclusion to this real-life fairy tale is that in the
end the sad sack can write his own book about his own misery.
Barthelme's message: the only way one can become a success
is if he boasts about and sells his failure (while, of course, remaining one). One can, ultimately, even teach a course on himself (and what a miserable person he is). Then he can become a
critic of the system by describing his own failure. A mockery of
the writer and teacher as moralist, the conclusion describes the
rewards of taking the failure-as-a-course: "Everyone who comes
to us from this day forward must take twelve hours of you a
week, for which they will receive three points credit per semester,
and, as well, a silver spoon in the 'Heritage' pattern. . . . The
instructions do not make distinctions between those lives which
are worth saving and those which are not."

One awaits Anita Bryant's resurrection.

XI *"The Captured Woman"*

"Why can't I marry one and live with her uneasily ever after? I've tried that."

In a series of random conversations and reflections, both funny and bitter, the speaker betrays the cold indifference at the heart of his (and his friends') romantic involvements. The story reads like a manual on "How to Catch, Placate, and Care for One's Lover, Although She Will Probably Leave You Anyway." His advice: hang photos all over the house, exercise, play chess, drink Jack Daniels, tie her up in sex play, mail her letters to her husband, go to church if she wishes, indulge her in abusing you, allow her to express how much she misses her husband and children.

XII *"And Then"*

"What we are trying to do is to get away from despair and over to ease and bliss."

The narrator has lost a part of his story (it has "fallen out of my mind"), and his "and then" phrase hangs in the "frangible air." The lost phrase is so real to him that it takes on an identity of its own. "It" and the speaker spend the day together. A wonderful dramatization of the creative process, all lines dissolve between art/life, imagination/reality, the word (story) and experience. The story has the flow and poetic logic of dreams—fusing persons, things, feelings, and ideas. Water, for example, becomes vodka, becomes beef broth with a twist of lemon, becomes herb tea with sour cream, becomes a glass of chicken livers flambé.

XIII *"Porcupines at the University"*

In earlier stories, a dragon walked the streets of New York, and King Kong attended a sophisticated party. Now, thousands of porcupines arrive in town and arouse the same indifference. Academics, accustomed to "busting people" while mouthing "de bustibus non est disputandum" worry that the porcupines will enroll and find the "Alternative Life Styles" course oversubscribed and cause riots. The porcupine wrangler, who lives with the American dream he's read about (in his "how-to" manuals), fantasizes reaching the "big time." A songwriter ("Git along theah li'l porcupines"), he would sit in New York's Muehlebach Hotel (really in Kansas City), meet fancy women, play his harmonica, and write more songs about "prairie virility."

When the dean and wrangler meet, they make a deal. If the latter will keep the porcupines from the university, the dean will try to introduce him to a Las Vegas booker (a former student), perhaps his ticket to the top—the "Sonny and Cher" show and possibly a "Golden Oldie." The story ends with the porcupines on the Cross Bronx Expressway and New Yorkers in their cars (products of both the university and the American dream) thinking: "What is wonderful? Are these porcupines wonderful? Are they significant? Are they what I need?"

The story satirizes the lost sense of purpose in once-purposeful institutions. The cowboys who drove their cattle across the frontier now dream of rocketing to fame by composing country music, and the universities that once taught the humanities now worry over riots, enrollments, and economics, and they send religion students to become agents in Las Vegas. New Yorkers still search for meaning, unable to recognize the absurd in their midst.

XIV *"The Educational Experience"*

In another lampoon on education (like "Heliotrope") and the myth of "organized knowledge," Barthelme parenthetically questions whether students truly wish to learn, rather than indulge in more earthy pursuits. If educators promise, "You will . . . be more beautiful . . . [with] a grasp of the total situation," Barthelme answers, "the total situation will have a grasp of you."

His educator-speaker is like a barker in a circus, selling a hodgepodge of subjects. There are, for example, "two major theories of origin . . . argued by bands of believers who gave away buttons, balloons, bumper stickers, pieces of the True Cross." Each specified course is a booth at the carnival: "We came to a booth where the lessons of 1914 were taught . . . wild strawberries there, in the pool of blood." But the students were using "the pool" as a "meeting place."

Education, nevertheless, is basic training—for the informational life: "We told them to keep their tails down as they crawled under the wire . . . of quotations, Tacitus, Herodotus, Pindar. . . ." Yet with all these provisions for important "life-lesson" courses (we "taught them . . . [to put] out the garbage") and the emphasis on "knowledge," the students already *know* about life, in the biblical sense. "Rotten of them," say their teachers, "to conceal their feelings from us." At one point, punning on the familiar "Is there life after death?" (or after college), they say: "Do you think intelligent life exists outside this bed?"

The story is filled with wordplay on popular college "culture" (i.e., the students listen to Vivaldi's "The Semesters"): all "quest" after truth. The only problem is that the Chapel Perilous is now a bomb farm. Barthelme sums up in a complex statement: "'The world is everything that was formerly the case,' the group leader said, 'and now it is time to get back to the bus.' Then all of the guards rushed up and demanded their bribes. We paid them with soluble traveler's checks and hoped for rain, and hoped for rodomontade, braggadocio, blare, bray, fanfare, flourish, tucket."

If educators maintain the world can be known, they also admit that their jobs consist of selling short and measured excursions through the world's bazaars. The payoff of the guards, however, adds a new and bitter dimension. In reality, and this the educators acknowledge, one must bribe the guards, the hired protectors of morality, the "system." One must cheat his way through, if it is his hope to come out of the process (to graduate) with fame and success, "braggadocio." But even then, he might only win the "tucket."

XV   *"Rebecca"*

Rebecca Lizard, a schoolteacher, denied by the court an official change in her "ugly, reptilian" last name (because "changing your name countervails the best interests of the telephone company [and] the electric company," goes home to her lover, Hilda, and they quibble because of the day's stresses. After some amusing dialogue on making the best things, as an "American ideal," the story touches on the warmth of their relationship: "Come, viridian friend, come and sup with me."

It is not until the end that one realizes that this is a story about the narrator, rather than Rebecca, whose problematic romantic life is totally guarded from the reader. As in "The Balloon" or "The Great Hug," fantasy—the telling of a story—is once again a necessary distraction. Barthelme writes: "The story ends. It was written for several reasons. Nine of them are secrets. The tenth is that one should never cease considering human love. Which remains as grisly and golden as ever, no matter what is tattoed upon the warm tympanic page."

XVI *"The Reference"*

An attack on the deviousness of political and business interactions, Barthelme devises an ingenious situation in which to work his satire. Arkansas, with its exploding population "enjoying free speech and voting their heads off," would hardly seem needy of reform. Nevertheless, someone is to be hired to "get the troops back on the track of tracks," to return the state "to its original tidiness."

The possibly unfit Shel McPartland is the candidate, but the story focuses on his "reference," Mr. Cockburn. "I have known him deeply and intimately and too well for more than twenty years," says Cockburn, about to rally all the psychological strategy he can to outfox his interviewer from the Arkansas State Planning Commission.

Barthelme satirizes his verbal ploys—his mixture of business and political lingo, straightforward language, and witty hyperbole. He also focuses on how, in the midst of all this, Cockburn is bold enough to reveal his own corruption, and by extension, McPartland's, who, we are told, "has a wide-ranging knowledge of all modern techniques, theories, dodges, orthodoxies, heresies, new and old innovations, and scams of all kinds."

Cockburn's strategies are fascinating. First, since he must appear honest, he admits the candidate's negative qualities: he "warp [whatever that means]." His next step, in the sophisticated sell, is to capitalize on his listener's lack of response to that admission (he perhaps is not even listening), and to emphasis his buddy's assets, while subtly repeating the "warp" problem.

Most important, Cockburn must say what the other wants to hear. Is the candidate, he is asked, concerned "with the mundanities?" McPartland is "sublime with the mundanities," he replies and explains: "You should see him tying his shoes. Tying other people's shoes." Yet, when the question arises as to whether or not he might be too good for Arkansas, he assures him: he's got a "certain common-as-dirt quality." With jargon for everything, the two speak as though in code (i.e., McPartland comes from a "bottom-edge state"). The perks must at last be negotiated: crab gumbo in the cafeteria, "ruffles and flourishes" of Muzak "upon entry and exit" from the building. Most impressive are the "ox stoptions [rather than stock options]." If McPartland stops one ox per week from mashing a child, he can become a media hero. After negotiating the figure to fifty thousand, and making it clear that McPartland has "a warp to power"— and that the reference, like any other agent, takes a ten percent commission—the deal is concluded.

XVII *"The New Member"*

Barthelme recalls Kafka and Pinter here, in portraying the so-called terror that lurks in the banal. His business meeting, conducted with impeccable parliamentary procedure, could easily be that of any executive committee (business people, bureaucrats, academics) that makes the decisions that determine a person's or nation's future. But as the story progresses, it becomes clear that these absolutely ordinary and insecure figures may be the gratuitously kind or malevolent forces of the universe concretized—the gods at Olympus, ruling with absolutely no justice, feeling, or idea regarding what to do with people. They could just as soon strike someone with pregnancy as with a snowmobile.

The "plot" concerns a stranger who has been standing outside their conference room window. Although he is also perfectly harmless looking, he is just as threatening to them (and their proceedings) as they are to their victims. Because they have no other way of dealing with him, they invite him in. He takes

over and decrees equally ridiculous but new commandments:
"The first thing we'll do is, we'll make everybody wear overalls."

A satire of all the literature that treats the precariousness of
the universe and the indifference of its "rulers," this is also a
parody of "the stranger" whose reasoned helplessness, instead of
pushing him to the limits of "the absurd," lands him at the top.

XVIII   *"At The End of the Mechanical Age"*

"The end of the mechanical age . . . [is] an actuality straining to
become a metaphor. One must wish it luck. . . . One must cheer it
on . . . give these damned metaphors every chance, even if they are
inimical to personal well-being and comfort. We have a duty to
understand everything, whether we like it or not. . . ."

The key to this very difficult story is its equation of the
mechanical age with the loss of imagination, specifically in the
form of metaphor. Barthelme delineates a marriage (which he
describes as "deeply enmeshed in the mechanical age"), whose
courtship, wedding ceremony, and eventual dissolution are portrayed in traditional structures (i.e., the romantic promises of
joy and eternal fulfillment during the courtship; God's presence
in the exchange of vows). However, this couple has no concept
of metaphor, and they treat everything concretely. The effects
are, needless to say, very funny.

The narrator, confused by all the supermarket's attractively
packaged detergents, "reached out blindly" and discovered a
woman's hand in his. A specialist on both cleaning products
and world matters (i.e., this is the end of an era), Mrs. Davis's
advice is to "huddle and cling," as we shall see, a far cry from
Arnold's "Ah, love, let us be true." (The story is, in fact, a contemporary version of "Dover Beach.") Although the narrator is
no "Jake" (her first husband), he can still offer marriage as an
"interim project." When it palls, their arrangement will automatically self-destruct.

He woos her with a sort of "Someday-Your-Prince-Will-Come"
song, whose lyrics, like his personality, are a hodgepodge of
familiar slogans and texts (from "The Windhover" and *The
Waste Land* to the Bible): a natty dresser with "a coat of
many colors" and "all major credit cards," Ralph (the prince)

"is striding to meet" her. Mrs. Davis also courts him with song. She sings of (Yeats's?) Maude, who waits to "heal" his *scrappy and generally unsatisfactory life* [italics mine]." Like Adam in Genesis, Maude is credited with the naming of the things in her everyday world—here, tools.

The songs are sung aboard a boat—during the forty days and nights of the flood (clearly the world is falling apart), but the minute they question the metaphoric meaning of their reality, the boat sinks. Their songs, in fact, seem to refer to death, rather than the dreams of life (tools would, after all, be "heaven" to a machine). Barthelme writes: "[The songs] are merely flaky substitutes for the terminal experience." Any distinctions between life and death have evaporated. We are one step beyond "Sleeping and Waking."

In such a world, with everything classified, with direct ties between signs and significations, God is also literalized. He is a regular guy who stands up in the flood, attends weddings, and spends most of his time reading meters, since "grace" is electricity in a totally mechanical world.

What is particularly engaging in the story is its portrayal of how these figures mechanically adapt to everything. During the flood, they enjoy "Scotch-and-floodwaters"; their inevitable divorce goes uncontested; their child is sent off to a T.V. ad's utopia, "that part of Russia where people live to be one hundred and ten." At the end, they shake hands like two business associates, their grace (electricity) still operative, with "standby generators ensuring the flow of grace." One assumes they will be reprogrammed shortly.

The vision begun in "The Big Broadcast of 1938" is complete. Scripts, which at least bore a human hand (although their material was derivative), have now given way to punched cards, all fed by the holiness of divine electricity. The eighteenth-century description of the universe as machine has materialized.

CHAPTER 11

"Great Days"

B ARTHELME develops a new form in several stories, which marks a new direction in his art. Familiar materials do recur, such as the parodies and satires ("Tales of the Swedish Army," "The Question Party," "Edward Lear," "Zombies"). "Abduction from the Seraglio" brings back the subject of art, with its possibilties for distraction and/or liberation (reminiscent of "Daumier"), though now in a more slapstick manner. Once again, frustration in love, indeed in life, and the loneliness of experience are the volume's underlying moods, alongside the redeeming affirmation that ordinary experience *of this world* is infinitely irresistible and preferable to the security and promises of any belief system.

Important to explore is the new technique in seven stories: "The Crisis," "Apology," "The New Music," "Morning," "Conservatory," "The Leap," and "Great Days." The form is that of dialogue, an outgrowth, it would appear, of the Emma-Julie conversations in *The Dead Father*. In the simplest of descriptive terms, one feels as though he had stepped into the middle of a personal conversation. Nonsequiturial utterances built around common themes, with recurrent, evolving, and changing imagery, create a polyphonic effect. Meaning accrues, as in music or poetry, through accumulations of tones, counterpoints, mood, images, and rhythm. Barthelme creates parallel voices that never announce their subject; ideas or feelings are buried within or around spoken words. The speakers alone know the particulars of their lives, and it is mood or perhaps a specific detail that becomes the substance of their story. The privacy of interaction, indeed the mystery of experience in even its most incidental aspects, is tapped. Barthelme has put aside the balloon, a totalized

194

image in itself, as an emblem of inexpressible private emotion. Now he pursues the virtually impossible task of expressing the inexpressible.

Many of the stories again develop at the level of language, but language now moves beyond the problems of sign and signification to approximate different dimensions of human response. The poetic techniques of *The Dead Father* continue, as he reflects experience in the terminology and metaphors (frequently literalized) of the several arts—opera, film, painting, and music. Once again, colors and chords, like the artifices of specific linguistic constructs, are as much a metaphor of felt experience as words, and often a more accurate reflection of one's experience, temporally and spatially. Barthelme has added to his verbal collage the more ineffable, infinitely suggestive techniques of poetry and musical composition.

Although these stories have different sets of couples, there is a unifying mood—a repeated sense that one can never really learn anything from the past, that all efforts at communication and change are limited by larger, inevitable patterns. What in the earlier stories was the limitation of words is now more clearly connected to the constrictions of personality, time, and history. Barthelme moves in and out of time to illustrate this. Our problem of touching one another is not merely a symptom of our time, but it is universal and historic in dimension. Thus, he retells old stories in the context of the contemporary sensibility. Montezuma, who might have been great friends with Cortés, meets him in his own time but with modern language and contemporary insights about experience. Yet they enact their fate against the historical context of their time (as history knows it). In "The Abduction from the Seraglio," as well as in "The Question Party," Barthelme recasts old stories again in contemporary language and in the contemporary *Zeitgeist*. What is most noticeable, in a story like "The New Music," with its mixture of old and new styles, is his vision that one only acts as if he were free, under the misperception that such things as "old" and "new" exist—whether in musical styles or adaptations to life and death. The only final certainty, as in *The Dead Father*, is one's illusory freedom in an absolutely unknowable universe.

The people in this volume, while not traditionally character-

ized, seem very human, and one identifies with their despair
and joy within the confines of past and present—their link with
the patterns of accomplishment and failure common to all
people of all times ("New Music," "King of Jazz," "Cortés,"
"Great Days," "Belief"). Barthelme has touched on the broad
issues of love, fear, faith, friendship, hope, ambition, death, and
despair—with a warmer tone. One will not take that leap in faith,
because the things of this world (the hideous, as well as the
marvelous) beckon. So too, if (and when) love disappoints, one
can recapture his childhood optimism, no less a part of the
human pattern than loss and failure ("The Apology," "Great
Days"). Emanating from the interwoven synchronic and diachronic lines is Barthelme's compassionate voice, as he portrays
the individual's struggles against the bonds of language, history,
human nature, and time.

I *"The Crisis"*

Told in the form of a dialogue, one speaker pursues images
of a political rebellion, "the crisis," whereas the other alludes to
a romantic relationship and business difficulties (other "crises").
The unifying image is "Clementine," both the leader of the
rebellion and the beloved: "—On the dedication page of the
rebellion, we see the words 'To Clementine' . . . —I loved her for
a while. Then, it stopped. . . . Is something wrong with me?"
The success of the two rebellions—personal (romantic and business) and political (military)—is intertwined in the alternating
statements: "Success is everything. Failure is more common."
Images of urban life connect the personal and political. The
rebels have, for example, captured "one zoo, not our best zoo,
and a cemetery"; "our frontiers are the marble lobbies of these
buildings. True, mortar pits ring the elevator banks but these
must be seen as friendly, helpful gestures towards certification
of the crisis."
Changes in the political and personal seem doomed, despite
repeated attempts at conquest: "Three rebellions ago the air was
fresher. The soft pasting noises of the rebel billposters remind
us of Oklahoma, where everything is still the same." Historic

questions remain: "Are the great bells of the cathedrals an impoverishment . . . or an enrichment?"

Barthelme's form here, begun in the dialogues of *The Dead Father,* would seem closer to poetry than prose. Eliot comes to mind in the imagistic fusion of the personal and historical. Even more noticeable, "The Crisis" resembles *The Dead Father* in its self-conscious portrayal of experience as linguistic artifice and in its use of the language, structures, and metaphors of the other arts for descriptive purposes. It begins, to repeat: "On the dedication page of the rebellion, we see the words 'To Clementine.' A fine sentiment, miscellaneous organ music next, and turning several pages, massed orange flags at the head of the column. This will not be easy, but neither will it be hard. Good will is everywhere, and the lighthearted song of the gondoliers is heard in the distance." If the language of narrative (i.e., words, traditional metaphor) is only an approximation of experience, perhaps Barthelme can evoke a more accurate metaphoric equivalence of one's spatial and temporal experience if he employs the language and media of painting and music.

Finally, if in stories like "The Balloon" and "Indian Uprising" he created extended metaphors—the balloon, the uprising—for the narrator's emotional state, one senses the same projection of emotion now through the medium of the dialogues. In the earlier work the image was fully realized, to be appreciated and enjoyed in its own terms; now, because the narrator's emotions seem more ambiguous and undefined, the crisis externalized in the story (and thus formulated in different voices) lacks even the shape of the balloon.

II *"The Apology"*

Two women play at ingratiating themselves to the world in order to distract themselves from time and the human plight. To apologize or not to apologize—that is the question. The first one thanks everyone (with an underlying hostility), and she tries to convince her friend to apologize (the corollary of thanking): "You are dumb. . . . Myself, I shower thanks everywhere. . . . Thank people . . . for what they are about to do as well as thank them for what they have already done, thank them in public and then take them aside privately and thank them again. Thank the thankless and thank the already adequately thanked. In fine, let no occasion pass to slip the chill blade of my thanks between the ribs of every human ear."

That Barthelme should focus his parody of one's survival in the universe in these terms reinforces his portrayal of our (necessary) use of language like children, for whom "Thank you" and "I'm sorry" are the phrases which most frequently organize and re-structure reality. The "plot" concerns the first woman's efforts to convince the other to apologize to her husband, in written or spoken form. As it is now, the latter sits passively by the window and anticipates his return. Although she says she doesn't care about him, her deepest thoughts are possibly otherwise. She says of a man standing outside the window, who may or may not be her husband: "Make him go away. Make the other return. . . . Have you no magic?" Only at the end, when he takes out his pistol, opens his pants, and seems about to shoot himself in his most vulnerable place, does she apologize—actually for every-thing: *"I'm sorry my stack of Christmas cards was always bigger than yours! . . . I'm sorry I slept with Sam! I'm sorry I married you and I'll never do it again."* The story ends: "Well. What's next? Do a little honky-tonking maybe?" and the apologist-con-vert answers: "We could. If you feel like it. Was I sorry enough?" "No," she is told, reminiscent of Beckett's couples who say: "What'll we do" "if he [Godot] doesn't come?" and "That's the idea. Let's contradict each other."

What is most fascinating about the story are the different spoken and written styles the women affect in enacting their roles. Since their role playing is entirely linguistic, changes in styles and vocabulary mark their adaptations to (or modulations of) role. Just as one cannot clearly explain (or clarify) her feel-ings toward her husband, so too language, in any of its styles, is clearly separate from experience, an inaccurate measure of it. (Two of the most inadequate phrases, for example, to reflect one's experience are "I'm sorry" and "Thank you.")

Drama then is at the level of language. In the beginning, the two use words and phrases like "Naw" or "screw it." They discuss the possibility that the husband might be drawn back in lit-eralized metaphoric terms: "The magnetic north of your brain may attract his wavering needle still." At a knock at the gate one says in mock-poetic language: "What is it makes you spring up so, my heart?" If, at the beginning, one woman described herself as "sitting on the floor by the window with only part of my face in the window," by the end, she is "sitting on the floor . . . with only my great dark eyes visible. My great dark eyes. . . . How pale the brow, how pallid the cheeks. . . ." *Barthelme* adds: "And so on." As we get into the form and mood of the story and the language becomes more euphonious and clichéd, it would seem as if things are getting better; but Barthelme undercuts their (and our) expectations for a happy ending. A final, jarring, and unequivocal "No" resounds at the conclusion.

III   *"The New Music"*

This is another story in poetic dialogue form, where characters and setting remain undefined. One gets the sense of the two old men contemplating past and future failures and successes (personal, sexual, social, military), the parents who failed to provide them "succor," and some perfect retirement home ("Pool"), which may come before or after death.

Barthelme chooses his title concept to represent the new-fangled ways—in terms as general as dreams and values to those more specific of sexuality, spontaneity, and the use of words— just about anything the reader wishes to associate with "the new" as opposed to the traditional. The new music has a magical quality; it offers hope in the passage of time; it ties all lost strands together. The lives of the two men are dull (one has to remind the other that he has just slept with Susie); they are so divorced from real feeling and sensation that they go to the grocery store and Xerox their food. They know that "if one does nothing but listen to the new music, everything else drifts, goes away, frays."

The story consists of the drifts and frays. "Did Odysseus feel this way when he and Diomedes decided to steal Athene's statue from the Trojans, so that they would become dejected and lose the war?" The motif of war then stirs private recollections and associations, which then suggest other personal motifs, perhaps mentioned earlier or to recur later, to be sloughed off and later reassembled in new contexts. One experiences the story like a musical composition, where a wealth of literary echoes culminate in a richly textured evocation of their mother who, in her own musical time (she is associated with Persephone, Demeter, and their Eleusinian mysteries), was as out of step with their music as they are with the current world's. Then, as now, "the new music burns things together, like a welder," or so it seems. "The new music says life becomes more and more exciting as there is less and less time." Now as then, however, their "Momma wouldn't have 'lowed it." But Momma's gone, as soon they will be. Evoking Hamlet's "undiscovered country" and Macbeth's "tomorrow and tomorrow," the new music in its dissonant way awaits the same fate as the heroic songs of time's long past.

IV   *"Cortés and Montezuma"*

"Bernal Diaz del Castillo, who will one day write *The True History of the Conquest of New Spain*, stands in a square whittling upon a piece of mesquite. The Proclamation of Vera Cruz is read, in which the friendship of Cortés and Montezuma is denounced as contrary to the best interests of the people of Mexico, born and yet unborn."

As we all know, history distinguishes the heroic liberators from the despotic invaders; depending upon a variety of contemporary political and social values, last year's fanatic may be tomorrow's martyr. Barthelme portrays the meeting of Cortés and Montezuma as it might have occurred in the past within the context of present historical "fact" and language. Written in the present tense, the story suggests that whatever their time and place, people are ultimately controlled by the forces of history. Free will cannot countervene inevitable patterns.

Cortés, a hero to the Spanish as Carlos I's Christian emissary, is simultaneously rapacious and destructive to the Aztecs, as he operates within the demands of his time and position. Montezuma is similarly "magnificent" and barbaric, both in his private and public ("textualized") roles. Courageous and kind to each other, they might have been, in another time and place, abiding friends.

Barthelme reconstructs their meeting as though Cortés were acting out his role in a history text; Montezuma responds according to his own historically defined, personal religious vision. The cadences are Hispanic: "Because Cortés lands on a day specified in the ancient writings, because he is dressed in black, because his armor is silver in color, a certain *ugliness* of the strangers taken as a group—for these reasons, Montezuma considers Cortés to be Quetzalcoatl, the great god who left Mexico many years before, on a raft of snakes, vowing to return." As each offers the other food, one resists because it is literally of human origin; the other pauses because it is *metaphorically* human: "Cortés declines because he knows the small pieces . . . are human fingers." Cortés sends Montezuma "food . . . like human food." The only stable reality of their world—not articulated by history and subject to negotiable point of view is nature—nonhuman and human; throughout, "little green flies fill the air"; Cortés and Montezuma like each other.

The shifts from the diachronic to the synchronic are striking to the reader, as is Barthelme's emphasis of the personal and yet often banal drama to be told, rather than the larger, traditional one recited by history texts. Montezuma admits, for example, that Cortés's priest, Father Sanchez, is busy "overturning idols," a modern idea, surely not a sixteenth-century phrase. Cortés and Montezuma, furthermore, are frequently portrayed "holding hands." Cortés sleeps with Doña Marina in a palace given him by his so-called adversary Montezuma, and Cortés then saves his life from a poisonous insect bite. Each could be the other's salvation. Montezuma writes his mother of his relief in observing the openness of the nobility's "disgusting ways." Grateful to see them "flaunt" their assertiveness and deceptiveness, he sees them outside their historical roles and no longer has "to *remember* them." He wonders "What has emboldened the nobility to emerge from obscurity at this time?"—a departure from history. Yet his modern, psychological answer is expressed through his own primitive perspective: "it is a direct consequence of the plague of devils we have had."

Cortés's men would break the myth and create new patterns of language: "Whisperers exchange strange new words," but instead they break through many more walls to find "invariably, only the mummified carcasses of dogs, cats, and sacred birds."

As they are victimized more and more by the patterning of history, we see that each is suspicious of the other. Montezuma has secret meetings with his "great lords," and each has employed a detective to watch the other. Moving in and out of

time, marked by changes in language, Montezuma admits that
"visions are better" than detectives. Punctuating everything are
the traditional "facts": Cortés is substituting images of the Virgin
for the Aztec gods; Montezuma is shrinking Spanish heads.

In the midst of all, and midway through the story, Barthelme
establishes our footing: "del Castillo," he writes, "will one day
write *The True History of the Conquest of New Spain*"; now,
however, he stands back observing all.

A proclamation arrives—drawn from the meeting of the lords—
denouncing Cortés and Montezuma's friendship "as contrary to
the best interests of the people of Mexico, born and yet unborn,"
contrary to the design of nature. (Who is its author?)

From this point on, the ending is predictable. On the one
hand, the friendship between the two leaders remains; they
even have gentle conversations about Christianity. But, still
dedicated to the pagan gods, Montezuma retains the art of
drama as a civilizing and moral force. Cortés dictates the remaining plot. Montezuma, aware of his role in history's script,
says to him: "Disclose to me the ending . . . of the drama."
(Oddly enough, earlier, Montezuma had received "new messages"—foreboding the future?—"in picture writing, from the
hills. These he burned, so that Cortés . . . [would] not learn
their contents." Had he accepted them, so to speak, the texts,
del Castillo's, for example, might have been written differently.)

Montezuma and Cortés go to Cotaxtla, the meeting place of
the Aztec legislature, where "laws" of the people are made. To
Cortés's surprise, Montezuma is not "absolute ruler." Here they
encounter more historical patterning, in the form of "pottery
figures" (Montezuma imprisoned not just by history's final
declarations but also by the politics of his particular culture).
Both laugh hysterically and dance around the room. Although
Cortés and Montezuma would indeed create a different conclusion, Cortés must "fulfill" his "destiny." He places Montezuma
under arrest (as he simultaneously offers that he "come away
with me").

At the end, Charles V, Cortés, and Montezuma, in chorus,
announce the inevitable conclusion: " 'Was there no alternative?'
Charles asks. 'I did what I thought best,' says Cortés, 'proceeding

with gaiety and conscience.' " "I am murdered," says Montezuma
as though he were a fictional figure, an actor in his own life.

At the end, in *our* present moment perhaps, "the ghost of
Montezuma rebukes the ghost of Cortés." Still "walking down
by the docks, hand in hand," Montezuma asks Cortés: "Why
did you not throw up your hand, and catch the stone?"—a
reference to Doña Marina's dream that Montezuma would
indeed be stoned, which Cortés ignored for his own "trust-
worthy" methods. History is perhaps a matter of which dream
one follows.

V *"The King of Jazz"*

Trombonist, and originator of sounds that have "the real
epiphanic glow," Hokie Mokie has at last become "king of jazz."
He is so distinguished that his pronunciation of a word "can
just knock a fella out." As he and the other local musicians at a
local gig prepare to play, Hideo Yamaguchi, from Tokyo, announces himself as "the top trombone man in all Japan." After
all perform, Hokie acknowledges Hideo's superiority and mod-
estly rejoins the group to play "sotto voce" with a "cup mute
on." Hokie is so "dadblangedest" "exciting," he reclaims his
crown. Each one, hearing his music in his own frame of reference and lingo, says: "that sounds like the cutting edge of
life . . . like polar bears crossing Arctic ice pans . . . like an oyster
fungus growing on an aspen truck . . . like prairie dogs kissing
. . . like witchgrass tumbling or a river meandering. . . ." Hokie
tells Hideo, who has decided to pack it all in and return to
Japan, "That's O.K. son. . . . It happens to the best of us."

Written in the journalistic style which creates our popular
mythology, this story parodies "the great leader"—musician,
artist, scholar, athlete, or politician—who wins his place by
ultimately facing and outdoing the rookie who threatens him.
A parody of any number of disparate myths within this basic
pattern—from the Grade B gangster movie, to the Oedipus/
Perseus/Achilles legends, to the Khrushchev-Kennedy encounter—
he pokes fun at the nature of competition, either on a grand or
small scale. The past will out. In characterizing his threatening

youth as Japanese, he also parodies the idea of Third World competition, as he gives the story an absurdly patriotic ending. What is, of course, funniest throughout is the blind worship paid the kingpin's every gesture by his "crritics" (to quote Samuel Beckett) and their adoration of all unimportant matters: i.e., "And he holds his horn in a peculiar way. That's frequently the mark of a superior player."

VI *"The Question Party"*

Language may not reflect reality; it may create it. Barthelme's footnote explains that this story consists of "some three dozen lines" added to a story published in 1850. It is about a party whose reserved and pompous guests make Joyce's people in "The Dead" look like celebrants in a vegetation ceremony. The spinsters and bachelors play a game in which, after a question is asked (in this case, "What is a bachelor?"), everyone writes down an answer; on this occasion Mr. Lynch (the name of a Joyce character) speaks of the "tedium" and "odium" of "sleeping with strumpets." At that point, a guest shoots him dead. The party continues and the guests determine—now Barthelme's anesthetized act that at the next party they must have something really exciting: they will invite Geronimo, chief of the Apaches. As for now, "No one will ever know that Mr. Lynch was the man who—How strange is justice! How artful woman!"

Indeed, in the 1850s, to use the word "strumpet" and to have admitted one's association with such—in the midst of the "gentle" sex—would have been "dangerous" enough and grounds enough for an honor-bound gentleman to use his pistol. In Barthelme's retelling of the story (as in "The Catechist," the diachronic contrasting with the synchronic), not only would the party continue in the same blasé way (with men and women similarly outspoken about the hardly shocking "strumpet"), but today's zombies would be shocked neither by language nor a shooting. The only hope for a truly "dangerous" party is the radical chic invitation of the exotic Geronimo, who, unlike King Kong in "The Party" (who socialized with everyone), promises to be at least "extremely cruel to everyone."

VII *"Belief"*

This is a rather moving portrait of the older set who, estranged from each other, their families, and the world around them, sit in Washington Square Park and talk of all subjects, their pasts, and their fantasies. Although the four bicker that each one's "belief" is the true comprehension of reality, ultimately the only reality is time and age.

Speaking of romance, Kathy, sentimental and superstitious, believes that if you say "rabbit" properly, you will be loved within the month. The men, concerned with more important cosmic matters, are of course no more in control of their lives than Kathy. They look "at the sky to make sure all of our country's satellites" are in the "right place." Jerome actually believes in nothing—neither magic, superstition, religion, or even concrete reality. He, now and always, has accepted "inner belief" alone: "I didn't believe in the Second World War . . . and I was in it." On hearing Jerome's derogatory mention of unions, Frank enters the conversation, his identity, he argues, a direct result of union activity.

As they continue debating, their roles reverse. Jerome admits his concrete "prostate" trouble, and Kate, playfully affecting his pose about subjective reality, says, "I don't believe there is such a thing as a prostate." Elise, who has obviously never had a lover, embraces Kate's romantic belief, and Jerome confesses that he has indeed believed one thing—a religious matter at that: *"It is forbidden to grow old."* To this Elise comments that although this is a pretty thought, "I could do without the irony," and Kate discards all her "rabbit" talk. ("She gazed about . . . at new life spouting in sandboxes and jungle gyms.") Jerome's comment—the ultimate illusion, as though one could through any belief control the reality of time—serves to puncture all their illusions; time remains, the ultimate nonnegotiable reality.

VIII *"The Abduction from the Seraglio"*

Mozart's opera, its heroine named after the composer's wife (connecting life and art) tells of Constanze's rescue from the

Turkish Pasha. Despite a variety of threats—mainly the Pasha's wooing—Constanze remains faithful to her Belmonte, who finally, disguised as an architect, rescues her from the seraglio. The Pasha ultimately aids in freeing them.

In Barthelme's extremely complicated story, this fiction is retold in contemporary terms. Thus his supermod characters treat each other like fictional or artistic entities (which they already are, as Mozart's characters), and they act (as in "Cortés and Montezuma") as if they know their historical (or literary) fate, even though they operate within a modern frame. But since they are also Barthelme's characters, they take on an additional autonomy. Once again, the synchronic and diachronic blend and separate.

(The mocked standard of beauty in Barthelme's story is the modern art medium of steel: "The only thing prettier than ladies is an I-beam painted bright yellow," says the Belmonte figure, an artist whose forms "better" everyday "digestible" items. He has, for example, made colored steel bread and 4,000 young steel artichokes. Since he finds the natural forms "too mannerly," he "roughens" them up in his art.)

It is at a creative impasse one Thursday (his record of Waylon Jennings is scratched) that this young sculptor decides to *distract* himself by rescuing Constanze. (Barthelme literalizes and elaborates the libretto in minute details.) Belmonte essentially turns a fictional reality into his more immediate reality (although we know all of this is taking place within the framework of Mozart's creation). He literally identifies with the heroic role; he motors to the seraglio (feeling "blindsided on the Freeway by two hundred thousand guys trying to get home from their work at the rat-poison factories, all two hundred thousand tape decks playin' the same thing, some kind of roll-on-down-the-road song . . ."), only to discover the literal equation of art and life. He sees the same wonderful (prefab) steel building as his own, except that it is larger and red, and it appears even more efficient. (Art—even within art—betters life.) It also has a picture of a watchdog pasted on it, and as we shall see shortly, art creates life. (The dog appears as an actor in this melodrama.)

In a sense, abducted himself by the seraglio, Belmonte steps completely outside of Mozart's (or the librettist's, Bretzner's) story, and tells us how "dumb" Constanze is, and he characterizes the Pasha, who made his ten million dollars a year, gross, as a Plymouth dealer. (Belmonte prefers the Pasha's "forms," his Plymouths, to the man—even more boxes within boxes.) He then learns that the Pasha successfully wooed Constanze with flank steaks, to which he admits, "If we're having Neiman-Marcus time, I can't compete." Aware that Constanze (like Snow White) has stepped out of her fictional role, he says, "She's in a delicate relation to the real," gathering together countless levels of artifice and reality suggested thus far. Constanze has, he continues, been "great" to him and even socially minded. He then says, threatened about the autonomy of art and the variety of meanings it has: "The really dreadful thought, to me, is that her real might be the real one."

As the story ends, he opens the door of the seraglio and the dog (the picture) becomes real, "carrying on in the way he felt was expected of him," another Barthelme "etc.", wherein language again draws attention to itself as an inadequate vehicle to describe "experience." Appropriately, with everything occurring on any number of different levels of art and reality, he hurls a "concrete porkchop" to knock down the dog. Like the speaker in "Daumier," he gets his Constanze back, and they step, momentarily, outside the frames of art, to walk "down the street together bumping our hipbones together"—another victory for the fancy.

Such ecstasy is short-lived, however, and he concludes: "There's no use crying over spilt marble." Constanze will undoubtedly return to her "frame," her "role," to future writers, readers, or patrons, and "She will undoubtedly move on and up and down and around in the world . . . making everything considerably better than it was, for short periods of time." Like the poet in "La Belle Dame sans Merci," he has returned to whatever reality he functions in, and she is back in her fictional/musical role. The story is about the creative/aesthetic experience, about perceiving and creating the work of art. It is about art's eternal, fixed (synchronic) dimension, and its diachronic, living manifestations. *Plus ça change!*

IX *"The Death of Edward Lear"*

Barthelme has frequently focused upon a society where intimate experiences become public confessions. Here, invitations
are extended on the occasion of Edward Lear's imminent death
(like Colby's in *Amateurs*). "People prepare to attend . . . as
they might . . . a day in the country." Lear's rambling comments
reveal his egomaniacal compulsion to maintain center stage. He
shows off his paintings and books, and then he just plain dies.
All agree it was "a somewhat tedious performance."

The reader is mildly startled by the ironic use of "performance" (since, especially in the case of death, one assumes a
distinction between "performance" and spontaneity). But Lear's
blasé witnesses have a different thought: "Something was understood: that Mr. Lear had been doing what he had always done
and therefore not doing anything extraordinary. Mr. Lear had
transformed the extraordinary into its opposite."

Barthelme satirizes the notion that one should die with heroic
stoicism. He also satirizes the relationship between actor and
his observer, between author and audience, between act and
perception. He parodies both the bards of dullness and their
groupies, who exalt in their guru's most private acts. The result
is a funny yet grotesque portrait of the symbiotic exhibitionism
evident on both sides.

The story continues: "As time passed," indeed the event gained
a different perspective in "historical light." Stories were told,
plays were produced, some "versions enriched by learned interpretation, textual emendation, and changing fashion." One
modification, however, was curious: "The supporting company"
played "in the traditional way, but Lear himself" appeared
"shouting, shaking, vibrant with rage."

A lampoon on the "distortions" of art, Barthelme ends with
an almost blasphemous play on Lear's name, recalling Shakespeare's figure's tragic rage, if not Dylan Thomas's pleas to his
father to "rage against the dying of the light."

X *"Concerning the Bodyguard"*

In our egalitarian age, we celebrate as heroes not only the

Willy Lomans but the Rosencrantzes and Guildensterns. We seek out and celebrate the humanity of all so-called major and minor figures, both real and fictional. One of society's most anonymous people who earns his living and reputation by means of his low profile is the bodyguard.

What Barthelme accomplishes here through his asking of questions—sociological, political, personal, trivial (i.e., does he scream at the woman who irons his Yves St. Laurent shirts?)—is the characterization of a bodyguard. In so doing, Barthelme destroys his very function—that of anonymity and inconspicuousness. He is no longer the totally forgettable personage.

Midway through the story he writes: "In every part of the country, large cities and small towns, bottles of champagne have been iced, put away, reserved for a celebration, reserved for a special day. Is the bodyguard aware of this?" One can only assume that the champagne has been iced in preparation of someone's imminent death. The story ends: "On a certain morning, the garbage cans of the city, the garbage cans of the entire country, are overflowing with empty champagne bottles. Which bodyguard is at fault?"

An Ionescoesque image, a bodyguard has obviously failed in his job; but it is Barthelme who has stripped him of his function and who thereby is ultimately responsible for his victim's death. The ordinary assassin/victim, power/weakness, sign/signified distinctions have been destroyed.

XI *"The Zombies"*

The story reads like an anthropological description of the mating habits of an exotic tribe, where mating is according to ritual and form, rather than romance, where morality among the zombies consists of the traditional "good" and "bad," and where secretive behavior also goes on behind the reforming clergy's back; gourmet foods are the fad. Barthelme's focus, of course, is not some strange South American or African tribe but contemporary America where, for example, women are sold for the highest price and where, "to accommodate" to their unappealing husbands, they turn to the life of fantasy. "No matter," they say before their weddings, "we will paste photographs of

the handsome man . . . on your faces, when it is time to go
to bed."

XII *"On the Steps of the Conservatory"*

Maggie and the pregnant Hilda (the literalized, modern-day
madonna) discuss Hilda's rejection from the elite conservatory,
"hostile to the new spirit." Told in the new dialogue form,
Barthelme uses the Conservatory to represent any selective
organization (i.e., from the American Academy of Arts and
Sciences to any local political organization) which arbitrarily
accepts and rejects figures who are not clearly distinct from one
another. The defiant Peace-Corps veteran, Hilda, talks to her
friend, a member, about the mysterious organization's "pro-
gramme"—from sex to art exhibitions. One could again speak of
the synchronic and diachronic, but whatever its variations, Barthelme pits the old against the new gardes and parodies as well
the novice who would ignore real life (her child) for the restric-
tions and artifice of the aesthetic life. Again, as in other dialogues,
the central image, the Conservatory, is developed by diffuse
allusion, rather than by more organized, extended metaphor.

XIII *"The Leap"*

—Fathoming such is beyond the powers of poor ravening noodles
like ourselves, who but for the—[grace of God . . .].
—We are but poor lapsarian futiles whose preen glands are all out
of whack and who but for the grace of God's goodness would—
—Do you think He wants us to grovel quite so much?
—I don't think He gives a rap. But it's traditional.

Initially funny and then wonderfully lyrical, Barthelme draws
two men who try to "make the leap of faith." As they examine
their consciences, they are able to speak only in the hackneyed
language of traditional religion (often misusing words): "We
are but poor . . . slovening wretches." But one of the speakers
("double-minded") cannot distract himself from reality and
subjects like overpopulation, disease, and suicide. In any case,
love, rather than God, calls them to the things of this world, both

the grotesque, as well as the beautiful, and they decide to postpone their "leap" to another day. In citing that day, the "double-minded" one gives a lush rendering of those worldly things that keep one's eyes downward. They will try again when:

—Garden peas yellow or green wrinkling or rounding. . . .
—The Brie-with-pepper meeting the toasty loaf.
—Another day when some eighty-four-year-old guy complains that his wife no longer gives him presents.
—Small boys bumping into small girls, purposefully.
—Cute little babies cracking people up.
—Another day when somebody finds a new bone that proves we are even ancienter than we thought we were.
—Another day when the singing sunlight turns you every way but loose.
—When you accidentally notice the sublime.
—Somersaults and duels.

XIV   *"Great Days"*

In this dialogue a series of moods emerges as two women talk of the strains of urban life, the search for vocational fulfillment, the need for friendship and love, and the inevitable process of aging—the joys and sorrows of the panoply of adult experience. The "subject" of the story is time, the dreams of adulthood, the ghosts of childhood, the hopes that survive amid poignant and painful loss. As ever, what they say bears the weight of literary history, especially echoes of *The Waste Land* and the hyacinth garden, which have haunted Barthelme's work. Each woman, at different points, says:

—He told me terrible things in the evening of that day as we sat side by side waiting for the rain to wash the watercolors from his watercolor paper. Waiting for the rain to wash the paper clean, quite clean.
—Took me by the hand and led me through all rooms. Many rooms.
—I know all about it.
—Figs and kiss-me-nots. I would meet you upon this honestly.

Like many of the other dialogues, "Great Days" is really a

poem, its statement-response rhythms reminiscent of the Greek chorus strophe-antistrophe, its polyphonic images and phrases similarly constructed to create and reinforce meaning. In addition, however, the women's responses to one another lack any rational consistency and are instead associational in nature. Barthelme brings his form close to stream of consciousness but in a unique style, as he utilizes two separate personae, somewhat like Beckett's dramatic couples who often function as a single consciousness. These blend, split, echo, and ultimately merge to suggest a universality in disparate, human experience. The voices, after a while, are almost impossible to define as distinct personalities.

The story begins and ends with images of childhood, as Barthelme suggests that childhood is pleasurable *because* it is a time of direct sensual experience—the joy of the moment, concrete, discrete, optimistic. With adulthood comes a sense of expectation and a need for purpose, and with this comes the pain of disappointment and loss, the failure to find purposes that are sustaining, the waiting for great days that only arrive a few times in a lifetime.

It is not that these days are not great, but they are few, and Barthelme laments that too much time is spent waiting for them, during which memories of pain and disappointment overwhelm. The pleasures of adulthood remain, however, ironically not so different from those of childhood. They are again the joys of direct sensual experience—for the adult, of sexuality and love, of "abandon." But one wants to return to the time (to quote Wordsworth) before "the years" brought the "inevitable yoke," before the "earthly freight" replaced "delight and liberty, the simple creed."

Much of the story alludes to women's lives in particular—"our many moons of patience and accommodation"—to their various attempts at fulfillment, their marriages, love affairs, children, jobs, household preoccupations, hobbies, and art, all ending in the plea: "toys, I want more toys." The wish for rain to come and wipe the slate clean recurs. Aging—"wrinkling"—the loss of youthful beauty, is inevitable.

Barthelme ends with the women playing a childhood game (interestingly, a word game). He affirms that the way out lies in recapturing the child's capacity for seizing the day as it comes, for enjoying the moment in itself, for (again recalling Wordsworth's "Ode") experiencing in adulthood "the innocent brightness of a new born Day."

XV   *A Final Comment*

New times bring forth changes in fundamental assumptions, and the artist both reflects and reacts to these changes. One ordinarily associates the avant-garde with those artists who create new forms and expound new visions toward these ends. If they succeed, they later become the established classics of their time.

Donald Barthelme is perhaps such an artist (to quote his phrase, "the new music"), as he reflects changes in contemporary consciousness, in its assimilation of the new (i.e., the pervasive influence of the media, science and technology, the desolating isolation of urban life) and its reinterpretations of recurring human dilemmas (i.e., age, loneliness, generational strife, epistemological questions). Barthelme's explorations of the role of language in human experience are unique and profound. His vision of our escape from the limitations of language—not only as a means of communication but as an emblem of human contingency—is valuable and hopeful.

To date, Barthelme has published over a hundred and fifty short stories and two novels. At forty-nine, his achievement is not concluded. Nevertheless, his accomplishments thus far are of such originality, richness, and depth, as to assure him a place among the most important writers of the twentieth century.

Notes and References

Preface

1. Despite all the labels and disagreements regarding precisely which writers belong to this "movement," there are several excellent introductions to the avant-garde: the pioneer work of Jerome Klinkowitz, especially his *Literary Disruptions: The Making of a Post-Contemporary American Fiction* (Urbana, 1975). See also Raymond Federman's *Surfiction* (Chicago, 1975) and Mas'ud Zavarzaden's *The Mythopoeic Reality* (Urbana, 1976).

Chapter One

1. Jerome Klinkowitz, "Donald Barthelme," in *Interviews with Innovative American Writers*, ed. Joe David Bellamy (Urbana, 1974), p. 46.

2. Ibid., p. 47.

3. Ibid., p. 46.

4. Richard Schickel, "Freaked Out on Barthelme," *New York Times Magazine*, August 16, 1970, p. 43.

5. "The Case of the Vanishing Product," *Harpers*, October, 1961, pp. 30–32.

6. John F. Baker, "Donald Barthelme," *Publisher's Weekly*, November 11, 1974, p. 7.

7. Ibid.

8. 27 (Winter, 1976):3–31. Page references cited in text.

Chapter Two

1. *Snow White* (New York, 1967), pp. 96–97; hereafter cited in the chapter as *SW*. Other references in the text are to *Guilty Pleasures* (New York, 1974), cited as *GP*; *Come Back, Dr. Caligari* (Boston, 1964), cited as *CBDC*; *Unspeakable Practices, Unnatural Acts* (New York, 1968), cited as *UPUA*.

2. *Phenomenology of Perception*, trans. Colin Smith (New York:

Humanities Press, 1962), p. 16. On speaking of his "deeper cultural sources," Barthelme has said: "I have taken a certain degree of nourishment (or stolen alot) from the phenomenologists: Sartre, Erwin Straus, etc." Cf. Klinkowitz, in *Interviews*, p. 52.

3. (New York: Doubleday, 1967), p. 129.

Chapter Four

1. He hurls the beer through the windscreen of a Volkswagen, driven by I. Fondue and H. Maeght (159), whom he associates with the scoutmasters who punished him when he was twelve and threatened him with the black horse, for not doing what was expected— for cleaning pots with Ajax, instead of mud. Earlier, he confused a nun, whom he thought followed him, with the great black horse, for which he "waited" since he was twelve years old (71).

Selected Bibliography

PRIMARY SOURCES

1. Novels

The Dead Father. New York: Farrar, Straus and Giroux, 1975.
Snow White. New York: Atheneum, 1967.

2. Short Story Collections

Amateurs. New York: Farrar, Straus and Giroux, 1976.
City Life. New York: Farrar, Straus and Giroux, 1970.
Come Back, Dr. Caligari. Boston: Little, Brown, 1964.
Great Days. New York: Farrar, Straus and Giroux, 1979.
Guilty Pleasures. New York: Farrar, Straus and Giroux, 1974.
Sadness. New York: Farrar, Straus and Giroux, 1972.
Sixty Stories. New York: G. P. Putnam's Sons, 1981.
Unspeakable Practices, Unnatural Acts. New York: Farrar, Straus and Giroux, 1968.

3. Children's Book

The Slightly Irregular Fire Engine, or The Hithering Thithering Djinn. New York: Farrar, Straus and Giroux, 1971.

4. Uncollected Short Stories

"Adventure." *Harper's Bazaar*, December, 1970, pp. 92–95.
"Alexandria and Henrietta." *New American Review 12* (1971):82–87.
"The Bed." *Viva*, March 1974, pp. 68–70.
"The Bill." *Viva*, November 1973, n.p.
"Blue Flower Problem." *Harvest*, May, 1967, p. 29.
"Captain Blood." *New Yorker*, January 1, 1979, pp. 26–27.
"Conversations with Goethe." *New Yorker*, October 20, 1980, p. 49.
"The Dassaud Prize." *New Yorker*, January 12, 1976, pp. 26–29.

"Edwards, Amelia." *New Yorker*, September 9, 1972, pp. 34–36.
"The Farewell Party." *Fiction* 6, no. 2 (1980):12–16.
"The Great Debate." *New Yorker*, May 3, 1976, pp. 34–35.
"The Inauguration." *Harper's*, January, 1978, pp. 86–87.
"A Man." *New Yorker*, December 30, 1972, pp. 26–27.
"Man's Face." *New Yorker*, May 30, 1964, p. 29.
"Momma." *New Yorker*, October 2, 1978, pp. 32–33.
"Monumental Folly." *Atlantic*, February, 1976, pp. 33–40.
"The Mothball Fleet." *New Yorker*, September 11, 1971, pp. 34–35.
"Natural History." *Harper's*, August, 1971, pp. 44–45.
"Newsletter." *New Yorker*, July 11, 1970, p. 23.
"Over the Sea of Hesitation." *New Yorker*, November 11, 1972,
    pp. 40–43.
"Philadelphia." *New Yorker*, November 30, 1968, pp. 56–58.
"Presents." *Penthouse*, December, 1977, pp. 106–110.
"The Story Thus Far." *New Yorker*, May 1, 1971, pp. 42–45.
"Then." *Mother*, November-December, 1964, pp. 22–23.
"Three." *Fiction*, no. 1 (1972), p. 13.
"Wrack." *New Yorker*, October 21, 1972, pp. 36–37.

SECONDARY SOURCES

1. Bibliography

KLINKOWITZ, JEROME, with ASA PIERATT and ROBERT MURRAY DAVIS.
    *Donald Barthelme: A Comprehensive Bibliography and Anno-
    tated Secondary Checklist.* Hamden, Conn.: Shoestring Press,
    1977. Impressive 127-page opus covering published and unpub-
    lished work from juvenilia (1948) through *Amateurs* (1976).

2. Articles and Selections of Critical Books

DAVIS, ROBERT CON. "Postmodern Paternity: Donald Barthelme's *The
    Dead Father.*" *Delta*, May 8, 1979, pp. 127–40. The novel ar-
    ticulates and denies "the function of paternity both thematically
    and structurally."
DICKSTEIN, MORRIS. "Fiction Hot and Kool: Dilemmas of the Ex-
    perimental Writer." *TriQuarterly* 33 (Spring, 1975):257–77.
    Barthelme is unique in creating recognizable characters and
    themes in fictions that function as artifices.
DITSKY, JOHN M. " 'With Ingenuity and Hard Work, Distracted': The

Narrative Style of Donald Barthelme." *Style* 9 (Summer, 1975): 388–400. Discusses the surrealistic transformation of materials in "Daumier"; sees style as a distraction against nothingness.

FEDERMAN, RAYMOND. *Surfiction*. Chicago: Swallow Press, 1975. Fascinating essays by and on the avant-garde, especially the subject of writing about writing.

GASS, WILLIAM H. "The Leading Edge of the Trash Phenomenon." In *Fiction and the Figures of Life*. New York: Knopf, 1970, pp. 97–103. Barthelme places himself in the center of modern consciousness: "his dislocations are real" in *Unnatural Practices*.

GILLEN, FRANCIS. "Donald Barthelme's City: A Guide." *Twentieth Century Literature* 18 (1972):37–44. Mass media and pop culture bombard the people of *Unnatural Practices* . . . and *City Life*.

GILMAN, RICHARD. "Donald Barthelme," *Partisan Review* 39 (Summer, 1972):382–96. Interesting speculations on Barthelme's imaginative/socially pragmatic vision.

GLICKSBERG, CHARLES I. "Experimental Fiction: Innovation versus Form." *Centennial Review* 18 (Spring, 1974):127–50. Excellent survey of experimental fiction from James Joyce through Barthelme.

GRIFFIN, ROBERT. *"Come Back, Dr. Caligari"* (audiotape cassette). "Cassette Curriculum," Deland, Fla.: Everett/Edwards, 1972. One of the best introductions to the technique of Barthelme's early stories.

HASSAN, IHAB. *Paracriticisms*. Urbana: University of Illinois Press, 1975. Presents Barthelme as "visionary" beneath his burlesque techniques.

JOHNSON, R. E., JR. "Bees Barking in the Night: The End and Beginning of Donald Barthelme's Narrative." *Boundary 2* 5 (1977): 71–92. Excellent discussion of the dialectical structure and linguistic realism of "Balloon" and "Glass Mountain."

————. "Structuralism and the Reading of Contemporary Fiction," *Soundings* 58 (Fall, 1975):281–306. A discussion of William Gass, Robert Coover, and Barthelme that includes a structuralist reading of "Me and Miss Mandible" and "The Catechist."

KLINKOWITZ, JEROME. *Literary Disruptions: The Making of a Post-Contemporary American Fiction*. Urbana: University of Illinois Press, 1975. Eminently intelligent survey of the avant-garde that serves as an excellent introduction to Barthelme's inventive use of language within a spatial fictional form.

LELAND, JOHN. "Remarks Re-Marked: Barthelme, What Curios of

Signs!" *Boundary 2* 5 (1977):797–811. Emphasizing *Snow White*, Leland argues that meaning in Barthelme lies between the "promise" and "lie" of signs.

LONGLEIGH, PETER. "Donald Barthelme's *Snow White*." *Critique* 11, no. 3 (1969):3–34. Discusses the "monomythic," psychological, Jungian dimensions of the novel.

McCAFFERY, LARRY. "Barthelme's *Snow White*: The Aesthetics of Trash." *Critique* 16, no. 3 (1975):19–32. About the failure of art, *Snow White* adopts decayed fictional forms to ultimately transcend them.

MALORY, BARBARA. "Barthelme's *The Dead Father*." *Linguistics in Literature* 2 (1977):44–111. An overview of Barthelme's work, including a close reading of the novel.

ROTHER, JAMES. "Parafiction: The Adjacent Universe of Barth, Barthelme, Pynchon and Nabokov." *Boundary 2* 5 (1977):21–43. Presents decay of language as the subject of the avant-garde (*Snow White* is discussed).

SCHMITZ, NEIL. "Donald Barthelme and the Emergence of Modern Satire." *Minnesota Review* 1 (Fall, 1971):109–18. Barthelme ironically celebrates the creative/destructive "consciousness" in the phenomenological world.

————. "What Irony Reveals." *Partisan Review* 40, no. 3 (1973): 482–90. Intelligent discussion of Barthelme's irony through *Sadness*.

SCHOLES, ROBERT. "Metafiction." *Iowa Review* 1 (Fall, 1970):100–15. Barthelme reinvents the "fiction of essences" to get to the "deep structures of being."

SPENCER, SHARON. *Space, Time and Structure in the Modern Novel*. Chicago: Swallow Press, 1971. A fascinating survey of "architectonic form" in the moderns from 1910 to the 1970s.

STEVICK, PHILIP. "Lies, Fictions, and Mock-Facts." *Western Humanities Review* 30 (Winter, 1976):1–12. Explains how the "myth-making imagination" mocks the traditional world of fact.

STOTT, WILLIAM. "Donald Barthelme and the Death of Fiction." *Prospects* 1 (1975):369–86. Discusses Barthelme's transformation of private values into public facts.

TANNER, TONY. *City of Words*. New York: Harper and Row, 1971. This excellent survey of American fiction from 1950 to 1970 discusses Barthelme's "redemptive" rearrangements of fragments.

WEIXLMANN, J. and S. "Barth and Barthelme Recycle the Perseus Myth," *Modern Fiction Studies* 25 (Summer, 1979):191–207. *Chimera* and "Shower of Gold" reflect remarkably different literary styles.

WHALEN, TOM. "Wonderful Elegance." *Critique* 16, no. 3 (1975): 44–48. Finds unified setting and character in "The Party."

WILDE, ALAN. "Barthelme Unfair to Kierkegaard: Some Thoughts on Modern and Postmodern Irony." *Boundary 2* 5 (1977):45–70. An outstanding survey of Barthelme's "ludic" and "suspensive" work and his humanistic joy in the phenomenological world.

ZAVARZADEN, MAS'UD. *The Mythopoeic Reality*. Urbana: University of Illinois Press, 1976. An excellent and useful survey of the avantgarde, including a close examination of Barthelme.

3. Interviews

BAKER, JOHN F. *"PW* Interviews: Donald Barthelme." *Publisher's Weekly*, November 11, 1974, pp. 6–7. A miscellany of interesting comments on art, the use of parody, etc.

KLINKOWITZ, JEROME. "Donald Barthelme." In *The New Fiction: Interviews with Innovative American Writers*, edited by Joe David Bellamy, pp. 45–54. Urbana: University of Illinois Press, 1974. Discusses a broad range of subjects, including Barthelme's youth, creative interests, and influences.

SCHICKEL, RICHARD. "Freaked Out on Barthelme." *New York Times Magazine*, August 16, 1970, pp. 14–15, 42. Fictionalized question/answer interview.

"A Symposium on Fiction" [with Barthelme, William Gass, Grace Paley, and Walker Percy], *Shenandoah* 27 (Winter, 1970):3–31. The writers comment on the purposes and techniques of contemporary art.

Index